"In *Bird Dream*, Matt Higgins cracks open this astonishingly dangerous sport and captures the spectacular adrenaline surges it delivers. . . . A riveting tale."
—*The Wall Street Journal*

"A compelling chronicle of the extreme sport subculture of those who love soaring, gliding, and plummeting to the earth from a wide range of deadly heights. Higgins has inherently thrilling material on his hands, but he does much more than merely describe the adrenaline-charged feats of jumpers. The book is a subtle study of the psychology of athletes engaged in a sport where death is a constant possibility."
—*Chicago Tribune*

"In *Bird Dream*, Matt Higgins offers an engrossing account of the men and women who pursue the most dangerous recreational activity imaginable, one in which a razor-thin line separates success from failure, life from death. . . . While Higgins fills *Bird Dream* with fascinating characters, living and dead, the focus is on two wingsuiters determined to achieve the ultimate goal of jumping from a helicopter or an elevated spot and gliding down to a survivable landing without a parachute. . . . Does either of them survive? You will find the answers to those questions in a book you will find hard to put down."
—*The Washington Post*

"Gripping . . . In a way that shocked me, the book is perversely entertaining when Higgins reveals the fates of many of the men and women he writes about with such admiration. Higgins manages to keep the reader hooked all the way through to the final page. In a truly intoxicating read that was hard to put down, Matt Higgins has managed to make real a world about as far removed from daily life as it gets."
—*The Daily Beast*

The breathtaking highs and life-threatening plunges of the most extreme stuntmen on earth. Keep your mixed martial arts, parcours, and BMX bikes; you haven't seen anything until you've seen the point-of-view video of these free-flying pilots soaring in their homemade wingsuits over some of the most extreme terrain on the planet. In this riveting journalistic account, freelance writer Higgins chronicles the evolution of the sport from simple parachuting to BASE jumping (the acronym stands for building, antennae, span, and earth, which serve as launch points) to the development of these soaring, superhero-like armored flight suits. . . . For anyone who finds these kinds of emotional and precise accounts of risk, ambition, and victory irresistible, this is a must-read. A highflying, electrifying story of a treacherous sport in which every triumph is an eye blink away from becoming a disaster." —*Kirkus Reviews* (starred review)

"[Higgins's] action-packed book introduces a global coterie of remarkable characters who have dared life and limb. He describes escapades from sixties stunt parachuting to more contemporary BASE jumping, in which one takes flight off of selected worldwide buildings and geographical points to the experience of wingsuit flying—the maximum challenge. The author recounts the huge preparations, financial investments, psychological motivations, personal setbacks, and extraordinary aerial accomplishments that have gone into these extreme sports. . . . An engrossing and exhaustively researched account of extremists who challenge failure and death on a regular basis. Highly recommended for ultimate jumpers in particular, sports enthusiasts in general, and all public libraries." —*Library Journal* (starred review)

"A new tribe of aerial daredevils write their deeds in blood and glory . . . Journalist Higgins sings the exploits and charisma of 'wing-suit' pilots. . . . The book is mainly a chronicle of death-defying stunts: mishaps are plenty grisly when wingsuiters traveling at 100 mph encounter anything denser than air, and the body count is high. . . . [A] tribute to the exaltation of defying death; one extreme parachutist 'felt somehow reborn into the world' on his first outing, 'as if scales had been stripped from his eyes.' These effusions won't move everyone to a conversion experience, but Higgins's account is hair-raising enough to hold the reader's interest." —*Publishers Weekly*

"Most of us dream of flying, but it is the exceptional person who actually tries it. Matt Higgins takes readers deep into the extreme and fascinating world of BASE jumpers and wingsuit pilots, those rare birds who risk their lives for a few exhilarating, gravity-defying seconds. *Bird Dream* is a beautifully crafted narrative, equal parts adrenaline rush and soulful meditation. From its first sentence, this book soars." —Susan Casey, author of *The Wave* and *The Devil's Teeth*

"Wingsuit fliers like Jeb Corliss and Gary Connery change the definition of 'impossible,' often at the expense of life and limb. Capturing the essence of such entrepreneurs of the extreme is like trying to grab sparks. In *Bird Dream*, Matt Higgins does just that with writing that is crisp, exhilarating, and exhaustively researched. A must-read about ultimate quests—and their costs."   —James M. Tabor, author of *Blind Descent*

"Some people dare to imagine human flight; others dare to don wingsuits and leap birdlike into the void. A breathtaking narrative of outsized courage and irreverent boundary breaking, Matt Higgins's *Bird Dream* captures human jumps that defy the rational mind, that duel with gravity's inexorable pull, and that tango with the ever-present threat of dismemberment and death."   —James S. Hirsch, author of *Willie Mays*

"Matt Higgins takes us on a thrilling ride with an international cast of visionaries, daredevils, and flat-out wingnuts who are pushing the limits of human flight. Higgins weaves a compelling tale that leaves us awestruck and inspired by those who refuse to be constrained by earthly boundries."
                                          —Joe Drape, author of *Our Boys*

"*Bird Dream* is *Born to Run* for the wingsuit BASE world. Matt Higgins has managed to straddle the difficult line between maintaining authenticity for insiders and opening this fringe lifestyle to outsiders. As a dedicated jumper myself, I found *Bird Dream* compelling and absolutely undiluted."
                        —Steph Davis, climber, BASE jumper, wingsuit pilot, and
                                       author of *Learning to Fly*

PENGUIN BOOKS

BIRD DREAM

Matt Higgins is a freelance journalist whose writing has appeared in *The New York Times*, *The Village Voice*, *Popular Mechanics*, *Outside*, and *ESPN the Magazine*. He lives in western New York with his wife and their sons.

BIRD DREAM

Adventures at the Extremes of Human Flight

MATT HIGGINS

PENGUIN BOOKS

PENGUIN BOOKS
Published by the Penguin Group
Penguin Group (USA) LLC
375 Hudson Street
New York, New York 10014

USA | Canada | UK | Ireland | Australia
New Zealand | India | South Africa | China
penguin.com
A Penguin Random House Company

First published in the United States of America by The Penguin Press,
a member of Penguin Group (USA) LLC, 2014
Published in Penguin Books 2015

Photograph credits appear on page 291.

THE LIBRARY OF CONGRESS HAS CATALOGED THE HARDCOVER
EDITION AS FOLLOWS:
Higgins, Matt.
Bird dream : adventures at the extremes of human flight / Matt
Higgins.
pages cm
Includes bibliographical references and index.
ISBN 978-1-59420-465-4 (hc.)
ISBN 978-0-14-312746-8 (pbk.)
1. Wingsuit flying.   I. Title.
GV770.28.H54 2014
797.5'5—dc23
2014005399

Printed in the United States of America
10 9 8 7 6 5 4 3 2 1

DESIGNED BY NICOLE LAROCHE

BASE jumping and wingsuit piloting are extreme and extremely
dangerous sports. The publisher does not advocate these sports to
readers and is not liable for any injuries that may result to readers who
decide to pursue these sports.

For Ann

It's wonderful to climb the liquid mountains of the sky. Behind me and before me is God and I have no fears.

—*Helen Keller*

CONTENTS

Part III
LANDING

AUTHOR'S NOTE

These pages are the result of five years of research, reporting, and writing, a process that required travel on four continents and exploration of internal landscapes I hadn't known existed.

For years I had been writing about so-called extreme sports, such as skateboarding, snowboarding, big-wave surfing, and free-style motocross. So it seemed natural to editors at the *New York Times* that I should look into BASE jumping, an activity that could hardly appear more extreme. It was during the course of my research that I discovered wingsuit flying and learned that some pilots had ambitions to actually land without a parachute. The idea captivated me from the start.

When I began, there was no guarantee that anyone would succeed in flying and landing without a chute. But to dwell on that possibility, it seemed, missed the point. The point was that in a unique and fascinating sphere of sports, men (mostly men, anyway) were willing to confront a stark choice: succeed or possibly die trying. The high stakes and commitment required by practitioners appealed to my most basic instincts as a journalist; the challenge, and joy, would come from uncovering their humanity.

In the course of examining the characters, culture, training, and courage required to perform a BASE jump with a wingsuit, I would come to meditate on questions concerning the nature of risk: *What kind of person not only approaches the edge, but then leaps off? Why are some attracted to scenarios that seem counter to the most basic instincts for self-preservation? Do they suffer from a deficit of fear? Is their behavior pathological? Which specific skills are required for survival?*

Bird Dream is an attempt to answer those questions and scores more encountered along the way.

BIRD DREAM

INTRODUCTION

Who are these that fly like a cloud . . . ?

—*Isaiah 60:8*

SATURDAY, JULY 16, 2011

On the morning that would make him famous, mountains upon mountains stretched to the horizon, and the air at seven thousand feet above sea level came cool and thin. An occasional gust bent thick grass on the ledge around his black boots. And more than a mile below, in a plush green valley, sun caught the waters of the Walensee and warmed cobblestones in a distant Swiss village along the lakeshore. It was one of those glorious days. The view, the sun and wind on your cheeks, made you grateful just to be alive.

"What do you reckon, ten miles an hour?" one of his companions asked Jeb about the wind. "Twelve?" Jeb was Jeb Corliss, a thirty-five-year-old stuntman and BASE jumper from California—"BASE" being an acronym for "buildings, antennas, spans (bridges), and earth (cliffs)," the primary objects that practitioners leap from. Jeb had plunged from the Eiffel Tower, the Golden Gate Bridge, Angel Falls, in Venezuela, and the Petronas Towers, in Kuala Lumpur, Malaysia; from countless mountainsides; and into a cave in Mexico more than a thousand feet deep. With a thousand jumps and counting, he was one of the leading lights in the most dangerous sport yet devised.

"More," Jeb replied, not taking note of the scenery, his mouth hard-set, conveying the seriousness of what he was about to attempt.

———————

HIS COMPANIONS on the ledge that morning were a Swiss graduate student named Gian, a British model with a West Country accent named Jessica, and an American reporter with a notebook and pen—and a case of nerves over what was coming. Jeb stood out among this group, as he tended to in any gathering. Rawboned, six feet three inches tall, and sharp-featured, he dressed all in black, from hiking boots to cotton pants to a spring jacket. On his head, a black knit beanie covered a scalp usually shaved smooth as a lightbulb but which was showing a bit of stubble this day. Modern mirrored sunglasses shielded his eyes. At his feet sat a black nylon stash bag, from which he had pulled gear moments earlier. Out came his parachute rig, helmet, a pair of goggles equipped with GPS sensors, gloves (all of which were black, too), the latest miniature point-of-view (POV) cameras, and, of course, his wingsuit.

Nearby on the ledge, the Swiss BASE Association had placed a comfort station consisting of a weatherproof black box containing cigarettes, rope, chocolate, and a logbook and first-aid kit. Above the box, a sign read:

SPUTNIK

After some misunderstandings with locals and negative press about jumping here the situation is relaxed right now.
Please use some common sense to keep it this way.
Thanks.

- This is an advanced BASE jump suitable only for experienced wingsuit pilots.
- Know your limits.
- Rockdrop is about 230 m/750 ft.
- Watch out for airtraffic.
- Please no close flybys on paragliders.
- No littering.
- Let the world know you have been here, write something in the book.

- In an emergency call Rega helicopter rescue: +41 333 333 333.
- The Mountain you stand on is called Hinderrugg, exit coordinates are 47.15323 N 9.302303 E.
- Enjoy the jump.

One mile below as the crow flies, other members of Jeb's team had assembled along a meadow dotted with wildflowers and echoing with the slow clang of cowbells. The meadow disappeared abruptly at the mouth of a jagged S-shaped fissure in the mountain, called Schattenloch Canyon, a feature known colloquially as the Crack. This seam twisted through the earth for a few hundred yards before ending sharply at a sheer cliff dropping straight into the valley to Walenstadt, the village from which Jeb and his accomplices had set out by car in the blue hours before dawn.

Two locals, brothers named Christian and Andreas Gubser, had volunteered to act as ground crew. An attorney and a surveyor, respectively, they had connected with Jeb on Facebook after seeing video of him jumping at the site months earlier. Their eagerness to help came from nothing other than a chance to witness something spectacular firsthand.

The brothers took up positions around the Crack, Andreas suspended in a harness tethered to a gnarled old tree on the edge of the ravine. Through a long camera lens he watched his brother, who, wearing a red Montreal Canadiens T-shirt, stood at the mouth of the Crack, clutching by their strings one red and one blue party balloon acquired from a nearby McDonald's. Stationed to Christian's immediate left was a father-and-son camera crew from Germany hired by the ABC program *20/20*. Their producer, Marc, waited below, on the outskirts of Walenstadt, with a camera to capture the final sequence as Jeb came in for a landing.

UP ON THE LEDGE, Jeb had pulled on a black wingsuit, an innovation that, aeronautically speaking, is more flying squirrel than bird or plane.

Wingsuits are not new; they have captured the imagination of storytellers since man first dreamed of flying. From Icarus to Wile E. Coyote, who crashed into a mesa on his attempt, the results have usually been disastrous.

Yet a new design, developed during the past two decades, has made them safer and more predictable. These modern suits feature two layers of tightly woven nylon sewed between the legs and between the arms and torso of a jumpsuit, creating vented wings with cells inside that fill with air and create lift, allowing for forward motion and aerial maneuvers while also slowing descent. Unlike skydiving or BASE jumping, in which trajectories are pretty much vertical, wingsuit flying creates a third dimension by providing glide. Pilots fly along a downward slope, expressed in a ratio of, say, 1:1—for every foot of forward motion, they descend one foot. Some have achieved ratios as high as 3:1, moving three feet forward for every foot of descent, similar to the glide of a parachute. As wingsuits, which cost about $1,000, have become more sophisticated, so have the pilots. The best fliers, and there are not many, trace the contours of cliffs, ridges, and mountainsides, in what's known as "proximity" or "terrain" flying. That's what Jeb was about to do at the Crack, the equivalent of a double-black diamond for difficulty.

Grasping a cable bolted to the mountain as a handhold, Jeb traversed a terrifyingly exposed stretch of ledge, the fabric between his legs restricting movement, and arrived at another grassy area; this was the exit. He had jumped here eleven times, the last time months earlier, rocketing over the head of Christian, who had been holding a pair of balloons as a target. The vortices in the wake of Jeb's wingsuit had ripped the balloons from Christian's hand and spun them into the Crack, making for stunning video footage, which had stirred a sensation on YouTube and lured the team from *20/20* on this day for another round of what everyone was referring to as a wingsuit William Tell.

THIS TIME JEB PHONED Christian to tell him to expect a jump in two minutes and secured the phone in a pocket. He pulled on a shiny black helmet with cameras mounted on booms like antennae. The helmet covered his head and mouth, and goggles shielded his eyes, making him look like those robot DJs from Daft Punk. He clipped more cameras to his suit. On his back he wore a parachute rig containing a single canopy. In the event of a malfunction, there wouldn't be sufficient altitude for a reserve.

"Ten seconds!" Jeb called to the others on the ledge, and then: "Three, two, one . . . See ya!"

Every jump is a drama in four acts. In this case, the first part, Jeb's launch, was unstable. He plunged head first, off-balance, an eight-second drop to the ground below.

Kicking his feet furiously like a swimmer, Jeb gained stability. Arms canted away from his body, legs apart, he resembled Leonardo da Vinci's famous Vitruvian Man pose. Air rushed into the vents on his suit, and his wings inflated. Jeb glided toward the meadow, gaining speed, mountain terrain and evergreen trees far below. Half a minute passed in flight as he made his approach, air roaring into his helmet like the sound of static. Soaring over the meadow, his shadow vanished beneath his suit, testifying to how close to the ground he was cruising.

Tall pines bracket the entrance to the Crack like goalposts. Aiming for them, he bore down on Christian's red T-shirt like a black bull to a matador's cape. Moving at 120 miles per hour, Jeb covered five hundred feet in three seconds, an unholy roar rising up as his suit sliced the air. He was bearing down on his target—fast!

Christian watched him approach, his trepidation growing. Feet apart, Christian steadied, balloons bobbing above him like thought bubbles. Jeb appeared low, possibly too low. A voice in Christian's head told him, *Dive! Dive! Dive!* and he lurched to the left, hitting the dirt hard on his chest and practically landing on a startled cameraman, crouched low, viewfinder pressed to his eye.

With a dark flash, Jeb burst past where Christian's head had been only a moment earlier. Six feet off the deck, the leading edge of his wing snagged the balloons' strings before they could float away.

Jeb did not flinch. Navigating the ravine in seconds, he emerged out the end, high above town. Reaching back with his right hand to grasp his parachute handle, Jeb pitched the pilot chute to the side, in one motion concluding the second act of his jump, and commencing the third, his parachute opening. His square black canopy bloomed instantly, snapping open like the crack of a whip. The final act of this jump, any jump, required landing, and as Jeb lined up, boots touching gently in freshly mown grass in a farmer's field, gray slab of mountain looming behind, he giggled over how close he'd come.

Up on the mountain, though, they were not laughing. Not the cameramen from ABC especially. They were galled that Jeb appeared to risk not only his own life but that of another man. Christian confessed to being shaken up too. "I think this jump goes bad," he said. "It's *so* close."

An element of near disaster would make for compelling footage, though, everyone had to admit. No one could anticipate precisely how compelling the sequence would prove once placed in a nice package and set loose online. Still, they knew they had something special. GPS readings told how Jeb topped out at 123 miles per hour during the 1:20-second flight, traveling a total of three miles.

*T*he following day, the jump over, footage secured, the ABC contingent departed, and Jeb sat in the lobby of the Hotel Churfirsten, across the motorway from the train station with a passel of wingsuit pilots, in town to test their skills from Sputnik too. None of them had their own camera crew in tow, with a producer, reporter, and personal ground crew. They weren't even staying at the hotel. They had shacked up at a campground, went without showers. They had only come to the hotel for the free wi-fi. In the lobby, they peered at laptop screens and smartphones, checking weather reports, sending e-mail, and updating social media, electrical cords snaking underfoot to feed at outlets, half a dozen conversations carrying on at once.

Jeb talked with two other pilots from California. At rest, he tended to crackle with nervous energy, head tick-tocking, legs pumping like sewing machine needles. He could be loud at times, delivering jeremiads in stentorian tones when excited or angry. Yet he was calm on this afternoon, passions stilled by the close brush with danger a day earlier, all of his quirks, tics, and contradictions went quiet and settled into a serene sort of winsome charm.

"China has forced me to become a little more scientific," he said, his voice slightly nasal, speaking in the patois of a surfer, which he is. He was referring to a stunt two months hence, in which he would attempt to fly through a gaping hole in the side of a mountain in central China. The stunt would be the first of its kind and the featured event during a daylong spectacular sponsored by the Chinese arm of energy drink maker Red Bull. Jeb had invited several of his friends and fellow pilots along to participate in the extravaganza. And he was treating his jumps that summer in Switzerland as training for a flight that would stretch his skills into unknown territory.

With a multimillion-dollar budget and a national television audience in China, the stunt would be the biggest of Jeb's career, a career he began with clandestine parachute jumps from the windows of high-rise hotels. But Jeb was finished sneaking around, trespassing, and operating in legal gray areas. The end had arrived in April 2006, when he had worn an elaborate disguise and attempted to parachute from the eighty-sixth-floor observation deck of the Empire State Building, where he was famously captured and handcuffed while dangling on a ledge a thousand feet above Thirty-third Street. His legal problems got him fired from his job as host of a show on Discovery called *Stunt Junkies* and prompted a reevaluation of his life. He had flirted with walking away from jumping, but the rise of wingsuit proximity flights drew him back. He kept seeing video of young pilots, kids he'd never heard of, making marvelous flights in the mountains. So he had been lured back to the new wingsuit thing.

Even during his days of cat-and-mouse with the authorities, though, Jeb's imagination had been fired by a grander ambition. In the first, formative years of the twenty-first century, he sought to achieve one of the last great challenges on earth. Jeb Corliss wanted to fly. Not like the Wright brothers, but the way we do in our dreams. He wanted to jump from a helicopter and land without using a parachute.

He was not alone. Around the globe, at least a half-dozen groups—in France, South Africa, Australia, Russia, and the United States—had the same goal. Although nobody was waving a flag, the quest evoked the spirit of nations' pursuits of Everest and the North and South Poles.

The landing, as one might expect, posed the biggest challenge, and each group had a different approach. In France, a wingsuit flier and champion skydiver figured that a pilot could glide to a stop on a snowy mountainside. "The basic idea is getting parallel to the snow so we don't have a vertical speed at all, there is no shock, and then *slide*," he explained, while also acknowledging the risks: "You might do it well one time and try another time and crash and die."

In South Africa, a costume designer for the motion picture industry turned wingsuit maker had a suit in mind that would allow pilots to land on their feet along a horizontal surface. "I think people will recognize this makes sense," she said. "Why didn't someone think of this long ago? I'm hoping that will be the reaction."

In the meantime, Jeb pursued his own plans, talking publicly about how he intended to land headfirst, on his stomach, at 120 miles per hour, using a massive landing apparatus that would borrow from the principles of Nordic ski jumping. The project would require millions of dollars, a team of engineers and scientists, and uncommon vision and courage.

"We laugh and we think those guys are crazy, but they're not," said a physics professor at St. Louis University who for thirteen years performed parachute-inflation research for the U.S. Army. "I will not be the one person who thinks that they're lunatics or they're stupid. These folks are very smart."

"Is it possible?" asked a gruff aeronautical engineer from California who had worked on projects for NASA and the U.S. military and who created his own concept for landing without a parachute. "Yeah! Anything's possible. It requires time, money, and innovation." He added: "Everybody wants to be the first one to do it."

For those inclined to wonder why—*why* dedicate many years and many millions of dollars in a perilous and uncertain outcome that could claim your life—Jeb possessed a ready answer: "Because everybody thinks that it's not possible," he explained. "The point is to show people anything can be done. If you want to do amazing things, then you have to take amazing risks."

And with his amazing risk at the Crack, Jeb appeared at last on the verge of assembling the final components—including funding—for what he called the Wingsuit Landing Project. In the coming weeks, before the summer was over, video footage of his close call at the Crack would go viral, luring many millions of views, as well as interest from TV executives eager to hear his proposal for landing.

Among those who marveled at the video footage from the Crack that summer was another wingsuit pilot, from England, who worked as a stunt-man for TV and film. This particular pilot had no access to major funding, and hardly anyone knew who he was. He could not claim a name or much reputation within the wingsuit world, although he had a record of per-forming a range of dangerous stunts safely. Yet he possessed vision and an obdurate temperament not easily swayed from a task. Inspired by what he had seen of Jeb at the Crack, by late summer this pilot would vow to be-come the first to fly and land without a parachute. His reasons were per-sonal, and he made no public announcement of his plans at first. That's why no one would see him coming. Jeb had no way of knowing, but this contender was quietly making moves, setting up a final, frantic finish that would nearly cost one of them his life.

Yet there was no hint of all that was to come as the pilots sat in the lobby of the hotel, debating where to seek refuge as the weather turned wet and windy in advance of an unseasonable cold front advancing across Europe. One of the pilots mentioned Arco, a charming small town at the base of a mountain in northern Italy. France, outside Chamonix, was also briefly considered. But some French jumpers had resorted to vigilantism against interlopers, and no one had the vital connections, so the idea was dropped.

While all of this was under discussion, the brakes of a touring bus sighed in the parking lot outside, and pensioners entered the lobby, gabbing loudly in Swiss German. An older woman, gray hair in a bun, finally waddled over to the pilots. "Are you da fly-ing boys?" she asked in lilting English.

"Yes!" Jeb said with great gusto. And pointing to Steph Davis, a rock climber and pilot from Moab, Utah, and one of the few women in the wingsuit scene, he added: "And the flying girl!"

The woman clapped her hands. Her companions, all male, were touring singers from Bern, she explained, and they had seen footage of pilots flying the Crack and wanted to offer a song in tribute?

"Sure," Jeb said.

As he and the other pilots listened politely, the singers belted out harmonies. None of the pilots had any notion what the singing was about, but it sounded traditional, authentic, stuff of the volk, evoking all the Swiss tropes. When the song was done, the pilots applauded the gesture with an understanding that, yes, their feats on the mountain had moved men to song. They could not imagine how, soon, footage of Jeb's close call at the Crack would, buoyed by a popular song, captivate the wider world.

IN THE END, fleeing wind and rain in Walenstadt, which grounded any chance at flight, Jeb and some of the others headed southwest into the Bernese Alps of Switzerland, winding up in Lauterbrunnen, an ideal redoubt in which to ride out bad weather, if only because of diversions. Lauterbrunnen is a fairy-tale town, located in a steep-sided valley with neck-straining views of the frosty peaks of the Eiger, the Mönch, and the Jungfrau, some thirteen thousand feet high. The gray cliffs bracketing the valley rise two thousand feet in some places and issue a series of thin waterfalls, filling the air with a magical light-altering mist and feeding a cold glacial stream, the blue color of a barber's antiseptic, which courses through town and down the valley to where cowbells clang in green pastures. The presence of so much moisture lends the valley air a faint mineral taste and, perhaps lyrical inspiration. Byron, who came to Lauterbrunnen fleeing the private storms of his own life, compared the largest cascade, Staubbach Falls, to the "long white tale of the pale horse upon which death is mounted in the *Book of Revelations.*"

Eventually, many in the valley would complain that it was the BASE jumpers who brought death to the valley as they launched from the cliffs. Jeb had been coming for ten years, staying at the Hotel Oberland, a modest, staid place on the main drag, with green painted shutters and geraniums in the window boxes. In that time, owners Mark and Ursula Nolan had gotten to know him well. A sturdy and gregarious Australian with white hair, Mark Nolan arrived while on a rugby tour and never left, marrying a local woman, building his business interests. Mark recalled that when Jeb first arrived, a decade earlier, he spoke so loudly on the terrace during dinner one night that other guests asked to be moved. Nolan had to request that Jeb turn down the volume. "He used to be crazier and take more risks," Mark says, "but now he's calculated, like an athlete."

The Oberland is a quiet place, where families feel comfortable staying. Much of the extracurricular action in town takes place down the road, at the Hotel Horner, a four-story wooden structure with a steep gabled roof and long eaves. You never know who you will encounter there, a guy wearing a T-shirt with the words "Fuck Normal Life" printed on the front, or a group of jumpers seated on a table on the porch, wielding a set of crotchety electric shears, giving each other Mohawks. Many jumpers lodge upstairs in rooms that start at thirty-five Swiss francs (about $40) a night. Lodgers pass most nights and days gathered at tables on the stone porch at the pub downstairs, nursing beers and rumors and gossip in the long, dull hours between jumps that inevitably make up the bulk of a jumper's life.

In the convivial atmosphere of rough wood and dim lighting on the first floor, regulars and repeat customers cultivate reputations and acquire nicknames, such as Black Simon, Jewbag, Special Tom, the Girl Whisperer, and Douggs. Still, an egalitarian spirit prevails, and newcomers are always welcome.

One summer afternoon, a smallish dark-haired kid bounded up the porch and stopped short. "You can't be Jeb Corliss," he said.

Jeb looked up from a table. "Hey, dude," he said. "How's it goin'?"

"I just arrived from Argentina," the kid said. Continuing into the bar, he announced that he had just met the famous Jeb Corliss outside.

No one inside was too impressed, not least because they already knew Jeb; that, and getting starstruck constituted bad form.

Yet that's what it had been like in the summer of 2011. Trainloads of newcomers unloaded in Lauterbrunnen and failed to observe established codes on which rested a delicate and hard-won relationship between visiting jumpers and a local community unconvinced they wanted them. Media coverage of fatalities in the valley had earned Lauterbrunnen a reputation as the place where jumpers go to die, a potentially serious problem for an economy promoting a tourist idyll.

From August 2010 through August 2011, seven jumpers were killed, bringing the total in the valley to twenty-eight over two decades. On July 23, 2011, *Berner Zeitung,* the daily newspaper in Bern, published a story beneath the headline "Reckless Jumpers Annoy Valley Dwellers." *Der Spiegel,* in distant Germany, followed, stating the case more forcefully: "Village Appalled by Thrill Seekers' Deaths." Both papers told of jumpers flouting posted rules governing their activities. Some had failed to pay for a registration card, the proceeds from which compensate farmers for meadows trampled when jumpers land there, affecting their silage.

Ruined grass was one thing, but much more serious were incidents in which schoolchildren witnessed jumpers screaming to their deaths from the cliffs. The papers told how some valley residents wanted jumping banned altogether.

Mark Nolan embodied the ambivalence. In addition to running a hotel, he worked on the local ambulance rescue, observing jumpers broken physically and emotionally on the valley floor. "I think they're selfish people," he admitted. "They're gone. Think about the people they leave behind— friends, loved ones."

Meanwhile, each summer more arrived. In 2010, an estimated fifteen thousand jumps took place in the valley. To Dr. Bruno Durrer, the valley doctor responsible for treating injured jumpers and scooping up the dead, the figures suggested that the sport was actually getting safer, at least in Lauterbrunnen. Durrer had been present for the first BASE fatality in the valley, on April 14, 1994. And his records showed 170 accidents since, with an average of fewer than two fatalities annually. Yet 2011 was shaping up to be an especially deadly year worldwide. Citing twenty-one fatalities that year, *Outside* magazine would deem BASE the "world's deadliest sport." Of those deaths, twelve involved wingsuits.

Even the doctor's support for jumpers had begun to waver following incidents in the summer of 2011. "It's that this year now we had crazy groups coming into the valley that didn't actually play into the rules," he explained. "And we have rules established here."

The rules required jumping only at marked exits, having at least the minimum required level of experience, and respecting the airspace of para-gliders and the helicopter ferrying skydivers to altitude. Enforcement was lax, however, and jumpers relied mainly on self-policing. "Now we had a few groups that didn't care about the existing rules," Durrer said. "They're ruin-ing the goodwill we have in the valley towards the BASE-jumping scene."

One of the doctor's patients was a former Marine from California who went by "Jewbag," and his example was instructive. A hard landing from an exit called La Mousse had left him limping out of the health clinic in an ankle splint while clutching anti-inflammatory ointment and pain meds. Durrer had instructed him to wait two to three weeks before jumping again. "But I'm only here a month," Jewbag said. "I'll be out there soon. I'm retarded."

Jeb had been incorrigible in his earlier days, too. He had a mentor who told him not to do certain things, which Jeb would do anyway. But he had learned to avoid some unnecessary risks, like jumping in foul weather. One morning, when the skies finally cleared and sun slanted in the front window at the Airtime café, Jeb scraped the last bites of egg from his fork and finalized plans to hike up to the High Nose, a promontory some two thousand feet above the valley floor and one of the more popular exits. Across from him at a varnished wooden table sat Joby Ogwyn, one of his closest friends that summer. Muscular, thirty-seven years old, with a nest of thick curls and an easygoing Louisiana twang, Joby was an accomplished high-altitude climber who had once been the youngest to scale the world's Seven Summits (the tallest mountains on each continent). He had been the youngest American to reach the summit of Everest, at twenty-four, earning an invitation to the White House, where he met President Clinton in the Oval Office. Next: he planned to launch from Everest with a wingsuit.

Joby had come to BASE jumping and wingsuits while hosting a show on the National Geographic Channel called *Adventure Wanted;* each episode revolved around his learning some new outdoor-sports discipline, from race car driving to bull riding to white water kayaking. He met Jeb at the Horner one night, and, given their shared background in television, they wound up hitting it off. It seemed only natural for Jeb to invite Joby to be a part of his project in China.

Stash bags slung over their shoulders, the two men made their way to the cable car station as parachutes and paragliders drifted from the cliffs behind them like tossed confetti. Somewhere unseen, the Air-Glaciers chopper thumped skydivers to altitude. At the cable car station they encountered other jumpers and joined them for a one-mile ride to Grütschalp, then a transfer to an electric train to Winteregg. From there, eight pilots hiked through thick stands of pine, and a logging operation, arriving twenty minutes later at an area of flat rocks where someone had placed a woodcut memorial in a notch reading STEFAN POR SIEMPRE, a reminder that men had died there.

Through the trees, the skies had turned the color of wet cement, and a rumble echoed across the valley, from either thunder or a distant avalanche.

Gearing up rapidly to beat the coming rain, they snapped POV cameras and clips into place. A quick call to the helicopter base and they were cleared to jump. With the chopper's flight path beneath the Nose, no one wanted a collision.

A short path wound to the exit, and any misstep would translate into a tumble straight to the valley floor, 1,910 feet below. In pairs, the pilots moved to the precipice, where two pine trees with knotty roots like rheumatic fingers gripped the rock. Beyond was a fifteen-second plunge to a certain demise. A length of climbing rope lashed to a tree provided a handhold on a vertiginous traverse to a slab of rock and dirt scarcely large enough to hold two people. The only thing between the ledge and the scenery of tiny farmsteads was an outcropping, a seven-second rock drop, and a hazard to anyone who didn't fly away urgently.

On the ledge, each man performed a final inspection of clips, fasteners, straps, and zippers, making sure cameras and GPS were activated. There were no histrionics or bravado, only supportive banter.

"Have fun!"

"Okay. You, too."

"Be safe!"

The first pair dove off, stable, arms wide, fabric on their suits fluttering like flags in a stiff wind until their wings inflated and went rigid with pressurized air. The pilots disappeared fast beneath the ledge, heading hard left, hugging the wall, in the direction of town.

THEY HAD ALL WOUND up in Lauterbrunnen eventually: the Italian beauty, the magician from Finland, the Australian computer programmer, the financial analyst from England, the professional skier from Norway, the former bricklayer in Florida, and an international collection of champion skydivers and professional stunt performers. Anyone serious about BASE jumping and wingsuits passed through the valley, their inheritance a hazy history of human flight that spanned centuries and continents and included many thousands of jumps, from before recorded time and through the Depression, a heyday of deadly homemade winged contraptions flown at barnstorming air shows around the world. Earlier trials were messy, ending in tragedy; it was not until recent times that science and skill had finally caught up with human longing.

Some would flirt seriously with fulfilling an ancient archetypal idea of flight. Much of their training was while falling from the big walls of the Lauterbrunnen Valley.

FOR SEVERAL WEEKS THAT summer, though, it was mainly rain that fell. When the weather turns, jumpers catch up on laundry and e-mail and paying bills. They read and watch movies, too. But when lonely or bored, they frequently lapse into a barroom routine, like skiers or climbers or anyone who spends too much time in mountain towns. In Lauterbrunnen, bad weather can mean brisk business at the Horner. Because he does not drink, such gatherings quickly grow tedious for Jeb, if he attends at all. One dark and rainy night when he remained holed up at his hotel, the bar action picked up early.

At the center, as he often is, was Douggs, a garrulous Australian with the Christian name Christopher McDougall. With his arms, back, and neck covered in lurid tattoos, his hair in a Mohawk, and his ears and eyebrow pierced, Douggs was a well-known character about town. He had overstayed his visa and was dodging authorities for as long as possible, hiding in plain sight. Returning home to Australia meant he would be back at work as a carpenter, or inspecting offshore oil platforms somewhere. Douggs did not love the work, yet he maintained a bright outlook on life, a philosophy he expanded on in a madcap, hilarious memoir, *Confessions of an Idiot*. His upbeat attitude and often deranged quips, delivered in a voice corroded from hard living, made him one of the more popular figures among his fellow pilots. Douggs had known Jeb for years, and it was a given that he would be invited to China to participate in his fly-through event.

Rain drumming the awning overhead, Douggs huddled in amber light on the porch at the Horner, brown liter beer bottle in hand, Aussie voice booming above the crowd. He was in his customary high spirits. "I get about one job every year or two, and we're gonna change that, aren't we, Joby?"

"Yes, we are," Joby said in his down-home Southern accent.

"That's all I want to hear. I don't care if it's a lie. I don't care if nothing happens. I just need a little hope to get me through. It gives you so much more drive to do stuff. Worst-case scenario, I'm going to live and jump off shit." Douggs laughed, eyes glowing, and added: "But I'd like to do *cool* shit."

Several members of the Red Bull Air Force, a cadre of parachute sport athletes sponsored by the energy drink company, had been haunting the Horner and the high cliffs around Lauterbrunnen all week. The Red Bull Air Force, in the minds of many jumpers, had coveted status, having mastered the art of getting paid for their stunts. They carried themselves with an easy grace.

Yet Jeb was the biggest name in the life, having fashioned a career with his black wardrobe, black talk, and appearances on television delivering homilies about mortality and living one's dreams. Still, his shtick tended to get under the skin of some of his peers.

"People only get to see his spiel during a documentary," Douggs said in Jeb's defense, "which is what he has to do to earn a living. It's done in a way that BASE jumpers will say, 'The shit he's saying, he brings down the sport.'" Douggs had a ready reply to such a charge: "The sport's down already. He imparts truth in a way non-jumpers will sometimes get shocked by, sometimes appreciate, sometimes get emotional by. He works harder than anyone, by the way. I tried it for a while. You've got to work your balls off to get one out of twenty projects. Most people can't sustain that. And he's in a position where he can now, whereas the rest of us have to go back to work."

Douggs and Joby agreed that Jeb's avoidance of booze and drugs had contributed to his success. "I wouldn't like to give him anything, either," Douggs added, muttering darkly and shaking his head. "Jeb on pills? Jesus!"

All week in Lauterbrunnen, Jeb had elicited mixed reactions. "Some people don't like him," a kiwi wingsuit pilot at the High Nose admitted with a shrug at the mere mention of Jeb Corliss's name. "I reckon he's good for the sport."

While out walking the valley one afternoon, Jeb happened to meet a Dutch jumper who had moments earlier plunged from the High Nose and was stuffing his parachute into a stash bag at the edge of a farmer's field. The guy introduced himself as Jens.

"Hi, good to meet you," Jeb said as they shook hands.

"You don't say *your* name?" Jens replied, an edge to his voice. "Everyone *knows* you?"

Taken aback, Jeb stammered a half apology, although Jens obviously knew exactly who he was.

"They're all jealous of Jeb because he's loud and American and one of the best," Mark Nolan would say of critics. "I don't think many could do what he does."

And yet the advent of online video had made the prospect of instant fame and glory, in the manner of Jeb Corliss, suddenly seem tangible for a fresh generation of pilots. "Someone like Jeb has slowly worked his way over fifteen years to get where he is now," Douggs said on the crowded porch at the Horner. "These new punks are coming in and trying to do it in six months. And they haven't carried their friends' dead bodies. They haven't dealt with the injuries, and they see YouTube and say, 'I want—'"

"'To go through the Crack,'" Joby said, completing the thought. "'I'm going to put my cameras on and go through the Crack like Jeb Corliss.' Bad idea. You might make it. Probably not. That's a super-advanced deal. He's doing multiple jumps to hone it down."

As the night wore on, conversation would veer in many directions, from the serious to the strange to the profane, banter steady as the rain. A man would threaten to expose himself. "Let me fluff it up for a second," he was heard to say. "I don't want to be embarrassed." A burst of laughter followed from the crowd. Cosseted under the awning in the close heat of human contact, cigarette smoke, and the occasional cloud of cannabis—the clink of empty bottles marking the passing hours—the crowd on the porch would grow more congested, the night gauzier. Outside, the pavement was slick with streetlight and gathering rain poured in torrents from the big walls, roaring like applause for the flying men and women of the Lauterbrunnen Valley, safe at least for another night.

Part One

TAKEOFF

Chapter 1
BEGINNINGS . . .

> We are not the sole authors of our destiny, each
> of us; our destinies are entangled—messily, un-
> predictably.
>
> —*Firmin DeBrabander, philosopher*

PERRIS, CALIFORNIA, LATE TWENTIETH CENTURY

For centuries, people have jumped off objects with primitive parachutes. During the Age of Discovery, in fifteenth-century Italy, Leonardo da Vinci sketched a pyramid-shaped device to save those who during fires were trapped in the upper reaches of stone towers, hundreds of feet above medieval settlements. Meant to be constructed of linen and wood, the parachute was among dozens of concepts that never made it further than the prolific polymath genius's drafting table.

The French would eventually give the parachute its name, which means *"to prevent falling."* But early constructions were crude, without manuals, tutorials, or design specs. And testing was dicey. In 1783, a physicist successfully plunged from the top of an observatory in Montpellier, France, with a design similar to Leonardo's concept. But attempts just as often went wrong. In 1837, a watercolor artist tested a two-hundred-pound creation, built in the shape of an inverted cone, from a balloon over an expectant crowd in south London. When the chute broke apart in the sky, the parachutist plunged to his death in a field.

By the twentieth century, structural steel construction had made the first skyscrapers possible, and a dozen vertiginous buildings had altered

Manhattan's profile. It was the job of Frederick R. Law, a steeplejack, to maintain the city's rising monuments to commerce, painting flagpoles on the likes of the Singer and Pulitzer buildings. During a period when work was slack, Law acquired the necessary permits and a camera crew and, on a February day in 1912, parachuted from the torch atop the Statue of Liberty, more than 300 feet above New York Harbor. His parachute was primitive by modern standards and lacked any steering mechanism, so Law swam desperately through the air to avoid a dip in the frigid harbor. Limping away following a hard landing on coping along the island's perimeter, he declined a request for an interview by the *New York Times*. But four days later, Law stepped from a taxi on the Brooklyn Bridge and parachuted 133 feet into an East River choked with ice as movie cameras captured the scene. A waiting tug rescued him. Two months would pass before his next act, a leap from the thirty-first floor of the Bankers Trust Building, at the intersection of Broad and Wall Streets. With stockbrokers and newsboys gaping, Law settled on the roof of the Sub-Treasury Building. According to the *Times*, he called over the edge to a stunned crowd on Nassau Street that he was unhurt and "feeling fine."

For the next fifty years, an occasional daring soul would make a fixed-object jump—a building here, a cliff or tower there, and the occasional bridge—but the resulting headlines and notoriety resulting from these stunts was fleeting. A new era had opened following the breakthrough in powered aircraft flight by Wilbur and Orville Wright in Kitty Hawk, North Carolina, on December 17, 1903. Two world wars would transform aviation, and beget recreational skydiving. By the 1960s a growing population of experienced and skilled parachutists would include some with a thirst for stronger thrills than exiting airplanes. Appraising the proportions of large fixed objects, they allowed their imagination to roam unchecked.

That is more or less what led two men to pose for a snapshot at a trailhead beneath towering ponderosa pines on a sunny July day in 1966. That day, an accountant named Mike Pelkey and a truck driver named Brian Schubert, both from Barstow, California, would launch from El Capitan, a hunk of cracked gray granite like an elephant's hide, rising three thousand sheer feet above California's Yosemite Valley. They wore bulky military-issue parachutes, and on the way down both men were battered mercilessly against the cliff by winds, ending up with multiple fractures. When their ordeal made national news, Schubert told a reporter for the *Los Angeles Times*, "I would suggest no one else do it."

It says something about a strain of skydivers that his warning served as a challenge instead. By 1971 a stuntman named Rick Sylvester would ski off the top of El Cap with a parachute (a move he repeated five years later on Canada's Baffin Island as a double for Roger Moore in the opening sequence of the James Bond film *The Spy Who Loved Me*). Then, in July 1975, a skydiver from Queens named Owen Quinn sneaked to the top of the North Tower of the World Trade Center while posing as an antenna repairman and plunged 1,368 feet into Manhattan, the sight of lesser buildings rushing up at him, like "jumping into a glass full of pencils." Months later, as workmen constructed the CN Tower 1,510 feet over Toronto, a member of the crew, Bill Eustace, parachuted off and was promptly fired.

Taking note of these pioneering jumps was a skydiving cinematographer in California named Carl Boenish, who had filmed scenes in *The Gypsy Moths,* a 1969 Hollywood production about a wingsuit starring Burt Lancaster, Gene Hackman, and Deborah Kerr. An original thinker who called his skydiving documentaries "film poems," Boenish avoided alcohol, drank buttermilk, and believed in the restorative power of avocados. Passionate and something of a proselytizer, he was, friends suggest, ideally suited to dream up a new sport.

On August 8, 1978, Boenish coaxed four skydivers from a skydiving center in Lake Elsinore to travel some 275 miles north to the top of El Cap so he could film them. They used the latest parachute technology and tracking skills in an attempt to build on those earlier jumps.

The resulting footage created a sensation. "We couldn't believe we never thought of that before," Nick DiGiovanni, a former Marine and surfer who was working as a jump instructor when he watched the film's premiere at the Lake Elsinore drop zone, recalls about his reaction to the jump. "Instead of going, 'That's nuts, we'll never do that,' everyone was going, 'Man, I got to do that.'

"That changed my life that night," DiGiovanni says. "As that film made its way around the world, it changed a lot of people's lives."

Boenish launched from buildings, towers, bridges, and cliffs, and coined the name BASE after consulting a dictionary and finding the definition— "a platform on which someone stands"—and noting how the acronym lined up. He issued registration numbers to certify those who successfully jumped from each of the four objects, completing the BASE cycle. He created an organizing body and published *BASE Magazine,* all to lend respectability to this new pastime. He "opened" countless sites around the world, trained legions of new jumpers, and boasted to friends, "In twenty years, we'll be shutting down the streets below the World Trade Center and they'll let us jump."

He failed to anticipate the reaction of property owners worried about liability, though, or concerns among the skydiving hierarchy that these crazy jumpers would ruin a reputation for safety. The United States Parachute Association (USPA), the national governing body for skydiving, advertised the sport as a sensible recreational pursuit with a sterling safety record. Any association with a bunch of cowboys flinging themselves from buildings and bridges appeared to run counter to those claims. The very notion of jumping off a fixed object strikes terror in the hearts of most people and seems counter to the most basic instincts for self-preservation. Moreover, by dint of making a BASE jump, you were often flirting with breaking some law.

Access to buildings or antennas often required trespassing. The National Park Service maintains jurisdiction over many of the cliffs in the United States suitable for jumping. Clashes with jumpers prompted the Park Service to invoke a preexisting ban on parachutes, meant to prevent hunters from resupplying with backcountry airdrops. Some continued to jump in defiance, stoking what would be a long-running feud with Park Service rangers determined to capture and prosecute BASE enthusiasts.

The USPA went so far as to expel skydivers who performed BASE jumps, but it eventually reversed course after the jumpers brought a lawsuit.

"They thought we were just stupid," one early jumper would say about attitudes among skydivers toward BASE jumpers. "We were just illegal bandits. We were like criminals."

His advocacy for BASE pitted Boenish against his friends in skydiving, making him a pariah in a sport he had done much to develop and promote.

"It's funny; in the beginning we didn't keep it to ourselves, because we didn't think we had to," DiGiovanni says. "We thought when people see this, 'This is great. This is an accomplishment. This is amazing that humans can do this.' [Boenish] didn't realize and none of us realized that it would be against the law, considered reckless endangerment. We thought it would be the opposite. The sport didn't go underground until that occurred. We realized that we can't tell people we're doing this, or they're not going to let us do it."

*I*t was from the parched high desert of the Peninsular Ranges, an hour or so east from Los Angeles and San Diego, that Carl Boenish recruited his intrepid El Cap jumpers. It's a region where, on average, less than ten inches of rain falls annually. The lack of precipitation in the region would present a peculiar problem in the late 2000s, when, in Perris (population 68,000), ground zero for California's mortgage default crisis, the situation grew so dire that civic leaders approved painting green the burnt-out lawns of abandoned homes, to restore a sense of community pride.

The climate may not suit grass, but sunny blue skies make for a fertile skydiving environment. Two drop zones, Skydive Perris and Skydive Elsinore, eight miles down the road, lure enthusiasts from around the world, many of whom stay on and work as instructors, or take jobs at the parachute lofts where riggers make repairs and repack chutes into their containers. Or they find employment at the related businesses attached to the airfields, doing whatever it takes to support their skydiving habit. It was from this population of dedicated, accomplished, and driven skydivers that an incubator for BASE would develop. It was not due to the presence of any particular cliffs, buildings, bridges, or notable antennas in the area; the advantages owed more to an emerging mental atmosphere.

No one has to make a BASE jump after all, except those who actually do. In a sport as perilous as BASE, in which those who die are said to have "gone in," practitioners owe their success to more than mere chance. They are assiduous in their preparation and planning. They are precise and deliberate in action. And they cultivate an ability to cope with sensations of fear so powerful they threaten to short-circuit brain function. A popular notion in the sport says that people fall into one of two categories: those who behave like jackrabbits and those who behave like deer. Caught in headlights on the road at night, jackrabbits hop free from danger, whereas deer freeze and get smashed to smithereens. Most jumpers, therefore, fall into the jackrabbit category; those who behave like deer don't tend to last long.

Anne Helliwell arrived into this environment in 1982, a recent émigré from New Zealand who came to the States on a German tramp steamer, in search of a skydiving life. "When I got here, I loved it so much I stayed awhile," Helliwell says about the Perris–Elsinore region.

Helliwell got her start in BASE when a skydiving friend asked if she wanted to watch a man parachute from a bridge. Afterwards, the guy asked Helliwell if she wanted to give it a shot. Following basic instructions, she leaped from the bridge, a photo capturing her perfect form as she fell. "I was just buzzing for a long time," she recalls. "I had to come back and do it again."

Cracking the jumping scene, though, proved not so easy. A newcomer needed a mentor, someone who not only would teach but would vouch for her in the secretive jumping community. Given the prevailing attitudes in skydiving toward BASE, this was best done with discretion. Jump sites were often referred to in code, to confound the authorities or wannabes. A newcomer might be told discreetly to meet at a time and place for a jump, with the understanding that she would keep the information private. Often the first object she jumps from will be a bridge with water beneath, to add an extra margin of safety, or a high cliff or mountainside where a few more precious seconds might allow for any errors to be overcome. Once at the site, she would meet experienced jumpers, forging contacts in an international network without headquarters, hierarchy, or membership rolls. No one knew how many other practicing jumpers existed, but probably not more than a few hundred worldwide by the mid-1980s. They were mostly a clandestine group. And when Boenish was killed, in 1984, while jumping a 3,600-foot cliff in Norway known as the Troll Wall, the sport—absent its greatest advocate—went seriously underground.

Helliwell knew of a few jumpers by reputation at the drop zone, but they were not inclined to let a woman tag along. Eventually she learned of a rendezvous point for a coming weekend jump and drove eight hours to the spot, in Northern California. "I showed up and they went, 'Oh, great, now we have to take her.' So they squeezed me in the back of the car. They said, 'We're going to blindfold you. You're not allowed to see where we're going.' There were four guys and me, and it was an antenna, and I was determined to be accepted in the group, so I made sure I wasn't a slacking girl coming up from behind. So I stayed in the middle, climbing. By the time we got to the top, we made our jump and it was great. From then on I was accepted. As a group we all went and started jumping things."

IN THOSE DAYS, jumpers relied on skydiving equipment. A standard skydive begins when a skydiver exits an aircraft at twelve thousand feet, wearing a harness and a container on his back holding two parachutes. In free fall, he accelerates to 120 miles per hour, which is terminal velocity, the maximum speed of gravity acting on an object relative to wind resistance as it plummets through the atmosphere. When the downward force of gravity equals the upward force of drag, this is terminal speed. It takes about twelve seconds to reach terminal velocity.

The second phase begins when he reaches behind his right hip for a handle on his rig, grabbing it and flinging it into the air. This releases a small parachute called a pilot chute. Caught by the air, the pilot chute inflates, creating drag and tugging a bridle made of a length of webbing connected to his parachute container, held fast by a pin or Velcro system.

Tension on the bridle from the pilot chute pulls hard, releasing the pin, causing the main canopy, folded and packed tight in the container, to spill out. As the lines stretch, the canopy opens with a resounding crack. Air rushes into vents along the parachute's leading edge, inflating cells that give the pressurized fabric the shape of a wing.

A skydiver typically deploys his parachute at between two and three thousand feet. That way if there's a malfunction, he has the option of yanking a handle to cut away the main chute and deploy a reserve.

This is where the main differences between skydiving and BASE equipment come into play. BASE jumpers frequently leap from objects that are less than a thousand feet tall. They seldom reach terminal velocity, and the lower altitudes involved in BASE leave insufficient time to deploy a reserve parachute in the event of a malfunction with the main. Therefore, a jumper requires one canopy that opens reliably and quickly and can be flown adroitly in the confined spaces that make up many BASE landing areas.

"A lot of accidents happened in BASE because we were using gear meant for another sport," DiGiovanni says. "We didn't have our own." Helliwell was determined to do something about that. She filled two pages of notes with specs gleaned from her own experience and those of other trusted jumpers in an attempt to design a proper BASE parachute. The gist of her scribbling called for a square-shaped chute (to improve handling) that opened both quickly and "on-heading"—that is, away from the object jumped.

Working at a loft where skydiving parachutes were rigged, packed, and repaired, Helliwell sat at a sewing machine and fashioned what she would call "the Gray Thing," owing to its unattractive color. It was "sewn atrocious," she admits, but looks weren't everything, and the parachute "actually flew quite well." With her parachute, she would partner with Todd Shoebotham, a jumper who had moved to California from Texas and ran a small business selling stripped-down BASE containers, pilot chutes, and accessories out of a catalog advertised in the back of a skydiving magazine. They called their concern Basic Research.

There was little business at first.

THE BEST GAUGE of the sport's size was an event that took place each October in Fayetteville, West Virginia, at a festival called Bridge Day, where jumping was permitted from the 876-foot New River Gorge Bridge. In 1986 more than three hundred took part, presumably a good share of the worldwide jumping population.

Spurred by popular media, skydiving was on the verge of a surge in popularity, though, and BASE would enjoy a spillover effect. The 1991 movie *Point Break,* directed by Kathryn Bigelow and starring Keanu Reeves and Patrick Swayze, depicted a group of California surfer/skydivers who robbed banks to fuel their lifestyle, a story that struck a chord with males of a certain age and bent. They were part of a whole generation that had been practically raised on amazing risks as entertainment, going back at least to Evel Knievel. By 1995 this generation would get its Woodstock when ESPN created a festival for radical sports in Providence, Rhode Island, called the Extreme Games, soon to be rechristened the X Games. Aggregating mountain biking, adventure racing, sport climbing, bungee jumping, street luge, skysurfing, skateboarding, in-line skating, BMX, windsurfing, and kitesurfing, the games were beamed to households around the world. And if audiences did not exactly comprehend the finer points of downhill mountain-bike racing, they could at least anticipate the possibility for serious carnage resulting from high-speed wrecks.

Around this time, Helliwell and Shoebotham noted a corresponding uptick in orders. They heard word of jumpers dying in such far-flung locales as Australia, Europe, and South America, all of which testified to the sport's broadening reach.

Indeed, there once had been a time when Anne Helliwell knew just about every jumper, or at least had mutual friends in common. By the late 1990s she couldn't make that claim anymore. As the sport expanded, Basic Research's business had made it so that anyone could plunk down a credit card and get fully outfitted, and this would present a dilemma for the company's owners. "We wanted to sell equipment," Helliwell explains, "but we didn't want to sell it to people to kill themselves." To help ensure that customers were qualified, she proposed training requirements, similar to those for skydiving. But the backlash from the jumping community was swift and noisy—they *liked* that their sport was loosely organized, and bristled at the suggestion of a sanctioning body. So Helliwell and Shoebotham created a strictly voluntary training program, with classes taking place over several days whenever enough students signed up. Their pitch to prospective students was plain and simple: "Can we help you out so you don't kill yourselves?" Helliwell says. "Teach you in the right way?" Students began to trickle in.

The point of the class was to prepare for jumping, but also for the inevitability of things going wrong. With problems occasionally presenting in rapid-fire sequence, and seconds to spare before impact, pausing to ask *What do I do now?* leads to certain demise.

Complicating matters are the altered states resulting from the physiology of fear. As chemicals course from the amygdala—a pair of almond-shaped nuclei, located within the brain's temporal lobes, where fear originates—blood coagulates and blood vessels constrict; heart rate and blood pressure shoot up; and hormones, including cortisol and adrenaline, surge through the body, tensing muscles for action. All of which attenuates the ability to think and reason clearly. Cortisol, in particular, interferes with complex thinking. Even simple problems become difficult during stressful situations, and simple problems in BASE jumping quickly turn deadly. So Helliwell and Shoebotham taught students not only to plan for perfect performance but to practice every conceivable problem scenario, making each motion an economy of choreographed muscle memory and reflexes honed by repetition.

DiGiovanni had assumed the role of unofficial historian for the sport and began compiling something called the BASE Fatality List, a catalog of deaths designed to serve as a memorial and an educational tool. "A lot of those people on the list, the first fifty or sixty, weren't strangers to me," DiGiovanni says. "They were people I knew. If you look at the first seventy-five fatalities, they're all sort of unique. After that, it's people making the same mistake over and over again . . ."

Just as in aeronautics and skydiving, incident reports on the fatality list testified to mistakes, miscalculations, and malfunctions you didn't want to repeat. Eyewitness accounts, interviews, and follow-up gear inspections amounted to cautionary tales. Where possible, Shoebotham and Helliwell acquired surviving video of a fatality and showed it to students as a lesson.

Together, this created a catechism spelling out the traits and attitudes of a serious jumper, which most students badly want to be. A serious jumper cares for his equipment, inspecting and double-checking several thousands of dollars' worth of essential gear—pilot chute, bridle, container, and parachute. He fastidiously packs his parachute. Because he carries only one, his backups are sound judgment and skill. He monitors weather conditions and interprets their meanings. He performs conservatively rather than pushing into more difficult mental and physical territory. He practices to maintain his training—in the language, staying "current," particularly as his next jump demands. He has familiarized himself with the jump site, through either experience or thorough investigation, by walking the landing area, memorizing the locations of any rocks, trees, buildings, fences, power lines, light poles, or roads that could present a hazard. He has consulted the weather forecast, paying special attention to specific winds at the area he's jumping. He knows that by failing to prepare in this way, he would imperil himself before he even reaches the exit point. He has also consulted local jumpers with expert knowledge. As a result, he carries a map in his mind of the landing area, exit point, and any salient physical characteristics in between. Armed with this information, he has a plan for every phase of the jump. He is prepared for any potential malfunctions and has formulated backup plans because a good jumper enjoys planning and preparation almost as much as jumping itself.

Once at the jump site, if he observes that conditions are not right, or if he's feeling uncomfortable for some reason, he understands that there is no one to save him. He has chosen an inherently perilous activity and will have to rely on his inner soundings for judgment and safety. It's possible that a more experienced jumper, if present, would offer advice, an admonition, or a cursory inspection of gear at the last moment. But just as likely, he may not. So a good jumper consults his own knowledge, experience, and an internal voice that may raise a critical question or provide some vague inkling that something is askew. If the voice is well tuned, the good jumper listens with a willingness to walk away or climb down from an object. He knows that a cautious, patient approach may keep him alive, because he accepts the maxim in the sport that says, *The only way to not die BASE jumping is to not BASE jump.*

GEARED UP at an exit, a jumper should already have an idea of the precise height of the object, which he can confirm using an altimeter or laser range finder. Often, though, he simply drops a rock and counts the seconds until he hears it smack ground. Consulting a printed table, he sees that by striking at six seconds the rock fell roughly 500 feet. That's how much functional altitude he has to work with. Seven seconds means he has 640 feet until impact; at eight seconds, he has almost 800 feet, and so on.

Ready to go at last, he will begin the first phase of a jump by leaping clear from the object and place his body in a position with belly down and shoulders level. As he falls more rapidly with each second, he encounters an increase in air resistance, which can be deflected off his body to "track," or glide, from the object as quickly as possible. With each passing second in free fall, he's accelerating. At one second, he's traveling roughly twenty-two miles per hour downward. By four seconds he's moving seventy-five miles per hour, wind whistling past. If the object is tall enough, at ten seconds he's howling along at 114 miles per hour. Five seconds later he has accelerated to roughly 120 miles per hour, terminal velocity, and he hears nothing but a dull roar, his exposed skin rolling in rippling waves.

With the ground coming up fast, he will begin the second phase of the jump by deploying his parachute, which starts by throwing the pilot chute, either clutched in hand or in a pouch attached to the back of his rig. Wherever he has stowed it, a good jumper throws his pilot chute to his side, into "clean" air—free from turbulence caused by his body—as if his life depends on it, because of course it does.

Several seconds pregnant with tense anticipation may pass, a situation similar to slamming the brakes in a car and waiting for the vehicle to screech to a halt, meanwhile ground rushing at him with increasing intensity. If the wait between throwing the pilot chute and the opening of the main canopy seems too long, a trained jumper switches immediately to emergency procedures, searching out a snag or some other problem. This nightmare scenario could be the result of a packing or rigging error, or an entanglement. Perhaps the pilot chute has been incorrectly configured or catches on some part of the jumper's body or has wound up in the burble of turbulence behind his back, a dead spot for pilot chutes where there's little air resistance. Whatever the problem, if he cannot correct instantly, he is finished.

In a proper deployment, when things go right, as the main parachute spills from the container and the lines stretch, the parachute's cells begin to inflate—two hundred square feet or so of pressurized fabric forming the shape of a wing. The force from a parachute rising off his back and inflating will swing a jumper beneath.

Even with his chute open, though, the danger has not disappeared. Chutes can open "off-heading," due to poor body position at deployment, a shoddy pack job, wind, or just plain bad luck. This means that rather than moving away from the object he's just jumped from, the jumper is flying fast under canopy straight for a cliff, building, antenna, guy wires, or bridge pilings, with only seconds to correct before smashing into rock, concrete, or steel. Worse, sometimes his parachute lines will be twisted, disabling the steering mechanism, which are toggles attached to lines that, in turn, are connected to the parachute and, when pulled, alter the shape of the canopy and affect its flight.

An excellent jumper will have planned for these scenarios, freeing line twists and steering his canopy to safety, taking into account headwinds, tailwinds, and other variables.

Even the landing, the final phase, can be fraught with peril. Under a parachute, hitting the ground at forty miles an hour would be a painful endeavor. So a parachutist flying a ram-air canopy performs a flare maneuver, say, a dozen feet off the deck, by pulling down on his toggles to convert forward speed into temporary lift, momentarily pitching the flight angle of the parachute upward. It's an act that relies on timing and precise action. Flare late or insufficiently and you hit the ground hard. Flare too early and the parachute will eventually stall, causing a fall straight down or backward, neither of which will be pleasant, even from ten feet. A poorly aimed approach or even a misplaced step can result in bones snapping, or worse. Only once both feet are planted firmly back on the ground can a jumper truly be said to be safe.

In addition to the mechanics of jumping, Helliwell and Shoebotham imparted ethics for their marginalized and misunderstood sport. One of the most grievous violations of ethics concerns "burning" a site, which basically means getting busted jumping at a banned spot—for trespassing or some other infraction—and leaving the place hot with surveillance so no one can jump anymore without getting caught. The other rules, such as they are, can be summed up simply: Perform jumps you can reasonably handle or you will get hurt or die; do not damage people, property, or the environment. In other words, leave no trace. If you are jumping a banned site and happen to get caught, "try to be courteous to the arresting officer," Shoebotham explained. "It may come back to help you out. Or at least might help the next guy who gets busted."

Helliwell told of a friend who, suffering from insomnia one night, rose from bed without waking his wife, grabbed his parachute, and headed to a high-rise hotel. Jumping unseen, he returned home, crawled into bed, and fell fast asleep. In the morning, his wife discovered the only evidence of his nocturnal jaunt: an open parachute stretched across the living room. That was the ideal jump.

Chapter 2
INTERNATIONAL LAUNCH

ENGLAND, MID-1990S

By 1995, jumping had made its way to England, specifically an army base in Dover, Kent, near the famous White Cliffs, where one day a paratrooper pulled some photographs from his locker. That day, a startled twenty-five-year-old private in the 3rd Battalion, the Parachute Regiment of the British Army, also known as 3 PARA, got his first glimpse of BASE jumping. That fateful moment set in motion a course that would illuminate the history of BASE. The private's name was Gary Bullock, and he insisted his fellow soldier take him along on his next jump.

First, Gary needed to learn to fly more agile square parachutes, unlike the round canopies used by the army. Round parachutes work fine, but they rely on drag. Like jellyfish in the air, they drift on currents and can scarcely be steered. A square parachute, though, is an airfoil, an inflatable wing that can truly be flown. Their maneuverability is essential in the tight quarters and time sequences endemic to BASE jumping. In skydiving, a landing takes place at the grassy infield of an airport, under controlled circumstances. BASE, though, can occur in dense areas where a landing zone may be populated with trees, buildings, power lines, and sometimes people. And due to the low altitudes involved, a jumper may have only a few seconds to land after opening his parachute. Following a civilian skydiving course in which he got acquainted with square chutes, Gary found himself one frigid February night along the Thames climbing an electricity pylon in the dark with three other jumpers. They were ten miles east of London and electricity hummed in high-tension wires overhead. In the distance, a corona of light suggested the city. The wires prevented them from climbing to the top of the tower and they stopped halfway up, 370 feet above the cold mud of the river's tidal flats, puddles shimmering in the moonlight. Their height was not unreasonably low, but it would require lightning thought and action, especially for a beginner.

It all happened so quickly that later Gary would be at a loss to recall the details of what happened. A flood of adrenaline washed away vivid memories as surely as a couple of downed cocktails. "When you're in the moment, it's difficult to capture everything," he would say. He did remember "amazing" emotions after all the men jumped and—when the endorphins wore off—throbbing pain from an ankle injured when he landed on a length of driftwood lodged in the mud.

Gary yearned to recapture the good feeling, though. Jumping again and again, he eventually sent away for a canopy designed specifically for BASE, built by a competitor of Helliwell and Shoebotham's, a California company called Consolidated Rigging. Having discovered a sport that suited his temperament and ambitions, Gary was fully committed to continuing.

HE HAD ALWAYS BEEN athletic. Gary grew up twenty miles north of London, in Hertford, a Saxon settlement that in more recent times launched the hard-rock band Deep Purple. Gary's mother, Hazel, worked as a school secretary. His father, Chris, operated a lathe at a factory, fashioning parts for submarines from polytetrafluoroethelyne, a material DuPont manufactures under the brand name Teflon.

Gary was the younger of their two sons. His brother, Jon, is two years Gary's senior. Yet it was Gary who learned to ride a two-wheeler without training wheels first. He was four. It was an early sign of a competitive streak. "Everything was a challenge as far as he was concerned," says Hazel. "If you told him something was impossible, he wouldn't believe you."

Gary raced up hills to beat classmates to the top. In archery classes, he burned to hit the bull's-eye. "I would have to be the winner," he recalls. "I always wanted to be first in terms of physical performance, because academics did not interest me."

He was galled when soccer and rugby teammates did not bring the same fierce intensity to training that he did, and quit in frustration. Individual sports suited his personality better anyway, because he had only himself to blame for failure. He and friends built ramps for their BMX bikes at a parking lot along the River Lea, launching over barges into the water. Soon Gary found another outlet for his restless energy, paddling kayaks in the very same water for the Herts Canoe Club.

Obsessive training meant that Gary performed well enough in local competitions to earn an invitation to a European kayaking championship in Austria. "Unfortunately, when the two boys were young, we were quite hard up," Hazel recalls, "struggling to pay a mortgage and so on." Gary cried when his parents explained that they could not afford to send him.

His disappointment soon hardened into resolve, and Gary vowed that money would never again stand between him and his ambitions. He delivered newspapers and knocked on neighbors' doors, lugging a bucket and sponge, offering to wash windows or cars. He worked at a sporting goods store on weekends. Some days he skipped lunch at school and pocketed the money his mother had given him.

By sixteen Gary had saved enough to cover half the cost of a school skiing excursion to Leysin, Switzerland, a resort in the Bernese Alps. His parents paid the other half. Although Gary had never been on skis, he wanted to avoid beginner's lessons. "I haven't done it in a while," he lied to his chaperones, "but no worries."

By observing others, he acquired basic skills and soon began linking turns. Returning home, Gary announced that he had discovered a sport worthy of his talent and dedication. He earned work experience and school credit helping out at an artificial ski slope fifteen minutes from home. In snow-starved England, they used Dendix, a short-haired bristle material that is to snow what Astroturf is to grass. It wasn't the Swiss Alps, but it got him on skis. And Gary loved it.

That was important. Gary and Jon understood that their father despised the long hours he spent on his feet in front of a lathe each day. Determined to plot a different course for their lives, Jon would earn a college degree in graphic design. Gary did not figure on college, though. He was not interested in a conventional career. Still, fresh out of school, he wound up as a gopher in an office. The job was a stopgap until Gary could figure things out. His wardrobe tended toward bright colors and loud prints, and he rejected the office dress code, showing up wearing ripped jeans and sneakers. During Gary's teenage years, Jon had watched a change come over his brother's personality. Outgoing and supremely confident, Gary spoke freely and generally did what he pleased. His parents found him beyond persuasion when he set his mind to a task. "There was conflicts between him and me dad," Jon recalls. "The pair of them would argue." Strong-willed himself, Chris met his match in Gary. "If you try to talk him out of doing anything," Chris says, "he would just go and do it anyway. That's the way he was."

Gary eventually shed the office job and returned to the dry ski slope, where he worked as the least experienced instructor on staff, a status he was determined to change. Every day at lunch, while the others ate and lolled about, Gary dragged gates out and set up a slalom course, bashing gates. He trained in his spare time, too.

Two months after starting at the dry slope, Gary entered a downhill race at Bad Gastein, Austria, a resort town in the Alps that had hosted the 1958 world championships. Inspecting the course, surveying all of the turns, bumps, and jumps, he paused to watch other competitors' training runs. They soared nearly a hundred feet from a jump.

On his first training run, Gary crossed the finish fifteen seconds behind the leaders, an eternity in competition. At the end, legs turned to jelly by fatigue and fear, he wiped out while attempting to stop.

The following morning, he woke up with a stiff and aching knee, which he wrapped tightly, and headed up the mountain, noting how fast the other racers were moving and how far they flew in the air. "Suddenly fear hit me," he says. "My God, I thought, I'm *doing* what they're doing."

Trembling in the start gate, he tucked for twenty seconds, sufficient time to build terrific speed, snow racing beneath his skis. He hurtled over the course's jumps in a dream and crossed the finish line. He remained far back in the standings, but Gary believed he could eventually compete.

The following winter, Gary started a run of five straight seasons racing

International Ski Federation (FIS)–sanctioned events, mostly downhill, competing in the federation's bottom rung. Without lessons or coaches, he would never win a single race or rank among the top five hundred in the world. He bluffed his way into races, never under the imprimatur of the British Ski and Snowboarding Federation. He faked eligibility, working up official-looking letterhead with the words "GB Ski Federation" attesting to his credentials. He failed to disclose that *GB* stood for Gary Bullock and not Great Britain, as FIS officials might assume. When caught, Gary talked his way into races on charm and balls. He took heart that he was competing on the same World Cup courses he had seen on TV, legendary places like Val Gardena, in the Dolomites, on the famous "Camel Hunches" of the Saslong run. "To be one of the guys pushing out the start gate, racing, and finishing was a high for me," he would remember.

Yet his was often far from the glamorous existence enjoyed by the stars of the World Cup series he saw on TV. Gary swapped odd jobs at hotels in exchange for a room. Often he slept in his frozen car. Each summer, he worked on construction sites in London as a hod carrier, hauling cement for bricklayers. It was backbreaking work, but the heavy labor kept him fit and helped finance the coming ski season.

One summer, five years into his racing career, Gary got the idea to operate a water-sports business in Portugal, hauling tourists behind a boat on tubes and floats. When the venture failed, he and a partner wound up deep in debt. The building trades were in recession that autumn, and there was no work. With the ski season fast approaching, Gary was out of money and ideas. So, on May 19, 1993, he did what legions of desperate men without options have done throughout the ages: Gary joined the army. He was twenty-three.

He had already begun researching prospects for a career as a stuntman in TV and film. A contact he made in the industry explained that he had learned all of the necessary skills to join British Actors' Equity and the Stunt Register while serving with the 3rd Battalion. An army recruiter noted that, with his skiing background, Gary was a shoo-in for the army's ski team.

In three years with the army, Gary would never once see a pair of skis.

It took little time to figure out that he and the army made an ill-suited match. Although he excelled at training and was a strong runner, with stamina, who shot well on the range, military culture struck Gary as surreal. He met men ten and fifteen years his senior who had joined fresh out of school and, to his thinking, appeared brainwashed into mindless obedience. Gary constantly ran afoul of his superiors and was not shy about telling them that "indeed their systems do suck and that they ought to get out a bit more." Such an attitude rankled command and would fail to endear him to fellow soldiers, who ganged up and slapped him around on occasion to teach the mouthy private some manners. In retaliation, Gary resorted to small acts of subterfuge. One took the form of becoming a vegetarian, just so the army would have to go to the trouble of furnishing him with special rations. After a few weeks of abstaining from meat, he actually noticed an improvement in the way he felt.

Still, Gary was fed up with the military by the time he discovered BASE jumping. And he would soon have other reasons to want to get free of his military obligations. The first arrived in the form of a petite blonde he met on a Wales beach while on leave in the summer of 1995. Gary had just made a jump from a nearby cliff and was ambling along the sand when a woman sunbathing caught his eye. She had her hands full with a toddler, and Gary stopped to watch her, wondering if a man was in the picture. After a spell, Gary strolled over and started a conversation.

Years later, Vivienne Lee would recall one of the first things Gary said: "How would you like to go sailing around the world with me?" She was twenty-seven years old and mother of a two-year-old daughter named Lydia. Vivienne had a house in Nottingham, a university degree, and a career as a personnel manager in recruitment for a bingo club. Her life to that point had been, in every respect, a conventional one. Everything about Gary, from BASE jumping to his confidence to the way he zigzagged through life, excited Vivienne. They would never sail around the world, but she joined him for a bonfire on the beach and on a skydiving camping trip. After Gary returned to the army in Dover, and Vivienne to her life in the Midlands, they kept in touch through the summer and autumn.

Gary continued jumping, launching from the White Cliffs at Dover, near where his regiment was stationed. He had dreams beyond what the military had in mind for him. In December, with Christmas leave approaching, he put the finishing touches on a plan that he hoped would bring a nice windfall—and the attention of the professional stunt world.

On December 20, 1995, the front page of the *Daily Mail*, one of Britain's largest tabloids, published a color photo of a man wearing a red Santa Claus costume and a BASE rig on his back, leaping from the roof of the twenty-eight-story London Hilton on Park Lane, in Mayfair. A headline blared, "Why Santa Took a High Jump off the Hilton." Inside, on page 3, six color photos depicted a sequence, beginning with the exit from the roof—where two models in a pantomime reindeer costume stood watching—and continuing to show a parachute opening a third of the way down the modern tower, to a final tumble on landing, in a field at Hyde Park. There, two waiting cops collared Santa, still wearing red hat and white beard.

The stunt had occurred a day earlier, on a hazy, mild morning six days before Christmas. The *Daily Mail* story explained that Saint Nick was actually twenty-six-year-old Gary Bullock, who had checked into the luxury hotel on December 18 and spent the night in a room. However, in the morning, rather than checking out like other guests, Gary sneaked to the roof, 330 feet above streets clogged with rush-hour traffic. Staring down on one of the city's most exclusive and elegant precincts, dressed as Father Christmas, two Australian women playing a reindeer, he jumped.

Gary was not the first to leap from the hotel. The first time occurred in 1985. And two years before Gary, in May 1992, Darren Newton, twenty-five, had famously died jumping from the hotel one night when his parachute opened and spun him 180 degrees off-heading, back in the direction of the hotel. He had smashed into a balcony on the eighteenth floor, causing his parachute to collapse. He plummeted through an awning, the metal frame ripping his arm off, and the mishap made newspapers across Britain.

"If you know what you are doing and are careful, it's really not dangerous," Gary told the *Daily Mail*, after he was freed following questions from police. Although not charged with a crime, he admitted that his superiors in the army might not be pleased. He was correct.

When Gary returned from holiday leave to Connaught Barracks, in Dover, the regimental sergeant major was waiting to chew him out, explaining that Gary would face a court-martial for bringing the regiment into disrepute. Gary weighed these facts as the sergeant major lit into him. He figured that what he had done had brought a little holiday cheer to the city during the yuletide season. Marched back to the barracks, Gary stewed as he was informed that he was about to be placed on every single duty until the court-martial proceedings, meaning, among other things, that he would receive no leave. He had already made plans to meet Vivienne for the weekend. "We had this wonderful relationship going," he says. "It was very young. I only saw her weekends, because I was in the military, based a couple hundred miles from where she lived."

His heart wrenched, Gary made up his mind in the barracks. Hanging his gear in a locker, he handed the key to another soldier whom he trusted, with instructions to wait a couple of hours before turning it over to someone in authority. He told the soldier to explain that the army's property could be found in the locker but that Private Gary Bullock was gone. Hopping in his car and driving to London, Gary hid out at a friend's house, where he called Vivienne to explain that he was AWOL and he wasn't going back. It was January 8, 1996, and Gary was about to begin life as a fugitive.

*T*he evasion techniques taught in the army would come in handy during Gary's days on the run. A month after his disappearance, he was captured attempting to sneak into England at the port at Dover, late on a cold February night on a ship from Holland, where he had been laying low. Customs and immigration officials saw that he was a wanted man during a standard passport check of passengers.

"Does the name 3 PARA mean anything to you?" arriving police asked.

"Not anymore," Gary said.

The cops took Gary back to Connaught Barracks, his mind all the while running at top speed, considering his options. Police released Gary into the custody of a guard he knew from his days in 3 PARA. By then it was around 3 a.m., and Gary refused to spend the night in the cells at the base. Instead, as the guard was distracted phoning the commanding officer, Gary made his move, hauled his fellow soldier down, snatched his passport, and bolted outside. Soldiers and guards in pursuit, Gary vaulted the front gate of the base and sprinted down into Dover, where he hid behind hedgerows, sneaked through gardens, cut across rooftops, and ducked into doorways, all while watching soldiers roaring through town in personnel carriers and Land Rovers, scouring the streets for a sign of him. By dawn Gary had made his way to Folkestone, a town eight miles down the coast, and phoned a friend in London for a lift.

Climbing into the car, Gary Bullock continued a life in hiding. Although nerve-racking at first, the longer he lived on the run, the more Gary realized that perhaps Big Brother was not as big as he had thought. Pulled over for speeding and given a summons, he arrived at the station to pay his fine. After showing his identification, he waited for the subject of military service to come up. But it never did. Still, there were close calls. Nine months after he'd run out of Dover, Gary and Vivienne were visiting his parents when police knocked at the door. "We'd all been sitting around quite happy that afternoon," Hazel recalls, "chatting and laughing, although he was AWOL and that was a worry all the time."

Gary bolted out the back door, past his startled father in the back garden, who was on a ladder inspecting the roof of a shed. Scaling a fence into a neighbor's yard, Gary continued down the block and out of sight.

Hazel trembled as she invited the police inside, where Vivienne, eight months pregnant with her and Gary's son, Kali, began weeping. The police took down Vivienne's name and address. By establishing another connection, the police tightened the net around Gary.

If Gary were to remain free, it was time to take added precautions. He and Vivienne paged through a phone book, scanning surnames for one that would suit their growing family. They rejected a few before settling on *Connery*, which had a nice ring to it. Some figured the name had something to do with a James Bond fetish, but it was nothing like that. "They weren't looking for a Connery," Vivienne says about the police. Filing the proper paperwork raised no red flags, and they thus became clan Connery.

GARY SUPPORTED HIS FAMILY with a small inheritance from a grandmother, with work on building sites, and by smuggling beer, wine, and cigarettes from France to sell at a profit in Britain. In the meantime, he studied to acquire the certifications to become a professional stuntman, visiting film and TV sets, introducing himself around while observing the trade. In November 1997, the paperwork came through and Gary was accepted on the Stunt Register, a division of Actors' Equity. To announce his arrival, he had dreamed up a scheme to impress his new colleagues, a BASE jump down through the center of the Eiffel Tower.

He arrived in Paris in December, snow swirling in the weeks before Christmas. The conditions were not ideal, and Gary would have been wise to call off the jump. Vivienne watched from above as Gary plunged from the first stage of the tower, three hundred feet high, through the middle of the monument, and opened his parachute as planned. Then, seized by a gust of wind, Gary flew forward, feet striking a curb, momentum cartwheeling him into a fence.

Security nabbed Vivienne as an accomplice, and handcuffed Gary and placed him in the back of an ambulance with broken ribs, a bruised lung, compressed vertebrae, and his foot and hip aching. He spent seven days in intensive care. "I was stupid to have jumped, and I know I was stupid to have jumped," he would say later. "It was a big ego lesson, which was great."

Taking pity on him, gendarmes eventually returned his passport and dropped all charges. Months later, in May 1998, fully healed and sitting in the garden out back of Vivienne's house in Nottingham, Gary was enjoying a warm day with the kids when Vivienne walked out with the phone pressed to her ear. She mouthed the name of a well-known stunt coordinator. Gary knew it was a job at last. He had an offer of regular work on a TV show about a high-tech, high-adventure crime-fighting team. Gary Connery, the erstwhile Gary Bullock, had his start as a stuntman.

Chapter 3

A CHILD CALLED X-RAY MUJAHIDEEN

I learned this, at least, by my experiment: that if one advances confidently in the direction of his dreams, and endeavors to live the life which he has imagined, he will meet with a success unexpected in common hours.

—*Henry David Thoreau*, Walden

AMERICAN SOUTHWEST, LATE TWENTIETH CENTURY

One bright day in 1997, Anne Helliwell was out at the Perris Valley drop zone, teaching tandem skydiving instruction, when a tall young guy with a shaved head walked up and, without preliminaries, launched into some questions about BASE instruction. Helliwell was accustomed to getting feelers from experienced skydivers. But novices generally found the prospect of jumping plainly daunting. Not this guy, though. "This guy came up to me," Helliwell would recall, "and it's more common these days, and he said, 'How many skydives do you require for somebody to go through your course?' We had a minimum of two hundred skydives. The reason for that is we need you to know how to fly your parachute. We can teach you how to jump off the object and save your life. When your parachute opens, you really need to know how to work that vehicle. Skydiving can do that for you."

Jeb Corliss, twenty-one, had amassed forty skydives at a small Cessna drop zone at Bermuda Dunes, near Palm Springs; it was not enough to begin training. "See you in a couple years," Helliwell told him, "or however long it takes you to get the jumps." Then she quickly forgot about him. Until her phone rang three months later. It was Jeb on the line, explaining how he had made more than a hundred jumps since their meeting, a staggering number in so short a time. Although this was short of the two hundred required to begin training, he wondered if she would make an exception and permit him to enroll.

Helliwell said she needed to talk it over with Shoebotham first. When he raised no objections, she called back. "You can start your class next week," she told Jeb.

AS A CARETAKER of his sport, Todd Shoebotham considered it his sacred duty to size up the students in his ground-course classroom at the Perris drop zone. He could spot a certain type of student from a mile away, the way they walked in, having paid $1,000 for the privilege of his and Helliwell's twenty-eight years of accumulated wisdom, already convinced of things they knew not a whit about. Their mix of energy, enthusiasm, and ignorance tended to make him nervous. He would recall thinking, *Whoa, dude, you're scaring me! You're not thinking about the consequences of your actions!*

BASE still occupied a radical fringe, even among skydivers, and each new injury or fatality tended to stir a tempest of negative attention that Shoebotham and other leaders would simply prefer to avoid. Intent on weeding out the kinds of characters who might go forth, do something dumb, get killed, and bring scorn on the sport, Shoebotham appraised a tall young man with a shaved head and tuning-fork tremulousness, bristling with big ideas of jumping iconic monuments and some of the most challenging sites around the world. It was brash stuff for someone who had yet to make his first jump. And Shoebotham asked himself: *Is this Jeb guy someone we should invite into our sport?* He decided to get to know Jeb, who was already an accomplished scuba diver. Jeb understood that to stay alive underwater, you needed a dive plan that defined the parameters of exploration and time spent at depth, taking into account a range of potential variables. It was a mentality and training that lent itself well to jumping.

"I remember most of the conversations where I got to know him a little bit, thinking, *This guy is not a whack or a kook,*" Shoebotham would say later. "*He has a character that we all need.* You need to be able to calculate this stuff. You've got to be able to think these things through, develop a plan, find flaws in your plan, reevaluate around that. I could see that in Jeb very early."

Still, Shoebotham would eventually regard Jeb as too much in a hurry at times. "Dude, slow down," he reminded him. "Don't go too fast. This sport is not forgiving. You mess up a little bit and it kills you."

If Jeb seemed in a hurry, it was because he was. He had endured a privileged but melancholy life, and in jumping he imagined a burnished future. In a sport few were willing to even try, Jeb was determined to distinguish himself. Shoebotham recalled that before Jeb had even made one jump, this student was certain he was going to love the sport, talking about his coming travels in which he would plunge from objects all across Europe. Aimless for years, Jeb saw in BASE something to order his life around.

Jeb Corliss had come into the world in Abiquiú, New Mexico, a remote former Spanish mission fifty miles north of Santa Fe. Surrounded by rugged red chimney rocks and desert blooms under a huge western sky, Abiquiú had attracted Georgia O'Keeffe, who favored the landscape and the light and maintained a home and studio there for most of her adult life. Beyond scenery and solitude, though, the town offered little else, and no hospital. That was why, as the time drew near for his pregnant wife, Gigi, Rick Corliss plunked coins into a pay phone and summoned an outback doctor to deliver their first child in a bedroom at a friend's house where they were staying. The baby was born on March 25, 1976, and in the spirit of the times there was some talk of calling him X-Ray Mujahideen. Tradition prevailed, however, and the child was given the Christian name J. Ray Corliss IV; everyone called him Jeb. He had an older sister, Sonia—Gigi's daughter from an earlier union—and before Jeb was out of diapers, Rick and Gigi would welcome Scarlett to complete their family.

Rick and Gigi were not in Abiquiú long, though. They never called any place home for long. They ran a business dealing in indigenous artifacts and folk art, traveling the world for, say, masks from New Guinea, war clubs from the Solomon Islands, human bones from a Buddhist sect in Tibet, and embroidery from the Golden Triangle of Southeast Asia. These items were a hit with wealthy collectors back in the United States, but it meant long stretches on the road. Children in tow, Rick and Gigi went from New Mexico to Palm Springs, where Rick's family was prominent, then on to India, Nepal, Pakistan, and Afghanistan, where Jeb celebrated his first birthday. There were camel rides and romps with monkeys. In India, the children watched in wonder as corpses burned on the banks of the Ganges.

The Corlisses' only son was willful and heedless of danger. At eighteen months, he wriggled free from a swim instructor and leaped from a dive platform, swimming to the side for another plunge. "That's basically what Jeb has been like since the beginning," Gigi recalls.

Once their children were school-aged, Rick and Gigi settled in Santa Fe, where Jeb was enrolled in Catholic school. Many of his classmates were Native American. He was blond-haired, blue-eyed, a new kid whose experiences and beliefs suggested he came from some other planet. He clashed with clergy and classmates over doctrine, which didn't mesh with his experiences abroad. "When a six-year-old child starts contradicting adults and other children, it's considered rude," Gigi says. "It's considered disrespectful. His beliefs clashed with others. He argued with other children, and they called him a liar."

By second grade Jeb was at public school, seeking a fresh start, furthering a pattern of dislocation that reinforced his status as an outsider. At home, Rick and Gigi were headed for divorce.

Jeb's imagination was his refuge. One day, riding in a car with an aunt, he gazed out the window, transfixed at the sight of birds perched on telephone wires, opening their wings and soaring. "When I get older, I'm going to do that," he announced.

His aunt explained that when he got older he would realize that humans cannot fly.

Jeb considered her words for a moment. "Maybe you can't," he said finally, "but I'm going to."

Gigi would remember that "he had real dreams about going up into these mountain areas and flying through earthworks and tundra and flying through massive cracks in the earth . . . Incredible dreams, anyway."

Jeb's reality, though, was less *Jonathan Livingston Seagull* and more *Lord of the Flies*. In the desert, he and other boys played a game called "rock war," from which participants staggered home with bloody head wounds. Rambunctious boys, they threw knives and ninja stars and jumped from bridges and rooftops. They attempted to capture rattlesnakes and scorpions. Left to his own devices, Jeb seemed to be regressing to a feral state. He grew ungovernable and did not respond to multiple groundings. He began to look dangerous to the parents of his friends, who barred their children from playing with the Corliss kid. Even Jeb's cousins weren't permitted to associate with him. "He had conflicts with his cousins, who were shooting birds with BB guns," Gigi remembers. "He was horrified. He admired snakes, and its life and its beauty, rather than wanting to stomp and kill it."

Soon Jeb's only playmates were those very snakes and spiders and the desert creatures he captured while scouring dry riverbeds around Santa Fe. Noting her son's loneliness, Gigi indulged these peccadilloes. He made a study of handling rattlers, anticipating when they were about to strike and maneuvering them so they couldn't. He was developing skills and a mind-set that would serve him decades later. He was fascinated by horny toads, and the way they shoot from their eyes blood containing a noxious chemical to ward off predators. Jeb could appreciate such a defense mechanism. His obstreperousness left him unpopular at yet another school. Without friends, he became an attractive target for bullies, who turned him into a punching bag. He tried threats, but the boys called his bluff and beat him anyway. Striking back was the only response that granted any breathing room. Still, each morning he woke sick with worry, girding for another assault. By fifth grade Jeb began to take a hard turn. When pushed, he shoved back. When another student landed a blow, he went ballistic. Fellow students learned to grant him a wide berth.

Yet one day, a group of boys pummeled Jeb in the schoolyard to teach him a lesson for some perceived infraction. Afterwards, vowing revenge, Jeb bolted into the school and seized the first solid object he saw, which happened to be an electric pencil sharpener. Stalking outside, he brought the object down on the head of the ringleader, then marched into the principal's office and confessed what he had done.

Alarmed teachers and school administrators reacted by isolating him from other students. They confiscated pencils, scissors, and books, anything they feared could be used as a weapon. They brought in specialists for testing. Finally the principal sat down with Gigi and urged her to consider homeschooling, noting that nothing about Jeb fit with other children. Gigi could not disagree.

Homeschooling cooled Jeb's rage, and he would never get in another fight again. Although Gigi tried enrolling Jeb in seventh grade at a public school in Palm Springs when they moved there, he lasted only a week. "I don't *want* to go to school," he pleaded, upset that some students had offered him a joint. "I don't want to know these people."

Back at home, Jeb spent long hours alone while his sisters were in school and his mother worked at a health food store and as an acupuncturist at a resort. He passed his days watching conservation documentaries on cable TV and studying with tutors. Asked about his career ambitions, he would mention something vague about working with animals. Mostly, though, he had stopped dreaming and could not imagine any future.

The Japanese media have identified a social phenomenon they've dubbed *hikikomori* ("withdrawal") that has resulted in a "lost generation," essentially legions of shut-ins who spend years of self-confinement in their parents' homes. He wasn't quite there, but Jeb Corliss was headed in that direction.

It was around this time that the physical being of the cute, towheaded kid began to transform. Jeb shot up in height, and his straight blond hair turned dark and curly, as if the mind over which it grew were struggling for outward manifestation. Walled off emotionally from the world, he cultivated animus. When his family encouraged him to see life as worthwhile, his standard replay was a defiant: "Maybe for you!"

A psychologist his parents consulted had earlier diagnosed "counterphobia," a condition in which people—often those who are extremely anxious—intentionally seek out the subject of their fear. Jeb caught snakes because they scared him, and he liked the way fear felt. Numb inside, he hungered for any feeling, which only intense experiences seemed to provide.

As it happened, circumstances would soon leave Jeb marinating in intense experiences.

A phone call would finally reroute Jeb Corliss's life. It came a few days after his sixteenth birthday, when he was living with his grandparents in New Mexico, studying with a private tutor. His mother and sisters had remained in Palm Springs, and Jeb hadn't heard from Gigi in a while. But there she was on the line, calling from Cancún. She wanted to know whether he could hop on a plane to meet her. She said she would explain once he arrived.

An angry, skinny, sensitive, pallid teenager with a wild nest of dark hair arrived in Cancún on a flight from LAX to meet Gigi and her new boyfriend, a man named Barry Fitzmorris. Tall, with shaggy gray hair and a sonorous voice, Fitzmorris resembled an old cowboy. He was something else entirely. Founder of a prosperous insurance brokerage, he was wealthy beyond anything Jeb was accustomed to, and he put everyone up in a luxury seaside resort.

Looking for something to bond over, Fitzmorris enrolled Jeb in a scuba certification course so they could dive together. One morning, a small boat motored out to Isla Mujeres, a popular reef in the aquamarine waters of the Caribbean. As everyone geared up, a squall came up, whipping the seas into confusion. The boat began taking water over the transom. Everyone on board clambered to the rising bow, nosing ever higher, until a voice called out to jump.

Jeb hit the water and the boat capsized, coming down feet from his head. He had other problems, though. He had fastened a twelve-pound weight belt around his waist. Sinking like a stone, he hit the sandy bottom fifteen feet below the surface. Frantically working to free the belt, he blacked out. When he came to, he was on the hull of the overturned boat, a man hunched over him, administering CPR.

When he relayed his ordeal to Gigi, she insisted that he would never dive again. But Fitzmorris argued that Jeb should try immediately, if only to triumph over any psychological trauma.

On a bigger boat, with better weather, Jeb earned his certification. Freshly credentialed, he and Fitzmorris bought cameras and underwater housings and ventured down to Cozumel for advanced instruction. Snapping pictures of pastel fish and eels in gin-clear water acted like a salve for the petulant teenager. With communication reduced to uncomplicated gestures underwater, his social anxiety vanished. In the water's warm embrace, Jeb discovered a comfort he had not known on land.

For eight months, Jeb and Fitzmorris would embark on an uninterrupted diving odyssey. They splashed in the waters off Belize, Cuba, and Costa Rica, where they encountered whitetip reef sharks. Nothing like the man-eaters of Jeb's imagination, they were beautiful and fascinating. Swimming in their presence summoned the old excitement of capturing snakes and scorpions in the desert.

Back home from his scuba sojourn, Jeb was watching *MTV Sports* one day, and there was a man standing too close to a cliff, suddenly sticking out his tongue and leaping. The sequence shocked, terrified, and exhilarated all at once. The jumper was a man named John Vincent, an oil worker from New Orleans. Long-haired, crackling with charisma, and insouciant in the face of authority, he had used suction cups to scale the Gateway Arch in St. Louis to jump, and at the World Trade Center he'd given security the slip to parachute from the roof.

For Jeb, who had dreamed of flying, here was something that came close. Not every man recognizes a glimpse of his destiny, or acts on it when he does, but when Jeb watched Vincent throw a gainer—an acrobatic maneuver consisting of a backward somersault while facing outward—from a cliff, he knew immediately what he was meant to do with his life.

He phoned a local drop zone for information. They didn't know much about BASE, but they suggested skydiving to start. The only problem was that Jeb needed to turn eighteen first. If he couldn't jump yet, Jeb figured at least he could study it. He scoured the library for any references but found scant evidence of its existence. This strangely brightened him. For one thing, if he were to jump, he would be joining an exclusive group.

Another motive was more morbid. "When I was sixteen years old," he would later say, "I became very suicidal, like actively pursuing things that could end my life."

"He was very depressed," Fitzmorris would recall. "I used to walk with him almost every day, and he would talk about how unhappy he was, how the only solution was committing suicide."

At the end of their Mexico idyll, Gigi and Fitzmorris had been married in Oaxaca, and Fitzmorris was building an eight-thousand-square-foot house with six bedrooms on a bluff over a private beach in Malibu for his new family. Before it was finished, Jeb moved into the maid's quarters to keep an eye out during construction. He was a seventeen-year-old security guard, living alone, waking each morning to the sound of workmen's saws and hammers. Making his way down to the beach with a surfboard, he spent hours bobbing in the Pacific, watching the traffic wend along the Pacific Coast Highway beneath the Santa Monica Mountains. He was waiting for waves, and something else, too, to come and propel him along in life.

When the catalyst finally arrived, Jeb did not like the form it took. Despite loud protests, his parents enrolled him in school in January 1994 so that he could graduate with a diploma. "He was freaked out by the prospect of returning to school," Gigi says.

He needn't have been. Colin McEwen was a private school with fewer than twenty pupils per grade. Jeb walked in for the first day wearing a T-shirt printed with a marine scene of coral reefs and sharks. His curly hair was shorn tight on the sides and rose high on his head, calling to some minds Herman Munster. "He was this tall kid with this bright shirt," recalls Shawn Stern, another student in his grade. "He was such an advanced scuba diver, and he had gone on a lot of fascinating scuba-diving trips, and his new father was super loaded and wealthy, so he always had the coolest, newest Nikon camera stuff. Jeb was interesting to all the kids right off the bat."

Jeb bonded with classmates over games of chess. He and Stern became fast friends. Jeb coaxed Stern to overcome a fear of the ocean, leading him on a swim beyond the breakers to deep water, where sea lions lolled on a navigation buoy. Stern would drive Jeb and Scarlett to school each day. Jeb eventually confessed that Stern was his first real friend.

For his eighteenth birthday, Jeb's grandparents bought him two tandem skydives at the drop zone at Bermuda Dunes. And in the spring he graduated, acceding to his family's wishes that he continue his education. That summer, tired of teasing about his bushy hairdo, he allowed his new friends to shave his head with a disposable razor. Nicked with cuts, his scalp was so bare it resembled a helmet. He nevertheless preferred this sleek look, which he embellished by wearing only black.

As his classmates headed off to college, Jeb enrolled in scuba training in Florida in hopes of becoming an instructor. He would repay the tuition by working in Fitzmorris's office. Equipped with a phone and a list of numbers to dial, Jeb began cold-calling companies in an attempt to gather information on their executives so that he might sell them insurance. No one had the slightest interest in talking to him, however, and his exasperation grew with each hostile hang-up. Unable to stand it any longer, Jeb marched into Fitzmorris's office, begging for another assignment. He had lasted thirty minutes.

Jeb worked off his debt around the house alongside Mexican laborers as they laid tile for the patio and pool, dug garden beds, and planted shrubs. His diving ambitions went unrealized. It turned out that teaching in the cold, murky Pacific off California delivered none of the joy he'd experienced in the warm, sight-rich Caribbean. His gig as a gardener ended, too, after another argument with Fitzmorris.

Jeb found work at a movie theater fifteen minutes up a canyon road from Malibu, in Agoura Hills. He tended the concession stand and ticket counter and worked his way up to operating the projector. "He didn't filter a lot," recalls another employee. "He was a very real person who said what was on his mind."

Jeb enrolled in classes at Moorpark College, a local junior college, but he had no career aspirations. At twenty, his life lacked a plot. Stern recalled his friend despondent and discussing suicide. "It wouldn't matter if I were dead," Stern remembers Jeb saying. Stern chalked it up to angst, but privately Jeb was still flirting with dangerous mental territory. Lacking any purpose, he truly didn't care if he lived or died.

Miserable, without fear of death, he had nothing to lose by risking his life. And it was then, toward the end of 1997, that Jeb strode up to Helliwell at the Perris drop zone. Back on Fitzmorris's payroll, working as a graphic artist and earning more than he ever had, Jeb could afford to ramp up skydiving training and enroll in Helliwell and Shoebotham's first jump course.

ONCE HIS CLASSROOM LESSONS were complete, Shoebotham put Jeb through several bungee jumps from a hot air balloon to refine his exit technique. Satisfied, he handed Jeb a rig and they rode in the basket of the balloon above a thick bank of fog that obscured the ground.

"Is this okay?" Jeb asked, scanning for some visual reference of the landing area.

Shoebotham explained that with a big open field below, Jeb would be fine.

"*Really?*" Jeb said, stepping to the edge of the gondola, gripped by terror. "If you say it's okay . . ." Launching into the marine layer, a strip of ocean fog trapped by hot inland air, he pitched blindly, his chute snapping open as the ground appeared. He skittered across the grass safely, and his training was complete.

Shoebotham recommended a bridge in Northern California for a first jump from a fixed object. It was best done after dark, he said, when no one was around. Jeb had questions, but Shoebotham cut him off. "Figure it out," he said.

Figure it out? Jeb thought. *Figure it out?! . . . Welcome to BASE jumping.*

—————

Jeb could think of no one else to ask for this errand but Stern, who steered a maroon Mercedes sedan—which he had inherited from his grandmother and promptly painted black—north along I-5, through the Central Valley. They picked up I-80 in Sacramento for the final thirty miles to the Foresthill Bridge, a metal truss 730 feet above the roiling waters of the North Fork of the American River, swollen with winter runoff from the Sierra Nevada. Jeb said little on the ride, and Stern suspected nerves. "I knew it was risky and dangerous," Stern says. "I don't know if I knew how risky or dangerous, but I think I knew pretty well the consequences and the likelihood that he could die on his first jump."

They checked in to a hotel in Auburn, a quaint town among golden foothills. They scouted the bridge and landing area, a narrow gravel road to the immediate left of the river, which would require precision, particularly in the dark. Jeb's equipment was minimal. He brought nothing but his parachute rig. He treated the jump as he would any skydive. He planned to jump after 1 a.m., and glow sticks to mark his landing were the only concession to the nighttime conditions.

That night, they parked along the approach to the bridge and crept like ninjas for the quarter-mile to the middle of the span. Each approaching set of headlights caused them to duck behind a concrete abutment separating the roadway from a pedestrian walkway. Uncertainty about the legal consequences only ratcheted up their nervous excitement. At the center of the bridge they huddled. "Let's do it," Jeb said, climbing into his rig and scaling the railing. Before heading up, he had set the glow sticks, and they gave off a faint green light more than seven hundred feet below. "All right, Shawn," Jeb called, crouching down, prompting Stern to lean over the rail and press the viewfinder of a camera to his eye.

"Later, dude," Jeb yelled into the night. Stern caught him with the flash from the camera for an instant before darkness swallowed everything and Jeb was gone. A second later, Stern heard the crack of a parachute opening, echoing across the canyon like a rifle report.

Sprinting back to the car, Stern encountered some hostile locals who had stopped their car on the bridge. They grabbed for his camera, but he brandished a pocket knife, and they fled. Arriving beneath the bridge and parking, he made the rendezvous on foot. Jeb emerged from the dark, teeth glowing in a stupid smile. He walked with an almost drunken swagger, words pouring forth. He sounded delirious with joy: *I threw my pilot chute immediately . . . flying blind . . . couldn't see the ground coming . . . impacted hard . . . pants and shirt torn . . . sliced the flesh from my palms . . . bleeding . . . never happier in life.*

Jeb had overshot his glow sticks and slammed into the ground. Back at the hotel room, he wrestled his canopy, repacking with bloody hands, smearing blood on the carpet, walls, and, somehow, the ceiling.

The next night at the bridge would be a virtual repeat, with Jeb overshooting the glow sticks and smashing into rocks along the river, scraping his knees, palms, and elbows. That was when he resolved to wear a helmet, kneepads, gloves, and other body armor. "When you eat shit," he told Stern about the difference between BASE and skydiving, "you eat shit hard."

The room resembled the scene of a murder, which, he would admit in retrospect, it had been. By jumping, Jeb had killed some aspect of his former self, some part that for years had prevented him from truly pursuing his purpose in life.

YEARS LATER, Stern would see the transformation clearly. "Here was something interesting about that trip, and it shows a little bit about how Jeb's brain works," he says. "The very first BASE jump he's ever done, before we even drove up there, part of the drive was going to be, we were to drive back through San Francisco so he could check out the Golden Gate Bridge. His first jump, we had to go see the Golden Gate Bridge, because he wanted to look at it and be next to it. Before he ever made his first jump, Jeb was already visualizing his incredible jumps. He was already starting to see where he was going to take himself."

What Jeb had to do on that particular day was get intimate with the Golden Gate Bridge in all its dimensions, take in its art deco ladder towers and coiled strands of suspension cable. He wanted to walk on its roadbed and trusses, run his hands along the round heads of its rivets and its peculiar dried-blood cast of paint, officially called "international orange." On the bridge that particular day, Jeb Corliss would reach for a destiny he was ready to seize.

If he could see a dozen years hence, he would see the many coming crashes in which he would break his back and ribs, and bones in both of his feet, legs, and arms. He would glimpse how some of his injuries would require weeks in the hospital. He would witness friends crippled and killed. All of which would be enough to make someone of lesser resolve consider quitting. But Jeb Corliss was beginning to consider the coming physical and emotional pain a worthwhile trade-off, because by risking his life he knew he would win something else: psychic relief and a growing sense of self-awareness and confidence. Already he was beginning to appreciate certain truths about himself. He recognized how, although fear caused most people to fumble, he hardly flinched.

Chapter 4

GIMME DANGER

As the new millennium drew near, and BASE jumping moved into a more prominent and public phase, science was making serious headway in describing how neurochemicals form the basis for a range of risky behaviors. For centuries man had understood intuitively the appeal of risking one's life, a sentiment Tim O'Brien summed up succinctly in "The Ghost Soldiers," "It's a hard thing to explain to someone who hasn't felt it, but the presence of death and danger has a way of bringing you fully awake. It makes things vivid. When you're afraid, really afraid, you see things you never saw before, you pay attention to the world."

Although more prosaic, science had lent its imprimatur, and a deeper understanding. A growing body of evidence suggested that preferences for risk can be traced partly to genes. Citing interplay between brain chemicals and physiology, geneticists said that those with a disposition toward risky thrills had at least partially been born that way.

Many of the discoveries were the result of the Human Genome Project, a thirteen-year effort to map the human genome, completed in 2003. And researchers studying genetic code homed in on sequences within the dopamine D4 receptor gene, known as DRD4. One of the most variable genes, DRD4 contains a large number of sequences that differ from person to person. These discrepancies are known as polymorphisms. Investigations into the relationship between DRD4 polymorphism and psychiatric and neurological disorders produced some interesting findings that suggested a possible causal relationship between this gene and a whole range of human behavior. Researchers published papers citing alleles—alternative forms of the gene—that correlated with everything from attention deficit hyperactivity disorder to schizophrenia, alcoholism, heroin addiction, and personality type associated with novelty seeking. The popular media would not be able to resist studies that associated DRD4 sequences with sexual promiscuity, and liberal political leanings, too. One journal called DRD4 "psychiatry's repeat offender."

There was little disagreement, however, about how dopamine, a neurotransmitter manufactured in the middle brain that promotes pleasure, acts as part of an internal reward system. As neural signals converge at a small group of interconnected areas of the brain called the medial forebrain pleasure circuit, dopamine plays a crucial role. Although the relationship between risk taking and dopamine remains the subject of continued inquiry, studies demonstrated that, at least for some people, dangerous scenarios feel *good*.

Through blood-chemistry analysis, clinicians discovered that those with a tendency to seek such intense stimulation have lower levels of monoamine oxidase, or MAO, an enzyme that plays a central role in breaking down neurotransmitters such as dopamine, serotonin, and norepinephrine. A protective enzyme, MAO regulates chemicals associated with arousal, inhibition, and pleasure the way a thermostat regulates the temperature in a room. As norepinephrine arouses the brain in response to stimuli, dopamine activates pleasure in response to arousal, and serotonin, in turn, counteracts norepinephrine and inhibits arousal. The resulting cocktail is tremendous arousal with tremendous pleasure. Although MAO is not completely understood, scientists agree that it at least plays a role in regulating the pleasure principle. Low MAO is associated with thrill seekers—hard-partying types, pioneers, police officers, social activists, and emergency workers. High MAO, by contrast, corresponds with depression and bipolar disorders.

One theory holds that those who have lower levels of dopamine experience a chronic state of low arousal in the brain's pleasure centers. For these people, novel and intense stimulation triggers a reward through the dopa-

mine pleasure reaction, and lack of stimulation, otherwise known as boredom, seems a fate worse than death. Although arousal and pleasure can be
stimulated by addictive substances such as heroin, cocaine, nicotine, or
alcohol, they can also be activated by dangerous thrills.

NOT ONLY IS RISK taking a genetic predisposition, but it's perfectly normal,
according to psychologist Marvin Zuckerman, professor emeritus at the
University of Delaware and a pioneer in the genetic aspect of arousal studies. Zuckerman calls people inclined to take risks "sensation-seekers." Beginning in the 1960s, Zuckerman and his colleagues organized sensation
seeking into a four-part scale, measuring the propensity for "thrill and
adventure seeking," with low sensation seekers on one end and high sensation seekers on the other. Zuckerman summed up much of his research in
a groundbreaking text, *Behavioral Expression and Biosocial Bases of Sensation Seeking*. In it, he defined "highs," as he calls them, as "seeking novel,
intense, or complex sensations and experiences and willing to take risks to
get them." His research revealed they tend to be impulsive, uninhibited,
and social and gravitate toward liberal political views. They enjoy loud
music, pornography, and horror movies, although vicarious thrills seldom
satisfy. They require *actual* risk—be it physical, social, or legal—to get
them juiced. Among them are big bettors, drug users, and practitioners of
adventure sports. Highs likewise hate boredom and need to up the intensity of activities in order to maintain their interest.

"It's called habituation," Zuckerman explains. "Any experience repeated
often enough loses its arousal. Even skydivers get bored. That's what leads
to things like BASE jumping . . . Because there's more risk."

There's more risk because events happen faster and there are fewer safeguards. But the risk is not exactly the point of the activity; it's the sensation
they're after. "They accept the risk for the sake of the experience," Zuckerman says, "the sensation. It's a matter of balancing the reward of the activity against the anticipation of risk . . . They need that to be fulfilled in their
lives."

One South African jumper has described the moment he approaches the edge as inspiring the most god-awful terror. The moment he jumps, though, all the sickness and fear simply drain away, replaced by rhapsody, "like a shot of morphine," he says.

In their most terrified moments, jumpers describe a sensation of sudden clarity similar to the enlightenment and consciousness of satori. In the present moment, the so-called *now,* they know that stepping off the building or cliff into the void could be the last thing they ever do. Tomorrow melts away, because it doesn't exist—there's a good chance it might not even happen. As far as yesterday is concerned, one jumper explains, "Who gives a rat's ass about your bills? All that matters at that moment is what happens in the next three seconds of your life. You become completely, 100 percent focused on everything that happens right at that moment. You can feel the hair on your body stand on end, and you can feel the wind touching each pore."

Car accident victims describe a similar sensation of time slowing. Psychologists call it tachypsychia, Greek for "speed of the mind," a false perception that our mental processes accelerate in times of stress. What actually happens is that fear allows subjects to gather more impressions, in greater detail, and only afterward does the resulting mountain of memories lend a distorted sense that time lengthened during a fearful episode.

Such altered states are the result of the physiology of fear, a time when the body shifts resources from rational thought and fine-motor function to pumping blood and oxygen to muscles, and gearing up for a brute-force reaction to a coming threat. Not everyone reacts the same way under such duress, though. Some summon superhuman strength and stamina. Others melt down under the strain, unable to perform even the simplest tasks.

The ideal response is what scientists call "the zone" or "flow state," a sweet spot of optimal performance that brings such intense pleasure that it can convey a feeling of being godlike. Psychologist Mihaly Csikszentmihalyi, a professor at Claremont Graduate University, who coined the term *flow state,* described it thus: "Being completely involved in an activity for its own sake. The ego falls away. Time flies. Every action, movement, and thought follows inevitably from the previous one, like playing jazz. Your whole being is involved, and you're using your skills to the utmost." Flow is not strictly related to sports, according to Csikszentmihalyi. It can come during any activity requiring intense concentration, when applied skills and a challenge achieve a kind of balance, delivering a fleeting moment of fulfillment.

Yet, paradoxically, it is the very unpredictability of what *could* happen that lights up the brain's pleasure centers like the Vegas Strip. This is what happens when a casino roulette wheel is spinning, or a blackjack dealer prepares to hit a player with another card. There's a possible financial pay-off, sure, but such fraught anticipation in those very moments of tense uncertainty provides its own rewards. And what is adventure if not an activity with an *uncertain* outcome? *The New Lexicon Webster's Dictionary of the English Language* defines adventure as "a dangerous or exciting incident, or a hazardous enterprise," and also as "a delightful experience." Indeed, adventure conveys both danger and delight.

Everyone defines adventure differently, of course. Some find satisfaction in waiting to watch a row of cherries line up on a slot machine; others need something stronger—say, stepping over the edge with a parachute. Still others obey the impulse to step over social boundaries, and some further, into extralegal territory.

Omer Mei-Dan is a BASE jumper, an internationally known orthopedic surgeon originally from Israel, and a professor at the University of Colorado School of Medicine. He described BASE jumping and surgery as exercises in control. "At the end of the day, it's a game of numbers," he said about jumping in a profile for the Colorado medical-school publication *CU Medicine Today.* "Can I live with a 90–10 or an 80–20 chance? I want to feel that I control almost everything that I can control." Mei-Dan likened jumping to surgical procedures he performed on players for FC Barcelona, one of the world's premier soccer teams. Some of the players he treated were earning $15 million and more. "It was a lot of pressure," Mei-Dan said, "and I like pressure."

For some, the pressure of treading to the margins, and launching beyond society's rules and safeguards, can serve as an act of self-discovery. Out there, you find out who you really are.

Such a moment arrived for Jeb Corliss on his sixth jump. He had been sizing up an antenna at a place known as the Conejo Grade, a few miles from Malibu, on the other side of the Santa Monica Mountains, at the base of a steep stretch of the Ventura Freeway outside Camarillo. Practically in his backyard, a jump there would satisfy the A in the coveted BASE cycle.

Consulting a sectional chart published by the Federal Aviation Administration depicting the altitude of objects that could pose a potential hazard to aircraft, he learned that the antenna topped out at three hundred feet. That was less than half the height of the Foresthill Bridge, and the minimum recommended by Helliwell and Shoebotham during training, because of the limited time to deploy and fly a parachute. The chart did not specify whether the height counted the hill the antenna sat on, however. To confirm, one night Jeb visited the antenna armed with an altimeter watch and a laser range finder. Parking his car, he walked alone along a strip of asphalt in the dark, traffic humming along the freeway. Climbing a chain-link fence topped by concertina wire, he scaled a ladder rising through the center of the antenna. At the top, his alti-watch and range finder confirmed the tower's height: three hundred feet above the ground.

There was a problem, though. Transmission equipment mounted on the antenna would be impossible to clear from the top. So he climbed down to where he could exit cleanly and measured again. The watch and the range finder read 260 feet.

The following day, he phoned Helliwell, who urged him not to jump. She said he wasn't ready, and that he could wind up in the guy wires in the event of an off-heading opening.

Jeb asked her how long it would take his parachute to open if he used a forty-eight-inch pilot chute and pitched immediately.

It could take 150 feet, she said, thinking that would be a deterrent.

Thank you, Jeb said, and hung up.

Subtracting 150 from 260 meant he had 110 feet to make any corrections, avoid guy wires, and fly his parachute to a landing. It was a sliver of time, offering no margin for error, but the jump was doable.

On the appointed day, Jeb packed his gear. Around dinnertime, as the sun dipped into the Pacific outside, he slung his rig over his shoulder and headed for the door. Gigi intercepted him in the foyer. In the six years since Jeb had vowed his intention to jump, she figured he would outgrow the fascination. When he didn't, she turned into a nervous wreck.

She had been waiting in his room when he returned from his first jump, at the Foresthill Bridge, tears in her eyes. When he went to the bridge again, she repeated her lonely vigil. Returning, Jeb found her sitting on his bed. "This is ridiculous," he said. "I'm going to continue doing what I'm doing, and you can't stop me. For you to sit here and waste your time with the worst possible terror inside isn't helping anybody."

So when they came face to face in the foyer, Gigi girded for another showdown. This time she would be firm. "I never tell you not to do anything and I never have your whole life," she began. "I never once told you not to do something. But this I'm telling you: Don't do this! I don't have a good feeling about this. I don't think you're ready for this. I think you need to get more experience for this. I don't think you're being smart—"

"Well, I'm doing it," Jeb cut her off.

"I feel so strongly about this," Gigi continued, her voice quavering with emotion, "that if you walk out that door, you're not welcome back. You will no longer live here and you will have to find your own place to live!"

Jeb considered her words—for about a second. "You're going to do what you have to do," he said with perfect equanimity. "I'm going to do what I have to do." Then he walked out the door and drove off.

That night, he ate alone in a restaurant and lingered until nearly midnight before driving to the antenna. Stern and a few other friends he called were not available. It was just Jeb and a new moon casting meager light on the shadows in the brush along the path. Over the hum of traffic on the 101, he heard rattlesnakes alert to his presence. Picking up a long stick, Jeb swept it in front of him to clear the way in case he encountered a snake. His heart drummed, and the merest hint of a breeze would have persuaded him to cancel. But the night was still.

He draped a carpet remnant over the razor wire along the fence, slipped over, and began climbing. With each rung, a reason not to continue tolled in his head. *He was alone. No one would alert help if he were hurt. The antenna was too low. He was too inexperienced. He could always come back. The antenna would always be there . . .*

He stopped beneath the transmission equipment, sitting with feet rested on metal supports, catching his breath and taking in the view of headlights and taillights floating along the freeway, the world oblivious to his presence. Pulling out his pilot chute, he stepped through the frame of the antenna and looked down at the glinting razor wire. *I cannot do this,* he thought. Watchful for signs, he noted a red light, marking the halfway point at 150 feet, flashing a steady message: *Stop . . . Stop . . . Stop . . .* As emotion strangled reason, he screamed into the night, "I'm not fucking doing this!" As his words echoed over the scrub terrain, his body pushed off involuntarily. Free from the tower, falling, he pitched his pilot chute immediately. *One . . .* Arms windmilling, he plummeted belly down, air flowing over bare skin on his arms and face, the road and cactus standing out starkly in the darkness. *Two . . .* The tower's guy wires and cross supports slid by in slow motion. Falling past the blinking red light, air rushed in his ears, roaring like a hurricane. Spotting the gleam from razor wire growing closer, he crossed his arms in front of his face, turned his head, and braced for impact. *Three . . .*

The force struck with such sudden violence that it knocked the wind from Jeb and left him seeing a constellation of stars. The only evidence he was alive was that he was upright and swinging, under canopy. Blinking, he watched the ground coming up quickly. With no time to grab toggles, he reached for a rear riser, connected to the parachute's rigging and steering system, and yanked hard, turning fast for the road and slamming into the asphalt, coming to a sudden stop on his back. Gazing up, the lights on the antenna seemed to blink red to a rhythm of blood squirting in his capillaries, which he could hear and feel with the utmost clarity. Sucking for air, his body went into nervous spasms. Senses hyperalert, Jeb heard insects crawling in the brush nearby and felt the presence of each molecule of air on his skin. Searching the darkness, he spotted rattlesnakes distinctly coiled among the cactus.

When Stern's phone rang late that night, he heard Jeb's breathless voice. "Dude," he said, "you don't understand . . ." Jeb always said, *You don't understand.* It was one of his favorite expressions. Shouting into the phone, he went on to explain how he felt a surge of power afterwards. He tried to convey to Stern what it had been like, the sensory experience of jumping this particular tower, but he was only beginning to understand the significance himself.

JEB CRAWLED INTO BED that night, but sleep would not come for two days. His mind reeled through the years he had wondered about jumping, and about himself. *Is this something I'm capable of? Is this me? Maybe it isn't . . .* At last he had the answer, along with some others. "I'm wired in a way where when I get scared, I operate better," he would say. "I think clearer. I move faster. My body works better." He was certain of something else, too. *He could do anything with his life. Nothing would stand in his way.* Not fear, not even for his life.

Within weeks Jeb had boarded a plane for Norway to continue training with Helliwell and Shoebotham outside the port city of Stavanger. They would jump from the big walls at Kjerag, an imperious gray slab 3,000 feet above the cold blue waters of Lysefjorden. A jumping club operated out of a tiny village called Lysebotn with the blessing of Norwegian authorities, luring jumpers from around the world in the summer months.

Back in Malibu, Gigi paced nights, and the Pacific roared on the beach as relentlessly as the storm of worry in her head. One restless morning, drawn to her balcony by a blood-red dawn, she spotted a swarm of bees blanketing the floor. Two decades earlier, pregnant with Jeb, she and Rick had rented a houseboat, a gingerbread barge, on Dal Lake in Srinagar, in the Kashmir Valley. It was autumn in the hills of the Hindu Kush, and they had hiked with porters in search of wild bee honey to collect for sale as part of their trading business. Back at the boat, the porters were packing honeycombs in crates when they were struck by a sudden swarm of vengeful bees from out of the mountains. The boat was pandemonium as everyone sought cover, but there was nowhere to go but overboard. Watching in wonderment, Gigi somehow remained untouched as men screamed and swatted around her. She would later reflect, "I always felt protected."

So when she saw the bees on the balcony in Malibu decades later, Gigi was seized by awareness that the cosmos, operating in its mysterious way, was sending a message. *The bees . . . Yes!* That's when she knew that Jeb would be fine, that what he was doing was not just okay, but it was a *great* thing. And just like that, she was released from worry.

For years after he vaulted the fence and fled the military in Dover, Gary strived to get on with a new life. If the army had been looking for him, they weren't doing so with any great gusto. He and Vivienne, the parents of a girl and boy, worked long hours to support their young family. Having gotten on the Actors' Equity Stunt Register in 1997, Gary advanced through the ranks. He took stunt work seriously and sweated to make it look realistic, gaining a reputation for professionalism and for saving money for productions with his efficient approach to scenes. In the industry he was known as "One-Take Gary," because that was usually how many times a director needed to shoot a fall or knockdown to nail it.

One day he was on location on Cephalonia in the Ionian Sea, working on *Captain Corelli's Mandolin,* a movie starring Nicolas Cage and Pené-lope Cruz, based on a book by Louis de Bernières about love amid a massacre during World War II.

One shoot consisted of putting a howitzer into action down a street while bullets stitched the walls of the buildings and explosions and fire rained from aircraft. During the course of filming the battle scenes, Gary recognized the face of a man on the set, but he couldn't place him. "I'm not sure where, but I'm sure we've met before," Gary finally said.

The man puffed out his chest and announced, "I used to be a sergeant major in 3 PARA."

Gary admitted that he, too, had been in 3 PARA. His service and the man's had overlapped by several months. Although they must have crossed paths somewhere in the battalion, the sergeant major had left before Gary took flight and gave no hint he knew about it. He told Gary, "I have something that will interest you," pulling from his pocket a piece of paper—a list of men currently serving in 3 PARA who would be joining them on set as extras when shooting resumed in a few weeks.

Gary looked at the list and recognized several names. His heart sank. If the men showed up on set, he was in trouble. When he returned for three more weeks of shooting, Gary pulled his cap low and avoided the 3 PARA contingent as best he could. It was no use; some of them recognized him, and were eager to talk. They made no mention of turning him in, but Gary guessed it was only a matter of time before the army picked up his trail again. He was two thousand miles from home in a Mediterranean idyll, working a job he had strived to obtain to support his family, and still he was looking over his shoulder.

Not that he had exactly been keeping a low profile. In 1998 he made a BASE jump by riding a BMX bike off a five-hundred-foot cliff at Beachy Head, a chalk headland in East Sussex, near Brighton. The stunt landed him in the papers and on television. Still, Gary was tired of running, and before returning home he made up his mind to do something about it.

Back in the UK after shooting for the film wrapped, Gary rang up a friend who worked as a civilian lawyer and explained that he wanted to bring the matter of his status with the military to a close. They wrote a letter to the adjutant, the head of personnel for 3 PARA. Among other things, Gary recalled explaining in the letter that he had friends in the press. *Toe the line with me,* he remembered writing, *or I'll go to the press with stories about bullying and the way the regiment deals with certain issues.* Two weeks later, an administrative discharge arrived for Gary in which the army determined his military conduct to be "UNSATISFACTORY." He was no good to the regiment, and a lost cause as a soldier. He was finally free.

It was a relief to no longer be on the run. Vivienne's mother was off his back, too, having been dragged into the deception once when the police showed up at her door looking for Gary. His parents also breathed a sigh of relief.

To further fix his future, Gary married Vivienne, and they settled in a seventeenth-century cider mill on two acres in rural Wales. Vivienne recalls that Gary did nothing to improve the interior of their home, but he did clear the woods to build the children tree houses. He bought them all-terrain vehicles and bicycles and led them in jumping from cliffs into the water. Living life with an eye to the next adventure, he eagerly pulled his family along. "When I was pregnant with our son, he would say, 'How would you like to go to Pakistan in November?'" Vivienne recalls. "'Hmm, I think I'm having a baby in November.' He was fun, different, and never a dull day. He taught me to ski, taught Lydia to ski, took us to Amsterdam in January time. When we would go out for a walk with Gary, a lot of people will walk on the trail along the path. Gary always goes off the beaten trail to climb on trees . . . When we went on family holiday, the parachute was always in the back. We would sit on the top of the car and watch Dad jump off and parachute down to us, and with the police after us, gather the parachute in and go off, and can't stop until we've lost the police."

Having put to rest the uncertainty surrounding his status with the army, Gary settled down to a life in the country—not for the quiet, necessarily, but for the promise of fertile ground to hatch future adventures.

Part Two

FLIGHT

Chapter 5

WINGS

> Any sufficiently advanced technology is indistinguishable from magic.
>
> —*Sir Arthur C. Clarke*

*T*hey come to Arco for adventure, too, the rock climbers, hikers, windsurfers, and jumpers, and they find it here in the Dolomites of northern Italy, on limestone cliffs favored by climbers, where a medieval castle clings high above narrow cobblestone lanes. Windsurfers skitter across Lake Garda, and from Monte Brento, jumpers enjoy a mile-high plunge into a broad valley. In the morning, they all meet at a café at the base of a cliff for the very best coffee and to share rides up the mountain to a trailhead followed by a hike to the exit.

Jeb Corliss first came here in the winter of 1999, having worked like mad as a graphic artist to afford another trip to the big walls of Europe. He was doing it, living the life. He had connected online with an excitable Frenchman named François, then met him at the airport in Geneva, and they traveled across Europe, jumping their way to Arco, where they encountered, among others, a group of Russians whom everyone called the Russian Mafia—and indeed, some were genuine underworld figures, brandishing big wads of cash and generally making everyone nervous.

One day up on Brento, Jeb and François watched as one of the Russians laid a garment on the snow, a thing that resembled a wetsuit, with webbing sewed under the arms and between the legs. No one had ever seen anything like it. "What are you going to do with *that*?" someone asked. The owner explained that what they were looking at was a wingsuit, and that he was going to jump with it from the cliff and fly.

With all eyes on him, the man geared up, stepped into the suit, and penguin-walked to the edge. Performing a countdown, he launched, plunging straight down at first, legs shoulder width apart, arms extended at right angles to his body. Subtly at first but steadily, he began to glide out over the valley. From the mountain they watched with intense concentration as the wingman became the merest speck before finally, a half mile distant, his parachute bloomed in the sky. "There's the future," someone remarked, breaking a stunned silence on the mountain, and yes, everyone had to agree.

As jumpers, they had all liked to think that BASE made them truly bird-like. Someone was always saying that the sport was the closest approximation to flying. You could *track* from a high terminal object, after all. But those who witnessed the Russian's flight were forced to reconsider their stance. His weird suit and webbed arms and legs gave him a distinct advantage. Jeb, for one, thought: *This dude's flying! This changes everything!*

Jeb was determined to get his hands on a wingsuit. His timing was impeccable. The Russian had fashioned his suit from a photo of one used by a Frenchman named Patrick de Gayardon. As it happened, two other men, Jari Kuosma of Finland and Robert Pečnik of Croatia, had recently taken de Gayardon's inspiration even further. Skydivers both, they had teamed up in a commercial outfit they called Birdman, taking orders for custom wingsuits. Pečnik brought experience constructing jumpsuits for skydiving, and Kuosma applied a degree in international business. "It was just such a big jump into the unknown," Kuosma would say about their venture. "We were doing something that we knew some people were doing before . . . but they were all dead."

*B*ird cults have preoccupied cultures throughout history, from Siberia, where shaman priestesses believed to be the very descendants of birds dressed in bird suits, to Central Africa, where Nyanga tribesmen donned bird masks to identify their bush soul, to Lascaux, France, where Paleolithic cave paintings showed, according to the scholar of mythology Joseph

Campbell, "a shaman . . . lying in a trance, wearing a bird mask with a figure of a bird perched on a staff beside him." Carl Jung had called birds "symbols of transcendence" and said the birdman shaman was on a quest to the realm of the unconscious by which he may achieve the ultimate goal—full knowledge of the potential of his individual *Self.*

Thus, flight as the highest expression of man.

Most discussions of wingsuits, though, begin at Icarus and Daedalus and wend through hundreds of years of records attesting to early winged men in China, England, Greece, Spain, Turkey, and Italy, where Leonardo sketched plans for a glider, and continue into the modern era, beyond the Wright brothers and into the wild wake of 1927, when Lindbergh piloted the *Spirit of St. Louis* from Long Island to Le Bourget Field, in Paris, demonstrating the range and potential of new flying machines to carry passengers around the world.

It is worth pausing there, though, at the dawn of a new age in aviation, to get acquainted with Clem Sohn, a skydiver from Lansing, Michigan, a performer at the barnstorming air shows during the Great Depression, billed as "the Michigan Icarus" and "the Batman."

The most popular acts during this era were low-pull contests, games of chicken with the ground among two or more skydivers who exited an aircraft at the same time. Whoever had the balls to delay pulling his rip cord the longest was the winner. The winner, of course, sometimes had death as his prize, a morbid prospect that was a guaranteed crowd-pleaser. Sohn had success as a low-pull specialist, but he soon devised a plan to guarantee he would be the shows' undisputed feature attraction.

Looking to the anatomy of flying squirrels and bats for principles to guide design, he built wings using airplane fabric and metal tubing, fastening them between his arms and the side of his jumpsuit. He sewed a tail fin between his legs. The result, weighing eight pounds, was a suit that on sight alone was enough to draw attention. Whether it would fly was another matter.

With a flair for showmanship, Sohn opened testing to the public on a winter day in 1935, in Daytona Beach, Florida. Stepping from a plane more than two miles above the palm-fringed coast, he dropped, according to eyewitnesses reports, two thousand feet in free fall and, gathering speed, spread his arms and legs.

As his wings deflected air, Sohn's downward speed slowed and he slanted across the sky. A report in *Time* noted how he bent his knees and somersaulted, banked left and right, leveled off, dove, and pulled up again. At six thousand feet he closed his wings and pulled his rip cord. Under parachute, he landed three miles from his starting point. According to *Time,* his flight had lasted seventy-five seconds, screaming through the sky at 130 miles per hour. Sohn and his wingsuit landed on the front page of newspapers across the country. Newsreel pictures of his flight sold for $300, a nice sum during the Depression. Suddenly in demand, Sohn earned what *Time* termed "a tidy living." Chevrolet sponsored him, its name stenciled on the underside of his wings. Newspaper reporters tailed him, chronicling his stunts. Sohn explained to them that he had grander ambitions: he envisioned a time when anyone would be able to don a wingsuit and take flight; when the military would use wings to drop paratroopers behind enemy lines; and finally a day when he would stall and *land* his wings without a parachute.

Imitators cropped up in Sohn's wake wherever he went. Without design standards or adequate training, many of these copycat wingmen wound up dead. Sohn suffered close calls, too. At a demonstration during the opening of London's Gatwick Airport in 1936, he spun out of control, and although he activated his reserve a couple hundred feet off the deck, Sohn struck a taxi on landing, breaking his arm and injuring his shoulder.

A year later, healed and at the height of his popularity, he arrived at the Paris Air Show, at an airfield in Vincennes, a Paris suburb northeast of the 12th arrondissement. The day was April 25, 1937, and the newsreels said two hundred thousand spectators had gathered under clear skies. Sohn was twenty-six. With his sandy hair, white jumpsuit, and leather helmet and goggles, he cut the figure of the dashing aviator as he slipped coolly into the open cockpit of a single-engine Farman. Before doing so, it was reported that he remarked, "I feel as safe as you would in your grandmother's kitchen." The crowd roared its approval as the plane sprinted along the airstrip and into the sky.

Sohn stepped from the cockpit at ten thousand feet and pirouetted into the air. A canister of chemicals attached to his leg emitted smoke, allowing those on the ground to trace his movements. He banked, somersaulted, and dove, gliding through the sky like a swallow feeding on flies, the newspapers said. They reported that his flight lasted nearly two minutes. At one thousand feet, Sohn drew in his wings and pulled his parachute's rip cord, but there was a problem and it did not deploy. Cutting away, Sohn reached for his reserve and pulled the cord. This time the chute and lines emerged but got snared in his wings. As his parachute flapped limply above, moans went up from the crowd and people turned away, the papers said, as Sohn thudded into a field. The crowd sprinted toward his broken body. Later, a witness told a reporter: "When I realized Clem Sohn was doomed, I felt worse than ever during the World War . . . The hush coming over the crowd was the most impressive thing I have ever seen . . . And when Clem Sohn hit the ground, it sounded like an explosion."

Sohn's death made newspapers around the world. Footage of his fatal plunge featured in newsreels. Yet grimmer developments soon seized headlines. The day after Sohn's death, the Luftwaffe terrorized civilians in Guernica during the Spanish Civil War. Before the decade's end, the Nazis would invade Poland, pounding cities and towns from the air with superior bombers. The war altered aviation irrevocably. The world's top aviators— including air-show stuntmen—were drawn into the conflict as instructors, pilots, engineers, and advisers. When the fighting ended, some resumed working in air shows, but it was soon obvious that their heyday had passed. The culture surrounding flight changed from a hell-for-leather approach to a precision pursuit. The new icons were jet pilots and astronauts, men selected for their superior abilities from among the most elite ranks of aviation. In this environment, amateur wingsuit pilots, with their crude contraptions, were relics, their main appeal the lurid spectacle of a potential fatality, a fact emphasized by those performing under names like Death Dodgers and Death's Angels.

In this climate, the USPA, the governing body for skydiving, first organized in the immediate postwar years as the National Parachute-Riggers, Inc., took a dim view of wingsuits, banning them outright at member drop zones, except with written permission. The danger and body counts resulting from wingsuits lent a bad name to a new sport striving for respectability. Wingmen would persist, using canvas, whalebone, wood, even fiberglass, but these materials did little to improve glide. Or they fouled parachutes. Some simply failed to catch on. It would require innovation in parachute design, and the passage of several decades, before a man with the right proportions of vision and courage provided the crucial link for wingsuits to move forward.

Early parachutes were round, dome-shaped designs, which are still in use today for military paratroopers and cargo drops. Round parachutes open easily and reliably. Yet they rely on drag (the slowing force of air resistance) and leave a parachutist drifting with little maneuverability, forcing a landing where the wind dictates.

A kite and balloon designer working on scientific projects for the U.S. military would change all that in the 1960s. His name was Domina Jalbert, and he patented the modern ram-air parafoil, a rectangular parachute with a profile inspired by an airplane wing. Air literally rams into vents on the chute, inflating individual cells, which gives the canopy a wing shape and provides lift. This allows a parachutist to not only control the rate of descent but glide much farther than with a round design. Handheld toggles connected to risers—lines that attach to the canopy—allow a parachutist to alter the way air enters a ram-air chute's leading edge, increasing control and maneuverability. Compared with a round canopy, a ram-air chute is so superior that skilled parachutists can land on a Frisbee-size target.

Patrick de Gayardon was one such skilled parachutist. Known as Deug (pronounced *doog*) to his friends, he was, by the 1990s, the most famous skydiver in the world. He starred at the early X Games in skysurfing, a discipline using a snowboard-like apparatus to ride air currents and perform freestyle maneuvers in free fall. Everything about him, from his attitude to his feats to his dark, brooding good looks, made him an ideal ambassador for his sport, and for consumer brands attempting to cash in on the cachet of skydiving to push their products. Reebok featured Deug in a TV commercial. "He was rippin' out moves left and right to 'Suicide Blonde' by INXS," reflected Troy Hartman, who was inspired to take up skydiving and later won a gold medal in skysurfing at the 1997 X Games. "It was insane!"

An Italian watch company called Sector underwrote many of Deug's projects as he jumped from the Eiffel Tower and skysurfed over the North Pole. He rode a snowboard off a cliff in Norway and parachuted to the ground. He plunged from a helicopter into Mexico's Sótano de las Golondrinas, or Cave of Swallows, and made a BASE jump adjacent to Angel Falls, in Venezuela, the world's highest waterfall. In 1995 he set a world record for the highest parachute jump without oxygen, plummeting from an Ilyushin Il-76, a massive Russian transport plane, 41,910 feet above Moscow, an altitude at which air temperatures were 67 degrees Fahrenheit below zero.

Deug laughed at danger and scoffed at skydiving taboos, chanting "Blue sky, black death!" Although he was number one, it was lonely at the top. "In half his mind, he was always in the sky," friend and camera flier Andi Duff recalled, "and that made it difficult for people to have a conversation with him—as soon as the conversation went away from skydiving, they lost him."

An inveterate tinkerer, Deug traveled the world lugging cases filled with contraptions for testing at the various drop zones he visited. By the mid-1990s the contents of his luggage included a wingsuit. Drawing on ram-air principles, he sewed two layers of tightly woven nylon—the kind used in parachutes—between the arms and torso, and between the legs, of a normal jumpsuit. When put in action, air rammed between the layers and formed the shape of small wings, providing lift and doubling time in free fall. Deug wasn't necessarily flying; he was more falling along a glide slope with a ratio of 1:1. Thus, if falling at fifty miles per hour, he moved forward at fifty miles per hour. A skydiver in free fall generally has a 0:1 glide slope, and parachutes achieve a 3:1 slope—moving three feet forward for every foot of descent. With some modifications to his suit, Deug eventually gained a glide slope of 2.5:1, slowing vertical speed to about thirty miles per hour while moving forward at seventy-five miles per hour. It was an incredible achievement that he was capable of a glide comparable to that of a parachute.

During public demonstrations of his wings, Deug buzzed journalists gathered on a lookout tower at Aiguille du Midi, near Mont Blanc. At the Grand Canyon, he jumped seventy-five times, sweeping closer to the cliffs with each flight. Above Chambéry, France, he exited a Pilatus Porter, a Swiss airplane designed for tight takeoff and landing zones, and flew alongside and reentered the plane while it was still in flight. Everywhere, he caused a sensation like Sohn had a lifetime earlier.

By 1998 Deug was thirty-eight and at the peak of his powers, but friends noticed he had grown glum and sloppy with safety, sometimes packing his parachute in haste. That spring he made his way to Hawaii, where he had an ownership stake in a drop zone on the North Shore of Oahu. He and friends stayed in a rented house equipped with a sewing machine, which he used to modify the deflector on his rig, a flap that creates more consistent airflow and improves wingsuit performance. A friend recalled Deug was lost deep in his work. "I disassemble, I unstitch, I sew, I reassemble, that's ugly," he recalled Deug saying. "I can't sew properly, but it works."

On the morning of April 13, Deug and friends climbed aboard a small plane at the drop zone. There are many powerful sensations associated with skydiving. The interior of a small aircraft provides none of the pleasant ones. The fuselage was dark, noisy, cramped, and heavy with the whiff of human sweat and fuel. As the plane edged higher, the view outside took in a sublime landscape of banana and pineapple plantations plotted on a narrow plane between a pale sea streaked with foam and the green wrinkles of the Waianae Mountains. On the load was Deug's friend Adrian Nicholas. Sheathed in wingsuits, he and Deug stepped from the interior into the square bay, howling with wind. Falling in succession like beads strung on an invisible filament, both men accelerated across the sky, playfully crossing paths. Nicholas could not help but notice the beatific expression his friend wore, eyes hidden behind streamlined sunglasses, hair plastered back by the wind. As Nicholas opened his parachute at 3,500 feet, Deug peeled away toward the drop zone to extend the flight.

The men appeared small as mitochondria to those squinting into the sky from the ground. But Deug fast grew more distinct, and at a thousand feet his friends could see him pretty clearly, handles in hand, chute trailing in an uninflated tangle. He let out a deep-throated scream as he approached the ground at terminal speed, then disappeared beneath the big green leaves of banana trees and was killed instantly.

An investigation would reveal that in his obsessive quest to improve equipment and performance, Deug had unwittingly disabled his parachute systems with the sewing machine.

HIS WINGSUIT would not die, though, and less than a year after Deug's death, Jeb Corliss got his first glimpse of a crude reproduction in Italy. Soon after ordering a custom suit from Birdman, a box arrived by mail at the drop zone in Perris Valley. Inside was a black wingsuit with black zippers, just as Jeb had specified. Using high-density nylon and double-reinforced stitching, the workmanship was clearly superior to the one belonging to the Russian jumper. But the suit came with no instructions, and when Jeb attempted to log his first jump in the flight manifest at Perris Valley, the staff had never seen a wingsuit before.

Unsure what to make of it, they asked if, once at altitude, he should jump from the planeload before or after the others.

Jeb was unsure. "Let me go last," he said.

Tumbling from the plane at thirteen thousand feet, he stretched his arms and legs wide. The wings filled with air, and he glided forward. At five thousand feet, an electronic altimeter sounded an alarm in his helmet's earpiece, indicating the time to pull. Unzipping his wings, arms free, Jeb grabbed the risers guiding his parachute and returned to earth. He would make ten jumps that day, each time gaining greater feel for the suit. Any slight movement of his head, arms, hips, or legs deflected air, producing an instant response. His heart soared. The sadness that characterized so much of his life had gradually ebbed till there was scant trace of those feelings. He was flying.

Chapter 6

THE WORLD IS A PLAYGROUND

> Fear cannot be without hope, nor hope
> without fear.
>
> —*Baruch Spinoza*

A round the time wingsuits arrived on the scene, the old guard of the jumping world, dedicated to an underground pastime with a tradition of secrecy and restraint, was coming to grips with a new generation intent on pulling off high-profile, public feats and basking in the publicity that followed. Training programs and businesses catering to jumpers meant that a novice no longer had to endure an apprenticeship of sitting around fires at night where beers were passed, listening to mentors telling old war stories that began, *There I was, sure I was either going to die or get arrested*... One no longer really required the imprimatur of his fellows in the jumping community to be on his way.

When jumping had been smaller and tight-knit, it was easier to get everyone to toe the line. "We used to use peer pressure to ostracize them," DiGiovanni says about those who violated the sport's codes of conduct. And if that didn't work, there was always vigilantism.

John Vincent, the jumper who inspired a teenage Jeb Corliss to pursue BASE, finally ran afoul of his fellow jumpers in Atlanta by leaping from a crane at a construction site and sending footage to a local TV news station for airing. Vincent did not know that others had been using the crane clandestinely. Their site burned, the other jumpers were bent on revenge.

Showing up at Vincent's apartment with pantyhose on their heads, like bank robbers, they rang the buzzer. When a groggy Vincent came to the door, he was seized, dragged inside, held down, and duct-taped. His attackers put plastic on the floor, bathed him in tar, and doused him with feathers. "Hey, man, we're your BASE buddies," they announced as they left, message delivered.

The incident had been filmed, and the footage, and talk of it, made the rounds, the lesson plain to any other would-be code violators. Eventually, though, not even the threat of a tar-and-feathering would chasten a new breed.

Perhaps it was inevitable that a personality type eager to see which objects they could get away with jumping from would also be curious about what else they could pull off. As one longtime jumper said, summing up the feeling: "I love the cat-and-mouse."

Another factor in the generational shift was a rise of new technology, namely development of small video cameras that could be attached to a jumper, and a World Wide Web on which footage could easily be disseminated. Suddenly it seemed possible for a man to make his name, and maybe his living, on daring jumps.

Exhibit A was an Austrian named Felix Baumgartner. Baumgartner had acquired skydiving training in the military and began performing parachute demonstrations for civilians in the 1980s for a then virtually unknown beverage company called Red Bull, with headquarters at Fuschl am See, Salzburg. With the backing of Red Bull, Baumgartner would make two record-setting jumps in 1999—the highest from a building (a 1,475-foot leap from the Petronas Towers, in Kuala Lumpur) and the lowest ever, a 95-foot drop from the *Christ the Redeemer* statue, standing sentinel over Rio de Janeiro. Handsome, articulate, fearless, Baumgartner stepped straight from central casting as a classic pitchman. In BASE, though, he was a creature without precedent, a figure who profited from high-profile acts that repudiated the jumper's ethic of "leave no trace" in favor of a "look at me" approach.

He was not the only one, though. In 1998 and 1999, an offshore oil worker from Norway named Thor Alex Kappfjell went on a spree in Manhattan. He parachuted from the Empire State Building and the Chrysler Building, eluding security and police and defying Mayor Rudy Giuliani. Kappfjell sold footage of his Empire and Chrysler stunts to the syndicated tabloid show *Extra* and made headlines worldwide. In interviews, he called the Empire State Building episode "my biggest dream for many years."

Giuliani called the antics "irresponsible," and Police Commissioner Howard Safir threatened to punish Kappfjell if he followed through with a vow to jump from the World Trade Center. "I know it gets a great deal of attention," the mayor said. "It's really a stupid and jerky thing to do, and it's a very dangerous thing to do, not only for him but for the people below."

Still, Kappfjell returned to New York months later. On March 25, 1999, he sneaked to the top of the South Tower of the World Trade Center and leaped from 110 stories into the city. Landing on West Street, he vanished into the World Financial Center. "It was fantastic," he told the *New York Post.* "I have no words to describe it." He told Oslo newspaper *Dagbladet* that he "jumped to applause from those on the roof and the street." Kappfjell again sought to sell footage to *Extra.* However, instead of sending payment, as promised, the TV show arrived at his room at the Hotel Carter with cameras and cops, capturing footage of the arrest of Kappfjell, his cousin, and a photographer.

Kappfjell would plead guilty to three counts of reckless endangerment and admit to sneaking into the country using his brother's passport after he had been placed on wanted lists by New York police. Sentenced to seven days of community service, he sued *Extra* for breach of contract for airing his Trade Center footage without paying him and for tipping off police to his whereabouts. Before the matter was resolved, however, Kappfjell was killed in Norway while jumping off Kjerag in fog early on July 5.

Helliwell and the old guard, who had done so much to emphasize values of maintaining a low profile to Jeb and other students, looked on such prominent and illegal jumps with dismay. "'Look at me on television and this bandit illegal thing I just did, and showing it to the rest of the world,'" she says. "The rest of us are kind of going, 'Oh, no.'"

Not everyone saw it that way, though. Some would see an alternative to a wage earner's lifestyle.

Although Jeb had acquired a wingsuit, he continued to devote himself to BASE adventures. At a café in Arco, he and François had discussed the subject of freedom. Their conceit: *What would you do if you could do anything?* Francois said he would jump from Angel Falls, in Venezuela, and in the spirit of spontaneity, he and Jeb decided that was what they would do.

They drove to Paris and booked flights to Caracas. After landing, they boarded a bus crowded with Indian peasants and their bawling babies and livestock, enduring a long overland drive on rutted roads to a town near Auyántepui, which means "Devil's Mountain" in the language of the local Pemon Indians. From the top of the mountain, Angel Falls spills 3,212 spectacular feet into Devil's Canyon, a brown squiggle through dense vegetation deep in the jungle in Canaima National Park. Located in the Guiana Highlands of southeast Venezuela, the park is larger than the state of Maryland. Characterized by canyons, flattop mountains, and dense tropical forest, the region remains as rugged, if not as remote, today as when it served as the inspiration for the setting of Sir Arthur Conan Doyle's classic *The Lost World,* a primeval place, largely unexplored, where dinosaurs had escaped extinction.

Posing as tourists, Jeb and François each offered a pilot $25 to fly a small plane over the falls, ostensibly to take photos. In their packs they stowed skydiving gear, and once in the air they secretly donned their rigs and instructed the pilot to fly to a higher altitude, all a precursor to the real jump they had in mind. François thrust $100 into the startled man's hand for his trouble and followed Jeb out the door. They parachuted to the top of Auyántepui, and that was where the improvisational nature of the trip began to go haywire. Unprepared to spend longer than a day out in the jungle, they had few provisions—little water or food and no tents or sleeping bags.

They slept on the mountain that night and in the morning hiked to the falls, only to discover the landing obscured by clouds. They waited all day for clear skies, and finally jumped that evening, a beautiful and long free fall to a trouble-free landing. But with darkness coming, they found themselves alone and facing another night in the jungle. Seeking shelter in a cave, they were devoured by mosquitoes during another long night without food. They would spend yet another night in the jungle. On the fourth morning, boats carrying tourists to the cataract finally arrived on the river. Bug-bitten, ragged, and starving, they used their remaining money to buy chicken and water from the boat's crew, greedily devouring it on the ride along the river to Canaima, deflecting questions as to what exactly they had been doing out there alone. They explained to the skeptical captain that they were nature photographers.

When he arrived home in Malibu, Jeb recounted his adventure for a baffled Gigi and Fitzmorris, neither of whom could fathom why he would go to such lengths for a thrill that lasted only a few seconds. "It was all about the preparation," Jeb explained. "It was all about going to the places, meeting the people. It was the entire experience. It's not about the sixteen seconds of free fall."

His parents remained skeptical of the value of his adventures, particularly as they concerned career prospects. They wanted him to come home and continue graphic design work. Jeb had other ideas; anyway, he was terrible at graphic design. Endeavoring to find out just what his footage was worth, Jeb phoned television producers about selling videos from Venezuela. A producer for the show *Real TV* agreed to pay $10,000, a baseline for further sales. Having figured out a way to make jumping pay, Jeb turned to plotting further adventures.

Soon he was in South Africa, where he and a jumper from Russia named Yuri brought their wingsuits and hooked up with a South African police officer named John, whom Jeb had met on Kjerag, the big wall in Norway where jumpers gathered each summer. In Cape Town they linked up with a righteous crew of South African jumpers and wound up on Milner Peak, a six-thousand-footer in the Hex River Mountains of the Western Cape. Milner Amphitheatre is a three-thousand-foot wall the color of a coppery sunset, with a monster ledge about two-thirds of the way down, making it a two-stage jump—a sixteen-hundred-foot plunge to a landing on a ledge, where you repack your chute, for another nine-hundred-foot finale. It was to be Jeb's first BASE jump with a wingsuit, and he and Yuri intended to clear the ledge in one fell swoop.

A Jet Ranger chopper whisked them to a ledge, and they rappelled a hundred feet down to a ledge. It was nerve-racking just getting into position. The measure of a wingsuit pilot at the time was his ability to fly far, getting maximum glide. And Yuri distinguished himself as one of the world's superior pilots, "a natural," in Jeb's words, who easily sailed over the monster ledge and pitched with plenty of altitude. When it was Jeb's turn, though, he struggled to find his glide, and became aware immediately that he would not clear the outcropping. Having planned for this possibility, he dipped hard left for a fissure gouged in the rock, dropping into a ravine, walls rising on either side as he traveled the trench the way Luke Skywalker had in his X-Wing on the surface of the Death Star in the climactic scene from *Star Wars*. Moving at more than one hundred miles an hour, Jeb burst through the end of the ravine into open air and pitched immediately, grateful to be alive. He had a lot to learn about flying a wingsuit.

Yuri headed home to Europe, but Jeb remained in South Africa to tour jump sites without his wingsuit. Wind canceled many of his plans, but from Durban, he and John drove an hour outside Pietermaritzburg to a place called Howick Falls, a three-hundred-foot plunge along the Umgeni River in the hilly midlands of KwaZulu-Natal Province. It was the rainy season, and the swollen river churned brown like chocolate milk.

John planned to film Jeb and a blond kid known as Rat as they jumped from the rim of the gorge adjacent to the waterfall, the river below providing a margin of safety if anything went wrong. Grabbing a handful of grass, Jeb tossed the blades to the wind, and they fell mostly straight down. Wind did not appear to be a factor. Only a malfunction would pose a potential problem. "In the analysis of risk versus reward, the risk didn't seem very high," Jeb would say later. "We decided to go ahead and jump."

As the more experienced of the two, Jeb jumped first, pilot chute in his hand for a quick pitch, given the relatively low altitude. "All right, bro," he announced to Rat. "Let's go."

Pitching without delay, Jeb nevertheless made a small but significant error with his body position as his canopy inflated. Because he had dipped his left shoulder, his parachute opened asymmetrically and swung hard to the left, ninety degrees, steering Jeb toward the veil of water pumping off the ledge. *Oh, no . . .* As he came in, legs out defensively, the water swallowed him and his parachute in one gulp, slamming Jeb into a ledge behind the falls in a seated position, insides crackling with the impact. In the ensuing chaos, rocks punched into his ribs and he plunged downward, a long fall headfirst into a cool green pool beneath the turbid water at the base of the falls. He knew he was deep underwater from the pressure expanding in his ears.

Kicking in desperation for daylight, he broke the surface and gulped air. He was a few feet from the waterfall. Slowly stroking for shore, bug-eyed with adrenaline, he paused in shallow water. In an area littered with large rocks, he rolled onto his back, exhausted. His parachute surfaced several feet away, rippling like some marine monster in the wash from the falls. Without strength to stand or crawl, his back throbbing with pain, Jeb hoped for a speedy rescue.

It took his friends an hour to reach him. When they did, John dragged Jeb as far as he could from the water, which wasn't more than a few feet. Jeb was heavy and waterlogged, and the rocks were slippery. Jeb lay shivering, small crabs scuttling from the rocks to feast on the raw, wounded flesh on his back.

Due to the coming darkness, a helicopter rescue was out of the question. It would be a long night. Three hours passed before a rescue team arrived. When it did, Jeb refused painkillers, out of his normal aversion to drugs and alcohol but also in the belief that he would be better able to determine the source of his pain if it was not blunted by morphine. On the rugged, dark terrain, it would take rescuers six hours to carry Jeb to an ambulance. They stopped to rest several times along the way, including once to pump Jeb with muscle relaxant when he experienced violent convulsions. He was too shattered to argue.

In the hospital, machines monitoring his vitals, Jeb lay shirtless in bed, tubes taped to his arms and disappearing into his nostrils.

"BASE jumping is fun, right?" John asked.

"Yeah," Jeb said weakly, waving a finger. "Ouch!" He had broken his back, sacrum, tailbone, ribs, sternum, and a knee and somehow chipped a tooth.

His resolve, though, remained intact. A doctor entered the room and said, "I'll bet you're never going to do that again."

Jeb responded in a voice quavering with emotion. "Dude," he said, "there's only two things that will prevent me from BASE jumping."

"What's that?"

"Quadriplegia or *death*!"

The doctor laughed.

Jeb would spend a month in the hospital in Pietermaritzburg, long enough to develop a romance with the daughter of a family friend from South Africa. She came to read to him in the hospital most days, and this would lead to an emotional parting when finally Jeb flew to LAX on a commercial flight, accompanied by a paramedic and nurse. They occupied nine seats in coach. He wound up spending one night at a hospital in Compton, and that frightful experience was enough to cure Jeb. He told his parents to get him home.

Within a week of arriving home, Jeb discarded a back brace and boarded a flight to Mexico, where his friend Omer Mei-Dan, the orthopedic surgeon, arranged for a jumping expedition to Mexico's Cave of Swallows. A one-thousand-foot sinkhole in the jungles of the Mexican midlands, the cave got its name from the groups of swallows that nest in the walls, flocking like a feathered tornado twice a day while leaving and entering the hole on their rounds. Yes, he was back.

At home again, Jeb began a yoga regimen to rehabilitate his injuries. He never thought he would practice yoga, but he had to admit that it worked. By and by, he began to feel better. His life was looking up. The entire ordeal in South Africa had been filmed, and would make Jeb a small fortune when he sold the footage to producers from *Real TV, Ripley's Believe It or Not!* and eventually something on cable called *Holy @#%*!*

Chapter 7

DWAIN, SLIM, AND DR. DEATH

> And immediately there fell from his eyes something like scales, and he regained his sight, and he got up and was baptized.
>
> —*Acts 9:18*

At the offices of Basic Research, in Perris, they were beginning to hear a lot of grumbling. Jumpers were calling up Helliwell and Shoebotham. *Who is this guy?* they demanded to know.

"He's definitely pushing the envelope," Shoebotham would explain. "But he's not doing it with carelessness. He's doing it because he's pushing himself; he's pushing the sport, but he's not doing it in a careless fashion."

Pushing the sport?! The guy needs to slow the fuck down!

Shoebotham finally confronted Jeb. "Okay, we've seen other guys do what you just did and die from it," he said. "We've seen kids come with a lot of energy . . ."

In addition to the problem of glory seekers, the old guard contended with a cult growing around some of the most progressive and dangerous maneuvers in free fall that anyone had ever witnessed. Jumpers were attempting half twists, full twists, half pikes, full pikes, full twisting triple flips, often from seriously low objects—slider-down stuff just a couple hundred feet off the deck.

Shoebotham was against the new acrobatics, or "aerials," predicting that they would only lead to a lot of injuries and death. And injuries and death would only draw a fresh round of negative attention to the sport. "In those early days, when I was really active, doing fifty, sixty BASE jumps a year, a couple hundred skydives a year, we were just going out there trying to survive," he recalls. "Not doing any fancy flips or anything, [but] belly to earth, open the parachute in the right direction, and not crash into anything."

Shoebotham argued with Jeb over aerials. "Why *can't* I?" Jeb said. "Who says I can't?"

"You're really pushing it. Just go out and fall safe off this thing. That's really where the sport is right now."

But Jeb saw the sport heading in a direction that Shoebotham wasn't ready to accept. The leaders of this movement were two Australians—Dwain Weston and Roland Simpson, whom everyone called Slim. They were the talk of drop zones and exit points around the world.

An accomplished gymnast and surfer, Weston trained assiduously, enrolling in high-dive classes, incorporating maneuvers into free fall. He worked as a software developer and brought the same attention to detail to his jumping, applying mathematical calculations to determine time spent in free fall, time to complete maneuvers, time to inflate his parachute. Weston combined an intellectual approach to jumping with a cocksure persona that left a profound effect on everyone who had occasion to meet him. He was known for his aphorisms: "Who has the guts to stand by and prove his convictions?" he would ask. "If you are not moving forward, then you are just moving backwards." His credo: "Today is a good day to die, blah, blah, blah . . ." His motto: "No ethics, no morals, no conscience, no guilt." Gary Cunningham, another Aussie jumper, who met Weston in the mid-1990s, noted that his friend appeared to lack something else, too— "the built-in survival mechanism called fear."

It was not so much that Weston wasn't scared. It was that he treated the edge as his playground; he enjoyed mastering dangerous thrills.

Outside Australia, though, Weston was more rumor than reality. Then, in the summer of 1999, word spread that he would be coming to Norway. The jumping community would have occasion to size him up. Cunningham accompanied Weston on that trip and would recall years later the shocked reaction. "Physically, Dwain was not really what most people expected when they first met him," he would write. "He was a short skinny guy that had shoulder length blond hair. A couple of times people had mistaken him for a girl (I guess from a short glimpse from a distance). On first sight some were surprised to realize he was the legendary Dwain Weston."

On the cliffs of Norway, Weston showed that he was the real deal. Soon he would take the international jumping scene by storm. Weston and his protégé Slim relocated to Portland, Oregon, where they fell in with a group of competitive jumpers with a wicked sense of humor. They called themselves Psilocybin Solution. One member of this group was Dr. Nikolas Hartshorne, a former medical examiner in King County, which includes Seattle. Hartshorne had a fondness for magic mushrooms. Known to acquaintances as Dr. Death, he had performed the autopsy on Kurt Cobain, and thus became associated with conspiracy theories surrounding the grunge icon's death. Dr. Death was the kind of person who inspired stories anyway. He possessed a morbid sense of humor and was rumored to have collected the hands of fetuses belonging to pregnant women he had performed autopsies on. People said he kept the hands in a jar of formaldehyde at home.

Karin Sako met the Psilocybin Solution crew on a jumping trip to Portland with Jeb, whom she had met through a mutual friend at Perris Valley. A rock climber, competition skydiver, and jumper, Karin is an attractive brunette with an easy smile, and she and Weston hit it off right away and soon became a couple.

The morbid vibe of the Portland crew was not for everyone, she says. Many were rubbed the wrong way. "They were having fun," she says in their defense, "and nobody wanted to die or get hurt. Never! There was never any of an attitude of 'Okay, seriously maybe today's the day I'm going to die and I'm okay with that.' It was never that heavy. It was like 'Today could be the day.' But any day could be the day."

Video of Weston's monologues speak to his satire. "The exit point does not look good," he says with his trademark lisp in one. "I've been advised by my ground crew that it looks bad for a jump. There's also wind, about five knots . . . A ninety left would be difficult. But in spite of all that *danger,* there comes a time when the animal inside says 'Let me be free,' and you must roll the dice and throw yourself into the unknown and see what happens, because that . . . that's truly living. Roger this, and maybe speak to you again down at the bottom. I may be happy or I may be in pain and agony, fucked up, or maybe dead. But that's the choices we make and we will live with them." Offering thumbs-up, he adds: "Rock 'n' roll!"

In another, a companion, breathless and screeching profanity, runs up after Weston has just landed a jump from an antenna. "Holy shit! Holy shit! You are a . . . fucking *psychopath*! You are the biggest psychopath I've ever seen in my fucking life!"

Another voice can be heard saying to Weston: "You're bleeding from the face."

"I went through a cactus on landing," Weston replied casually, absently licking his fingers to wipe the blood, adding: "But I got through the wires."

Given his reputation, many jumpers were eager to measure themselves against Weston. One jumped simultaneously with Weston from the Perrine Bridge, four lanes of traffic rumbling 486 feet over the Snake River in Twin Falls, Idaho. It is the only bridge in the United States that is legal to jump 365 days a year. On the way down, Weston slashed the air like a blade with acrobatics while his accomplice remained upright, eyes locked on Weston for some signal that he would pull. Weston continued twisting and somersaulting, finally flicking his chute at the four-second mark. His partner reacted instantly, 4.8 seconds into the jump. But it was too late, and he hit the water at eighty miles per hour, smashing three vertebrae and tearing his rectum; he lived. All Weston got was wet.

In Weston, Jeb saw a model. A friend would say later, "For sure, Jeb fucking loved the guy. He wanted to be Dwain. For me, [Dwain] couldn't get hurt. He was in amazing shape. There were those reference points: there was our standard, and then there was Dwain. He really was immortal."

Weston encouraged Jeb to rely on experience over luck. He explained the advantage of enrolling in high-dive training if Jeb was serious about performing acrobatics. Both Weston and Slim trained with an Olympic-level diving coach in Portland. The calculus was simple: From a high-dive platform you can practice a hundred exits each day. It might take you an entire year to make a hundred exits as a BASE jumper.

Through an acquaintance, Jeb arranged a meeting with the diving coach at the University of Southern California, a man named Hongping Li. Li was a national champion from China and a competitor at the 1984 Olympic Games in Los Angeles, where he finished fourth on the three-meter springboard. He agreed to take Jeb on as a student, placing him in a class with those of equal experience, all of them children. Jeb was twenty-three years old. Standing six foot three in his Speedo, he looked like Gulliver in Lilliput at the pool. It was humbling.

The youngsters proved superior in every way, from flexibility to relative strength to skill. And the kids let him know he was not their equal. A girl called him a pussy one day in front of the other students when he hesitated on the five-meter platform, contemplating a coming jolt of pain from striking the water wrong.

But Jeb worked hard to improve. What Jeb learned at the pool he applied on jumps around the world, traveling with a cohort of fellow jumpers and friends. One of them he had met while hiking Kjerag. His name was Iiro Seppänen, and he was a professional magician from Helsinki who looked like the Hollywood central-casting idea of a Nordic villain—tall, handsome, square-jawed, with cold blue eyes. Kjerag requires a two-hour walk, and Seppänen spilled the details of his life. The son of a politician and a journalist, he began practicing magic at age ten and by sixteen had left home to join a traveling circus. He parlayed his act into a career touring the world, selling out hockey arenas in Europe, and performing live shows in Las Vegas, Barcelona, Cape Town, Los Angeles, Beijing, and New York and for television audiences on the likes of the *Late Show with David Letterman*.

Despite having money waving from each hand and a new woman on his arm in each destination, hopscotching cities and living out of hotels, performing three hundred magic shows each year had begun to wear. "This was not the life I was meant to live," he told himself.

He had performed some Houdini-inspired escape acts—suspended from burning ropes while wearing a straitjacket; chained underwater holding his breath for three minutes; bound, a sword of Damocles suspended overhead from a burning rope. He had been shoved from an airplane, hands tied, breaking free and deploying a parachute before becoming a human pancake, a stunt that required learning to skydive. "Once I tasted the freedom and had the feeling of free fall, I said, *Fuck magic*," he says.

His next escape act: he wound up living in a tent at a drop zone in Zephyrhills, Florida, where no one had a clue who the tall guy with the funny accent was. Relieved of the pressure to perform, he lived simply under the Florida sun. It was there that he discovered BASE jumping. "It was one of those things where you know, *This is something I was meant to do*," he says.

Jumping clarified things: *If I indeed die after this jump, have I lived the life I set myself to live?* He didn't think so. As he jumped, he began to see the world differently, as if scales had been stripped from his eyes. So much of life seemed like magic, an elaborate sleight of hand. Jumping was real, and it rearranged his mind. It was surprisingly easy to turn from his former life. He pursued happiness, and jumping was one way to get there. He developed powerful bonds with other jumpers. They were not necessarily the tie-dyed, tattooed, pierced longhairs, or the nearly *touched* you might expect. They were characters, but that wasn't it exactly . . . If forced to put his finger on it, he would say that those willing to jump from buildings and mountains were not likely to be limited too much in their daily lives. All those books about the power of *now* suddenly made perfect sense, too. If you could overcome fears of death enough to jump, then you could bust out and break free finally of the Rube Goldberg devices that trapped one in the mechanisms constructed to manage life. Iiro learned a lot through this period and felt somehow reborn into the world.

And that's more or less where his head was when he met Jeb on Kjerag in the summer of 1999. Jeb was not exactly socially gifted, but he was not as weird as some people Iiro had known in the circus, either. It turned out that Iiro had met Jeb's sister Scarlett in Malibu while visiting Finnish director Renny Harlin and his wife, Geena Davis. Iiro had been in Jeb's house, in his room, and handled the albino python he kept as a pet.

Jeb had discovered a stash of booze Iiro had bought for Scarlett and poured it down the drain. They had a good laugh over that on the mountain. Parting in Norway, they arranged to meet in West Virginia in October, during the annual gathering of jumpers at Bridge Day, and this would be the start of a North American odyssey. From Bridge Day they drove to Manhattan, both of them requiring a *B*—a building, the toughest object—to complete the BASE cycle. Sneaking into a thirty-story high-rise under construction on Park Avenue one night, they launched, and Iiro was nearly struck by a taxi when he landed in oncoming traffic. Convinced the cops were after them, Jeb hid in the back aisle of a bodega until his friends fetched him.

The next day, they took off for Niagara Falls, Canada, jumping from the observation level of the Skylon Tower, five hundred breathtaking feet above the brink of the falls. Separated on the ground, Jeb encountered a security guard who had called the cops. Soon the police and a newspaper reporter showed up. A photographer snapped a shot of the police writing Jeb a ticket for criminal mischief, in the amount of $65 Canadian. Afterwards, the officer gave Jeb a lift back to his hotel and asked casually, "Who was your friend?"

Oh, shit! Jeb claimed he didn't really know—they had met on the Internet.

At the hotel, Iiro had cleaned out their room but Jeb hooked up with him outside at their car. Iiro had ditched his gear on landing, with police in hot pursuit, and had injured his ankle while launching over a wall and finally shaken his pursuers by darting in front of a moving train and hiding out in a stand of bushes. He would have misgivings, though, about abandoning $2,000 worth of canopy, container, and harness. He wondered if Jeb would be willing to retrieve his gear, since he had already been captured.

"It's a waste of time, bro," Jeb said. "There's no way it's there."

But when they arrived at the parking lot, the parachute, container—everything—remained right where Iiro had ditched it.

They returned to Manhattan and the New York Palace Hotel, a glass-and-steel tower sprouting from the seed of an elegant nineteenth-century stone mansion in midtown. Located across Madison Avenue from the rear of St. Patrick's Cathedral, the hotel is the height of luxury, room rates starting at $600 per night. Jeb jimmied open the window of his room on the fiftieth floor using needle-nose pliers. The small size of the window aperture required dexterity developed during yoga to slip his long body through and steely nerves to remain steady on the thin ledge. The slippery glass skin of the building descended to a rooftop some five hundred feet below, and stray traffic crawled along Madison Avenue. Clad all in black, crouching like a gargoyle high above the midnight city, Jeb launched, chute snapping open in the wind. Steering his canopy, he sailed past office windows lit for overnight cleaning crews, but no one spotted him as he settled onto the street and disappeared into a desolate city, making a clean getaway. Seeing the difficulty of slipping through the small opening, Iiro passed on following his friend out.

It was clear that high-rise hotels offered the best way to avoid the hassles associated with jumping from private buildings—from the need to outfox security to the risk of trespassing charges. Hotels don't figure on their guests exiting through the windows of the upper floors, so it barely rates a consideration.

In Las Vegas, they booked a room at the Circus Circus Hotel and Casino, a place Hunter S. Thompson described as "what the whole hep world would be doing on Saturday night if the Nazis had won the war . . . the place is about four stories high, in the style of a circus tent, and all manner of strange County-Fair/Polish Carnival madness is going on up in this space." The spectacle outside was stranger yet. From a window five hundred feet above the Strip, two guests leaped in quick succession, opened their parachutes, touched down in a parking lot, and hightailed it out of there, security already in hot pursuit.

Iiro injured his ankle again on landing. Rather than go to a hospital, where he might encounter the police, he hobbled into a gentlemen's club and killed time and his pain with cocktails and lap dances. Jeb got away clean. But a girl he was seeing, filming the stunt from a nearby parking garage, was captured by a hawkeyed security guard. When Jeb found out, he turned himself in. Security sat him at a table in a windowless room and told him he was going to prison for trespassing. When he pulled a room key from his pocket and explained that he was a paying customer, they changed tack and said he had endangered the lives of others. Jeb explained that he had a video camera mounted on his helmet that would show such a claim was untrue.

"Are you a law student?" security asked.

Jeb smiled. "I kind of am."

"You can tell it to the police when they get here." The cops arrived four hours later; collaring BASE jumpers did not rate high on their list of priorities. They checked Jeb's license for outstanding warrants, and when he came back clean they returned his driver's license and explained to security that they couldn't charge him because no laws had been broken. The guards' faces collapsed, and Jeb walked free, although he would henceforth be as unwelcome at the Circus Circus as the most notorious cardsharp.

Jeb didn't care. Jumping took him further afield. To mark the millennium, on New Year's Eve Jeb jumped with fourteen others to set a world record from the Petronas Towers, in Kuala Lumpur. Next he was in South Africa to film scenes for a documentary on BASE jumping. He continued to Paris and performed a double reverse flip inside the Eiffel Tower from 320 feet. He fell 140 feet in three seconds, and pitched in time to swoop below the latticework arch, 180 feet above the ground—an astoundingly difficult jump that required months of training and impeccable timing to pull off. Scattering pigeons as his boots skidded to a stop on the Champ de Mars, he embraced a female security guard and screamed, "I'm alive!"

"Yes," she said, "and you're in trouble." But the police let him go with a warning not to jump again.

As his skills sharpened, Jeb's stunts grew more complex and audacious. He, Iiro, and Arne Aarhus, the host of an extreme sports show in Norway, traveled to San Francisco. Gates bar pedestrians from the Golden Gate Bridge at night to prevent suicides. When they opened at 5 a.m., the jumpers walked onto the span at dawn wearing yellow hard hats. The bust factor on the bridge was high, and Iiro was on a tourist visa, so he offered to film rather than jump. Other aspects of the jump spooked him, too. "You're going to die," he told Jeb.

"I'm not going to die," Jeb said. "You're going to film it."

In the purple light of morning, with fog on the bay, Jeb and the Norwegian walked along thick suspension cables rising five hundred feet to the top of the tower, next to a blinking red aircraft beacon some seven hundred feet above the water. Video would show Jeb gripping his knees tight to his chest as he tumbled backwards, plummeting, a mere speck against an enormous sweep of bridge and sky. Opening his body, arms and legs extended like a black *X*, he pitched and swung like a pendulum as he descended beneath his black parachute.

Iiro's camera caught the reaction of a spectator who just happened by on the bridge. *"Sheee-ut!"* the man yelled at the sight. "That's a hell of a free climb! Damn!" Leaning over the rail, the onlooker let out a *"Woo-hoo!"* in the direction of the drifting parachutes. By then sirens were wailing on the bridge.

"Hide! Hide! Hide!" Iiro screamed into a handheld radio. And for seven hours they did, behind scrub vegetation on a dirt slope beneath the bridge, on the Marin County side, as cruisers circled below. Finally, Jeb and Aarhus slipped away, sitting through a forgettable movie and returning after dark to retrieve their gear. It was all starting to seem, well, *easy*.

Back in Las Vegas, Iiro would strip the insides from a mammoth stuffed dog and place his and Jeb's rigs inside, in order to slip them past security at the 1,149-foot Stratosphere Tower, part of a hotel-casino and the tallest structure in the city. Their friend from Norway, Aarhus, had devised his own secret method for smuggling his gear inside. They met in a bathroom a thousand feet above the paved and dust-parched landscape of Vegas, donning their rigs and emerging onto an observation level, hustling away from guards and up a flight of stairs. Scrambling over a fence, they walked onto the glass roof of an observation deck. Startled tourists glanced up at the sound of their feet. "Awww . . . ," someone said. "Look, there goes one of them there!" All three men jumped, Jeb balling into a triple reverse flip, and floated to a parking lot across the street. Stuffing their billowing parachutes into a waiting car, they split, breathless and sweaty with excitement.

Months later, at Bridge Day in October 2001, fall colors setting the gorge aflame in red, orange, and gold, Jeb launched from a platform jutting off the span. He spun into a double inward front flip, legs straight, tucked to his chest, helmet buried in his knees. Folded like a pocketknife, he opened for a half twist, and tucked tight again into a double outward backflip.

It was a stunning maneuver, the sum of his hours of high-dive training. Jeb stole the show with his moves and one of those who approached along the riverbed to offer congratulations was Slim. Only a few men in the world could have pulled off the sequence, he said. Alas, Slim was no longer one of them. He walked with help from a crutch, due to permanent injuries resulting from an off-heading opening that slammed him into a cliff in Australia. He had sustained two broken legs, three broken vertebrae, a broken collarbone, and a punctured lung and shattered pelvis. Although he would return to jumping six months after the injuries, Slim would never be the same. For the remainder of his life, even walking would be difficult.

At Bridge Day, Jeb gushed about the praise from Slim. "He was the excited little kid," Iiro recalls.

It was around this time that Helliwell encountered Jeb on a frigid winter morning on a mountainside in Arizona. As she and others looked on in amazement, Jeb approached the edge of a cliff, stood in a handstand, and sprang off. "And he was doing it well," she remembers. "He looked trained. He wasn't just throwing some maneuver. He was approaching it the right way."

To Helliwell, here was proof of a profound transformation. "The student," she says, "became the master."

Chapter 8

CHECK, PLEASE!

> Only those who will risk going too far can possibly
> find out just how far one can go.
>
> —*T. S. Eliot, preface to Harry Crosby's* Transit of Venus

*H*aving achieved the status of a master, Jeb was a candidate to take on a student, and she would find him in the winter of 2002, down in Cape Town. Karina Hollekim was one of dozens of competitors from five nations at an event in South Africa called the World Championship Extreme Air, partly put on with help from Omer Mei-Dan, Jeb's friend the orthopedic surgeon and BASE jumper from Israel. Each athlete at the multidiscipline competition had been selected for some specific skill that lent to the team's overall strength. A professional big-mountain skier from Norway, Karina is a tall, striking blonde, the kind of woman who turns heads. Yet whenever the athletes from the various teams mingled, sharing meals and riding together in a bus to competitions at sites around the Eastern Cape, while everyone was looking at her Karina's eye was drawn to a tall guy on the U.S. team with a head as bare as a baby's. At mealtime, the guy talked like . . . well, unlike anyone she had ever known, holding the others spellbound with stories of adventure and BASE jumping around the world. Other times, though, like on the bus, he would withdraw, sitting alone, earphones plugged in, his head bopping, not necessarily in time to the music but to some other internal rhythm. He appeared to be tuned in to some separate personal frequency ricocheting around his skull. There was something, well, *different* about him, and it wasn't just his black wardrobe. She asked the other athletes about this Jeb Corliss. "I had never heard of him before," she remembers. "I spoke to the other Americans and the team-mates on my Norwegian team. They also spoke very highly of Jeb, especially his skills as a BASE jumper. I also saw some of the videos he had taken himself and I realized he was a very skilled BASE jumper."

To Karina, Jeb was somehow apart from other jumpers. "I didn't trust them completely, because it was all based on whether you had balls or not," she says. "And they wanted to show off, in a way. I felt like Jeb wasn't really showing off. He was doing it for himself. When he was on travels, trips, or expeditions, he could go on his own. It wasn't about showing off for anybody."

Karina had been captivated by jumping ever since she saw video of two climbers launching from the twenty-thousand-foot Trango Towers, in northern Pakistan, some years earlier. She had nurtured a childhood fantasy of flying, shirking terrestrial bonds and an anvil's weight of terror, strife, and insecurity that those who encountered her would never have guessed at. Soaring above all of life's petty hassles and responsibilities seemed pretty appealing. To Karina, BASE jumping looked like one way to capture that elusive feeling.

She had begun skydiving the previous summer, and she finally worked up the nerve to ask Jeb if he would teach her to jump. He said yes—if she ever came to the States. But he doubted whether she would follow through. Chicks were always asking him to teach them to jump. They didn't mean it, it was just something to say. If circumstances hadn't intervened, perhaps Karina never would have followed through either, but then she got sick in South Africa, winding up in a Cape Town hospital with a stomach tumor after competition ended. All the other athletes had returned home except Jeb, who had stayed on to fly his wingsuit from Table Mountain, and he visited with Karina every day, sitting and talking for long hours. "So we kind of got to know each other fairly well throughout those days in the hospital," Karina says.

Back in Norway, Karina finally had surgery for what turned out to be a benign tumor. Once fully recovered, she called Jeb in May to take him up on his offer of introducing her to jumping.

He picked her up at LAX and drove her to his place, out back beyond the patio and pool of the big house in Malibu. There, Karina confessed that she had actually only made 23 skydives, not 223, as Jeb had been led to believe. Jeb took a look at her skydiving jump log and was like, *What the . . . ?* Annoyed, he fixed her with a look and said, "I don't know if I'm able to take you BASE jumping. With twenty-three skydives, I'm not sending you on a suicide mission."

Then he had an idea. To evaluate her readiness, Jeb took Karina to Perris for a series of skydives. Her athletic background was an asset. He could see that much. In free fall, Karina demonstrated aerial awareness and tracking ability. She handled her canopy in flight and nailed the landings. Satisfied, Jeb booked them tickets to Twin Falls, Idaho, to begin training at the Perrine Bridge.

That first night in Twin Falls, Karina came down with food poisoning and curled up on the bathroom floor of their hotel room. It was humiliating but Jeb was nice about it. While her strength returned, she learned to pack a parachute. Once well enough, she visited the bridge to observe other jumpers scaling the railing, eight hundred feet above a green river, the Snake River, the one Evel Knievel planned to launch over in his Skycycle X-2 before that stunt turned into a debacle. Passing motorists roared by, honking and shouting encouragement, issuing thumbs-up out open windows.

After two days of rest, Karina was well enough to try. She wore a wetsuit, which left her feeling uncomfortable, not exactly ladylike. She carried a round parachute on her back. Landing in the river, she would be scooped out by a waiting rescue boat. Car horns blared, this time for her as she made her way along the bridge. Jeb followed with a video camera, firing questions to gauge Karina's readiness. Probing for some sign of nerves, he was shocked to observe that Karina appeared the very picture of cool confidence. He did not know that, as she scaled the railing and stepped onto a lumber plank set up as a launch platform, clutching a pilot chute in her right hand, thoughts swirled like the river's currents: *Hold tight! This is unnatural! You shouldn't do this! You don't want to fall from this bridge!*

Jeb coached her from the other side of the railing, barking commands. The particulars would be difficult to recall. But she remembered the basics. *Three, two, one . . . See ya!* Pushing off with both feet, Karina delayed two seconds before pitching, her round chute opening with a *whoosh*. Pulled into the rescue boat, dripping wet, she wondered if that was it. *Is this BASE jumping?* It had been a blur. *Was she changed somehow?*

For four days, Karina would launch from the bridge, her awareness and impressions expanding and intensifying each time. By accretion, internal voids of which she had been only dimly aware began to be occupied, and she understood at last what was meant by fulfillment. Her training at the Perrine ended suddenly when, on a two-way jump with Jeb, he broke an ankle while landing downwind along the riverbank.

On crutches, Jeb continued to coach, taking Karina to a dam in the Sierra Nevada. Because he could not get around easily, it was up to her to walk the landing area alone beforehand and get acquainted with the terrain. She couldn't do it. She was frightened—not of the jump, but of the dark. Reaching the landing zone would require walking through a wood at night. This brave girl was petrified of the dark.

So they drove to Auburn, where Jeb delivered instructions from a walkie-talkie as Karina made her way alone onto the Foresthill Bridge in the dark and dropped into the canyon.

"He had something about him that made me feel very confident about his skills, and he was also very honest and very direct, maybe to the point of morbid in the way he spoke about BASE jumping," Karina would remember. "From the point I came to the U.S. and started learning, he was very direct about the fact that I would get injured and could get hurt through BASE jumping. I would see other people die, most likely some of my very good friends. And potentially, very likely, I would die doing it myself if I kept on doing it. He was always talking about death and people dying and accidents and stuff that I never really talked about. The way he put it out there, it forced me into making a decision about whether this was something I wanted to do or not. If I wanted to do it, I had to do it 100 percent."

At times, a fed-up Karina would say, "You're always so negative about it. You're always putting an emphasis on worst-case, and it's not always like that."

"I'm not *negative*," Jeb would reply, voice rising an octave. "You're walking through a minefield, and I'm going to tell you there's a minefield out there. If you need to get to the other side of the minefield for whatever reason, you need to get to the other side, fine, I'll help you. But even with all my help and doing everything right, you can step on a mine, [and] there's nothing I can do for you if that happens."

THAT SUMMER, circumstance would offer an object lesson for what Jeb was trying to convey. His ankle healed, he returned to Lysebotn and jumped Norway's big walls at Kjerag with Karina. When they parted the first week of August, Jeb headed to Switzerland and the Lauterbrunnen Valley.

The valley had fast gained a reputation in the jumping community for the big walls and permissive attitude of the locals, who decades earlier had grown accustomed to extreme sportsmen—climbers, skiers, and paragliders—lured to their town. An added appeal for jumpers came in the convenience of cable cars and trams rising from the valley floor to Mürren, Wengen, and Winteregg, all of which offered jumpers short hikes to the exits. That summer, Karin Sako was there with some of the crew from Portland—Weston and Dr. Death, Nik Hartshorne.

For a week, Jeb and Weston "had a friendly one-upsmanship going," Sako says. But Weston always seemed willing to go further. When Jeb balked at jumping in the rain one day and began walking back to the cable car, Weston raised him on the walkie-talkie. He told him everything would be fine and called him out for a lack of courage.

"Dude," Jeb barked into the radio, "you're better than me. I know that. Go ahead, call me a pussy."

Weston argued that eventually Jeb would have to jump in marginal conditions, so he might as well learn.

But Jeb spotted the flaw in such reasoning. Continuing back to the cable car for a return trip to Lauterbrunnen, he understood that you never had to jump in marginal conditions. You never had to jump, period.

Days later, though, Jeb would be called to account for his own reckless conduct. Flying his wingsuit, he had pulled low over the pasture, practically going in before his parachute popped open. Dr. Nik brought the episode up one night over dinner with Sako and Weston and some other jumpers. "Jeb, we like what you do," he said. "But you've got to be more careful, because we'd like to keep you around a little longer."

"I get it," Jeb said. "I know."

Dr. Nik had been thinking a lot about the future. He'd been saving up to marry his girlfriend and was debating whether to buy a new Jaguar or pay off his student loans first.

"Bro," Jeb said, "why wait? Pay the student loans later. You never know how long you're going to live." He had a good point, everyone agreed.

"I have to be responsible," Dr. Nik explained.

"Buy the Jaguar!" Jeb insisted. Everyone agreed that buying the Jaguar would not be a wrong decision, exactly.

As dinner broke up, Dr. Nik had not yet made up his mind. Everyone agreed to get up early the next morning and jump the High Nose, a promontory just beyond Staubbach Falls. It is almost two thousand feet above the valley, but a nasty ledge looms about a seven-second rock drop, or 640 feet, below the exit.

The next morning, August 6, Jeb overslept. Making his way down to the street, he figured he would wait for the second load so he could join the others on the cable car. Through a light rain he spotted Sako and Weston approaching up the street. "So are we going to go do a jump?" he called out.

They didn't reply until they were nearer, their faces uncharacteristically somber. "Naw," Weston said finally, "Nik died."

His canopy had opened 180 degrees off-heading, sending Dr. Nikolas Hartshorne sailing straight for the cliff. He had managed to land on a ledge, but, forward motion arrested, his parachute deflated and he fell backwards, striking the cliff several times as he tumbled to the valley floor. He was thirty-eight.

Two months later, reunited at Bridge Day in October, Jeb and Karina stood in the shade along smooth river stones nine hundred feet beneath the graceful steel arch when a cable TV reporter approached and made a proposition. She was compiling a program on illegal sports that would include street fighting, drag racing, and, if they were willing, BASE jumping from a building. Her producer would pay, she said, if Jeb and Karina would jump for their cameras. Jeb said he knew just the place.

A few weeks later, he and Karina were in Manhattan, waiting out the weather, passing time in Central Park and sitting through movies and Broadway shows, basically behaving like a couple, although they weren't despite Jeb's growing feelings for her.

One night, once the skies finally cleared and the wind died down, sometime after midnight, Jeb crouched on a thin ledge fifty vertiginous stories above Madison Avenue. He had disabled the locking mechanism on the window of his room at the New York Palace Hotel with needle-nose pliers, just as he had done years earlier with Iiro. Opening the window as wide as possible allowed him to maneuver his long body through the narrow opening, and invited the city's familiar music inside—car horns, the percussion of speeding tires on potholes, whinnying brakes, and a distant rumble from a truck's diesel engine.

Earlier in the evening, staff in the opulent lobby had stared as a crew hauled video equipment to the elevators, to the room where the bald guy and the blonde were staying. They were unaware of what was about to occur from the upper floors. Like . . . *were they making a porno in there or what?* Accomplices waited in the streets, and Gigi fretted in her room, several floors below. A conspiracy requiring weeks of planning and the right weather conditions had entered its final phase.

Jeb was dressed all in black, from his helmet to a rig on his back containing a single parachute. From the ledge, it was a six-second plunge to a fatal impact some 170 yards directly below. And although he had jumped from the hotel once before, that act had stretched his skills and composure to their limits. "Remember, you don't have to do it," he called to Karina, seated on the bed.

"I know," she said.

The small window of the hotel required backing out first. Clinging to the frame by fingertips, Jeb performed contortions that only years of yoga practice could have prepared him for. As he faced forward at last, size 12 boots balanced on a thin sill, the building's slippery skin descended hundreds of feet toward the suggestion of a rooftop. "Fuck," he said, sighing. "Fucking sketchy exit point, dude." After a deep breath, he added, "All right."

Clearing his mind the way he had trained, he banished any thoughts of tremors bobbing his legs like sewing machine needles, the dryness in his mouth, perspiration on his hands, his heart's hard-thumping rhythm, and an acid panic rising like an elevator in his throat. In a city of millions, friends and family nearby, he stood alone on the ledge, utterly focused.

"Five seconds," he said, which Karina repeated into a handheld radio to the rest of the team.

Exhaling, Jeb called, "See you, guys," and jumped, commencing a precise choreography: *One* . . . Flinging his body backward, he executed a flawless gainer, fear draining as his mind tightened to the task at hand. *Two* . . . Air rushed ever louder through his helmet as he plunged into the night. Reaching behind his right hip for his pilot chute, he grabbed it and flung it into the air. *Three* . . . Caught by the air, the small chute inflated, tugging on a bridle connected to his parachute container, held fast by a single pin. Tension on the bridle pulled hard on the container, releasing the pin. As he fell faster, objects below gained size and detail in the first stage of a powerful sensation known as ground rush. *Four* . . . The main canopy, folded and packed tight in the container, spilled out, catching the air and inflating with a resounding crack that startled Gigi in her room.

She and Fitzmorris had just happened to be in New York that week on business, and Gigi had maintained a late-night vigil, white-knuckle-gripping a two-way radio, eyes gazing at the silhouette of St. Patrick's. She had switched the radio chatter off earlier to provide quiet as Fitzmorris slept nearby, in preparation for a meeting in the morning. So she was startled by the sudden appearance of a black parachute bursting open before her eyes, causing her window to shudder as if buffeted by a strong wind. Legs buckling, Gigi dropped to her knees, overcome by a feeling she would describe as "breathtaking, like an out-of-body experience . . ."

Outside, under an open parachute, Jeb descended slower, hovering feet-first thirty stories above an orderly grid of floodlit streets. Reaching above his head for toggles, he tugged hard left, sweeping ninety degrees in that direction. Lined up over Madison Avenue, desolate in the early hours except for a few cars and trucks inching along like insects, he traveled three city blocks. The lonely pavement rose to meet him until finally his boots skidded to a landing in a bus lane beside orange construction barricades, parachute deflating nearby like a sigh. Without the sound of air whooshing in his ears, the city's sound track returned at heightened volume—a rhythm of clunking metal from a delivery truck, whinnying brakes, and horn echoes.

He quickly gathered his parachute as a cluster of cars approached up Madison. A yellow cab edged toward him, stopping with a weary shriek. "Are you okay?" the cabbie called in a foreign accent through an open window.

"How's it going, man?" Jeb inquired, as if greeting an old friend.

"Where you came from?"

"The sky," he said, with a trilling laugh, hustling away hugging his parachute down a darkened East Forty-eighth Street, where he hailed a different cab and disappeared into the night.

On the walkie-talkie, Karina made it clear she had no intention of following Jeb out the window. The footage from the Palace Hotel jump would never air anyway; nervous corporate lawyers pulled the plug. And in a few months, Jeb and Karina would part after he confessed his growing affection and she expressed her wish that they merely remain friends. This brought to an end twelve intense months during which Jeb mentored Karina and made more than four hundred BASE jumps in sixteen countries. Having arrived at the top of his sport, Jeb was at loose ends, and exhausted.

Neither he nor his fellow jumpers could anticipate how, soon enough, the deed of one man would invigorate them and alter expectations, and their destiny, in the coming decade.

Chapter 9

SKYDIVER OF
THE DECADE

SWISS ALPS, SPRING 2003

Looking back, his early life would make his later deeds seem almost preordained, like he was meant to fly. The pattern started early for Loïc Jean-Albert. He was raised on Reunion, a lush volcanic French island territory in the Indian Ocean east of Madagascar. He grew up racing sailboats in the tropical waters offshore, where under sail he had learned to read air currents, scanning the skies and the roll of the swells as if he were studying a second language. The son of skydiving instructors, Loïc began jumping from planes at age fifteen, applying lessons and principles from sailing to tracking and maneuvering through the skies, catching and deflecting air resistance. By eighteen his skills were sufficiently advanced that Loïc was selected for the French national skydiving team for eight-way relative work, a discipline in which participants create choreographed formations—like synchronized swimmers in the sky. He moved to the French Alps to train and was responsible for maintaining the team's equipment, spending much of his time sewing, drawing on his experience repairing sails. It was in this capacity, in Gap, France, in 1996, that Loïc met Patrick de Gayardon, the world's leading skydiver and inventor of the modern wingsuit, who admired the lanky teenager's talent, resolve, and easygoing manner. The two became friends and began jumping together outside of team activities, trading ideas, sharing their dreams and ambitions. Loïc became a protégé of sorts to the older man, trailing Deug, packing his rig, sewing his wingsuit. Learning at Deug's elbow, Loïc was one of the first to build and fly a modern wingsuit, incorporating principles from sail construction into wingsuit design. He continued his mentor's work after Deug died, founding a wingsuit-manufacturing company he called Fly Your Body.

Testing designs for this company, Loïc honed his skills as a wingsuit pilot. By 2000 he had begun pushing into new realms. Rather than attempting to maximize glide to soar as far away as possible, free from the danger of a collision with a cliff, he wanted to see how *close* he could come to terrain. Jumping from a friend's Pilatus Porter, he buzzed mountains around Megève, a ski-resort town in the Rhône-Alpes region of France, near Mont Blanc. In Italy, he made a BASE jump from Monte Brento and hugged the big wall with his wings. When he was featured in a skydiving film, *Crosswind,* cruising cliffs on Reunion, the footage sealed his reputation. At a time when a pilot's skill was measured by how far he could travel from his exit point, Loïc's approach turned the sport on its head. "He was an artist," Jeb would later say.

Using his body as a brush, the terrain as a canvas, with precise strokes, Loïc traced memorable, heart-quickening lines. His masterpiece, though, from an aesthetic point of view, would be a stunt he had trained months for, scouting and selecting a snowfield in Switzerland with an ideal slope of thirty degrees. And on a bright March day over Verbier, Switzerland, Loïc, twenty-five, was at last ready to put his plan into action.

On that day, a white chopper lifted off, thudding into a cloudless blue sky above the Pennine Alps in western Switzerland, where daggers of rock and snow rise fourteen thousand feet into the atmosphere. Inside the helicopter, wearing a UN-blue helmet and headphones, Loïc sat calmly in a white-and-black wingsuit.

As the helicopter hovered a thousand feet above the peaks, he stepped onto one of the skids and into position. Falling toward a blade of rock, belly first, wings filling with air, he edged forward gradually until he was nearly on top of a pristine snowfield. Adjusting his body position, Loïc glided forward faster, accelerating to more than a hundred miles per hour, roaring through the air, his angle matching the slope of the muscular frozen landscape. Head up, feet down, body canted at a forty-five-degree angle,

Loïc resembled a fast-moving Nordic ski jumper moments before touch-down. Except that the gap between his body and the snow never changed. He appeared immune to gravity, his shadow on the snow resembling the skirted figure that restaurants place on the door of the ladies' restroom.

Two accomplices on skis lay ahead, along a glaciated strip of mountain. Stopping, they turned to watch, waving their poles as Loïc ripped the air a mere six feet overhead, near enough that if they had tried, they could have reached up and touched him with the tips of their poles.

Hewing close to the mountain, Loïc hurtled away, running out of ter-rain where the snowfield ended at a cliff. Gaining altitude as the ground dropped away, he pitched his pilot chute and descended under a canopy colored to match his helmet. His feet finally touched down in another snowfield, unblemished but for two ski tracks.

It's hard to understand the significance at this late date, but in the ensu-ing months, video of Loïc's run made the rounds in the skydiving and BASE-jumping realms, studied and deconstructed with the kind of intense concentration associated with the Zapruder film. Online forums and drop zones crackled with word of Loïc. "Amazing . . ." a typical poster on Drop-zone.com wrote, "just stoked . . . can't go back to work . . ." In recognition of his achievement, Loïc would eventually be named Skydiver of the De-cade by *Paramag* magazine.

In the aftermath of Loïc's close flight, discussion focused on the pros-pects for landing a wingsuit without a parachute. Not everyone agreed that it could be done, or that it was even worth attempting. But those who felt otherwise seemed convinced that, now that he had shown the way, it would not be long before Loïc or someone else with the proper proportions of brains and balls made a serious attempt. A new era of wingsuits was about to begin.

W hile Loïc had been in Switzerland in March 2003, the buzz surround-ing wingsuits had lured a curious Gary Connery to California, where he and a friend made a jumping junket in which his friend would make his first skydives. Gary preferred the United States over the UK for skydiving. One factor was weather. Another was culture. In the UK, he'd roll his eyes at the drop zones when he encountered what he considered a bunch of failed rock stars telling one another failed-rock-star stories. In the States you simply showed up, signed a waiver, and were on your way.

When they arrived at Perris Valley, Gary inquired about making a wingsuit flight. "I hadn't discussed it with anyone," he would later recall, about the potential for landing, "but I was aware that other people were discussing it. But I needed to then experience wingsuit flight before I could make a considered assessment of whether it could be done or not."

At Perris, Gary walked right up to the manifest, where you check in for each skydive, and explained that he wanted to try a wingsuit. He had the required experience, but it was recommended he use another parachute than the sport canopy he owned, because if he pitched while unstable, he would likely wind up with line twists, necessitating a nasty cutaway. Gary bought a secondhand parachute someone was selling on consignment at the shop at the drop zone and paid to have it rigged.

The following day, he picked up his new canopy, signed his name in the ledger at the manifest, and met his instructor. The instructor took Gary through a ground course, explaining all they would do in the aircraft and in the air. Gary would make five jumps that day. The first four, he kept it simple, gaining a feel for the suit, and the necessary body position. His head slightly down, something he needed to correct, but he was ready to attempt some more advanced maneuvers. For the fifth jump, the instructor explained that he wanted Gary to look at him. He would be to Gary's left. Then they would make a left-hand turn together, and look at each other, before making another left-hand turn. In that way, they would make a descending corkscrew pattern before finally pulling.

Once at altitude, Gary and the instructor checked out of the plane together, tumbling past the tail. When Gary looked around, though, his instructor was nowhere in sight. He looked left. Nothing. He looked right. Nothing. He finally spotted the man far below.

Alone, Gary went through the drill they had discussed, making left-hand turns before dumping at four thousand feet. He was somewhat unprepared for the force of his chute opening in full flight and performed a front somersault through his lines. Still, he had no other problems and on landing Gary walked up to the instructor. "What happened?"

The man admitted that Gary had flown so well that there was nothing more he could teach him. He had passed the lesson. *Just keep going,* the instructor urged.

THOUSANDS OF FEET UP, the ground hadn't appeared to be moving, but Gary had felt the glide, and the possibilities for landing without a parachute. As a stuntman, he had leaped from ledges a hundred feet high before and landed in hundreds of empty cardboard boxes at more than fifty miles an hour, the crumpled cardboard absorbing all the energy, allowing him to walk away without a scratch.

Could he fly accurately enough to land a wingsuit in stacked boxes? Grabbing a pen and paper, he sketched out a box rig, outlining a rectangular shape and a target for landing. Quick tabulations told him that he would need eighty-seven thousand boxes to build a rig the size of a soccer field and as tall as a basketball hoop. More calculations told him he would need about $250,000—for the boxes as well as to rent a helicopter and pilot and to put on a large-scale production for what would amount to a world's first in aviation—in his words, the "Holy Grail of human flight."

As his mind expanded on the subject, Gary came to believe that landing would be similar to summiting Everest: everyone knew that Sir Edmund Hillary had been first, but few could say who had been second. From Neil Armstrong to Roger Bannister, everyone always remembered the firsts, and the chance to etch his name among the immortal warmed Gary's blood.

Landing in boxes would not be altogether different from his stunt work. All he needed was sponsorship to cover the costs, and additional training. Vivienne would recall her excited husband walking in the door at their house in Wales with talk of his wingsuit flights. "When he came back from California, he said, 'That could be landed,'" she said.

Yet beyond Vivienne and a few close friends in the stunt industry, who weren't sure what to make of his plans anyway, Gary said little about his ideas. If he was going to proceed, it would be in near secrecy. Later that month he traveled to Empuriabrava, on the coast in Catalonia, Spain, home to the largest drop zone in Europe, where he practiced flying for a week, trying to get a feel for his capabilities.

By May 9, 2003, Gary was back in England. That morning a crowd gathered at Trafalgar Square, in the center of London, among the many missions and consuls belonging to the nations of the world wishing to be near the arms of British administrative power. The crowd gazed up at Gary, perched on a 170-foot platform atop Nelson's Column for a stunt conceived by the Act for Tibet organization, a group protesting Chinese occupation of Tibet. The group had recruited Gary in order to draw attention to their cause.

Arriving at the square early on a Friday, Gary and accomplices handed out pamphlets apologizing for any inconvenience and asking citizens to be "patient and understanding." At 5 a.m. British Summer Time, he and three activists began scaling the monument's gray Corinthian column, like rock climbers. An hour later, they reached the platform. They unfurled a fifteen-yard banner depicting the Dalai Lama and draped Tibetan prayer flags over the statue of Admiral Horatio Nelson that crowns the monument. Gary wore black nylon pants and a blue nylon Windbreaker, a white bandanna printed with a pattern on his head, and a parachute on his back. At last ready, and with rush hour at a pitch, as morning commuters streaming along the streets around the square stopped to stare, Gary jumped, arching his back, bending his knees and elbows, hands positioned to grab his risers as soon as his parachute opened. He had three seconds to get his chute open and operating or he would hit the ground at more than sixty miles an hour.

To ensure the chute opened, he used a static-line setup, in which a cord attached to the platform would pull his parachute from its pack as soon as Gary fell a few feet. Working as designed, his chute popped open, a blue-and-gray pattern. Gary flared immediately, feet hitting the ground as onlookers screamed in a mix of shock and delight. It was all over in seven seconds, and as he gathered his parachute, constables from the Met moved in to arrest him.

"I know I'm coming with you," Gary said to police as reporters fired questions. "Can I get my parachute in the bag?"

No worries, the inspector said.

Gary explained to reporters that although he was "frightened," he had jumped "for a good cause." He described being "scared shitless," adding, "You'll have to excuse me—I'm in a different space at the moment."

Gary was bundled into a van and driven to Charing Cross Police Station, only a few blocks away on the Strand. He was booked for causing criminal damage. Later, an inspector visited Gary's cell, carrying a tray containing tea, toast, bananas, and a copy of the *Evening Standard*. On the front page was a photo of him under canopy, flying in front of Nelson's Column.

The inspector was a Buddhist from India, where the Dalai Lama lives in exile, and he was intent on making Gary's stay as comfortable as possible. He encouraged him to visit the nurse, a pleasant and attractive young woman who fixed Gary another cup of tea. In the end, Scotland Yard treated Gary as well as the metropolitan police had and did not pursue charges. They were not interested in Gary Connery, for jumping Nelson's Column or anything else.

VIVIENNE HAD ALWAYS BEEN tolerant and supportive of Gary's stunt work and ambitions, but the demands of his career, especially long periods of separation from his family, had created tremendous strain at home. Traveling from job to job, Gary had once not returned home for four months. Often he crashed on friends' couches in London in order to be closer to work on set, rather than driving three hours on dark rural roads back home to Wales. These were especially lonely times for Vivienne. "So while we would keep in touch by phone, at night I had little children, an eleven-year-old and an eight-year-old," she says. "I was very busy. And working—I worked in social services and also buying property."

Gary had made few friends in Wales and felt no particular attachment to the place, except for his family. He worried that one night, pushing hard to get home to his family following a long shift on set, exhausted and racing along winding lanes, he would exceed his capabilities and crash, possibly killing himself.

So, toward the end of 2003, the Connery family cut their losses in the country and moved closer to London, packing up all their things, including a framed print of Peter Pan that Vivienne had given Gary as a gift. It was a reminder that when he struggled with his role and responsibilities as a husband and father, Vivienne viewed Gary as a boy who had never grown up, holding fast to youthful dreams of flying.

Chapter 10

WHATEVER HAPPENS, HAPPENS . . .

> I began to live truly independently of everything that could place limits on my inclinations. As long as I respected the laws it seemed to me that I could despise prejudices. I thought I could live perfectly free.
>
> —*Giacomo Casanova*

COLORADO, OCTOBER 2003

In the months after Loïc's close flight above Verbier, Dwain Weston, the man who had done so much to alter BASE with his progressive acrobatic maneuvers, was bracing for life-altering changes. That summer, he had traveled to Europe for a last hurrah, jumping his way across Switzerland, Norway, and Austria. When he returned, he was to decamp from Portland for a new job at Boeing Defense, Space, and Security, in Seal Beach, California. He would be performing classified work, developing software for use in satellites manufactured up the coast in El Segundo. He would move in with Karin Sako at her place in Huntington Beach and settle into a standard nine-to-five schedule, with two weeks of vacation each year. Working at Boeing had been Weston's dream, and living at the beach would allow him to surf every day. "The ocean was his church," Sako says. The downside to the coming changes: BASE jumping was about to take a backseat in his life.

As a result, when he arrived at the airport in Denver during the first week of October 2003, Weston was, in the argot of skydiving and BASE jumping, "not current." He was rusty. He was there for the Go Fast Games, a three-day festival put on by an energy drink company called Go Fast that would feature speed climbing and BASE jumping at the Royal Gorge, outside Cañon City, Colorado, a hundred miles south of Denver in sagebrush country. The finale called for Weston and Jeb to fly wingsuits together from a plane and buzz the Royal Gorge Bridge, the world's highest suspension bridge, a thousand breathtaking feet above where the Arkansas River carves a course deep through Fremont Peak. A half mile wide, the span features three-hundred-ton cables strung between 150-foot towers. Organizers of the games had built a platform extending from the deck for jumpers to launch from.

Part of the Weston legend rested on his assiduous preparation. In the early part of the summer, he had written in a magazine article: "It is no secret that over the past five years I have pushed the limits hard. Although I train extensively and arm myself with the latest knowledge and technology, I have used these things simply to survive at the very edge, rather than allow myself any margin for error."

But if his recent hiatus gave organizers and other athletes cause for concern, they did not share it at the time. During a decade of jumping, Weston had never sustained a serious injury. "Every time he succeeded with one thing that we felt was the very limits of what you could do, he would then step it up and train for something even more extreme," his friend Gary Cunningham recalls. "After awhile we gave up worrying about him and just accepted that he was invincible, as he did many extreme jumps and made them look easy."

Others were too much in awe of the man to suggest caution. "He was a god," Jeb would say. "He didn't even have a close second."

But Karin Sako had expressed her concerns before the trip. She knew everyone would expect Weston to be the best, and he would be loath to disappoint. She knew he was unfamiliar with the new wingsuit he'd brought to the event. There was also a subtext to Loïc's flight at Verbier that could not be ignored. Months before meeting Weston, Sako had dated Loïc, and that fact weighed on Weston's mind, friends would say. Weston was proud; he had prominent buttons that were easily pushed. "Just go and just have fun and make good decisions," Sako had told him before he departed for Colorado. "Just remember, you don't have anything to prove to anybody at this point in your life and your career. Just go and enjoy yourself."

The first two days of the festival went off without a hitch. Climbers scaled the gorge, jumpers launched from the platform into the narrow canyon, and Weston confirmed that his acrobatic maneuvers had lost nothing during his time off.

The night before his planned wingsuit flight, he called Sako in California and left a message. He said he was being safe and having a good time. "I'll be home tomorrow night, back in your arms," he said.

On the appointed day of his flight with Jeb, the plan called for the two to exit an airplane and swoop past the bridge. Wearing his customary black suit, Jeb would sweep beneath, while Weston, clad in the bright yellow wingsuit he had bought recently, would soar above the span.

In the belly of a plane lifting toward three thousand feet, Weston donned goggles and Jeb pulled a shiny black helmet snug to his skull. As their ears popped, dulling the prop's whine, Weston, wind blowing back his hair, appeared uncharacteristically nervous.

Jeb thought to ask if his partner was okay. Did he want to call off the jump? If it had been anyone but Weston, Jeb would have spoken up. Instead he bit his tongue and let the matter drop from his mind and concentrated on what came next.

Minutes later, standing in the rear of the plane, wind roaring through the open bay door, Jeb was ticking through a final mental checklist when Weston grabbed his hand. Between the prop noise and the wind and the helmet covering his ears, Jeb had to stoop, pressing his head to Weston's mouth. "Jeb," he shouted, words carried off in the wind. "Just remember, whatever happens, *happens*."

Stunned, Jeb shook his head. Weston had seldom breathed a trace of doubt on more difficult jumps and now he sounded just spooky. But no more was said. There was no time to talk. The time had come to exit.

When the pilot signaled their position, both men bailed out in quick succession, tumbling past the tail as the plane floated away. Jeb glimpsed Weston's distinctive yellow suit in his peripheral vision for a moment, aware that the first part of the jump had been executed without hiccups; they had not collided with the plane or each other. Turning his attention toward the bridge, he spread his arms and legs, pressurizing his wings, scanning for markers to guide him to his target. The canyon loomed below, and, according to the rough flight plans they had plotted earlier, his course would carry him beneath the steel-and-cable span. Although comfortably on target, even a slight lapse at a hundred miles per hour could send him crashing into the bridge or the canyon's granite walls. Focused, he was vaguely aware that somewhere above, Weston had his own target.

Hundreds of spectators had gathered on the bridge, watching as Weston screamed out of the sky, the yellow of his suit stark against the gray belly of clouds in the background. As he neared, his suit cut through the air with the sound of tearing paper.

He moved at a steep angle, knees slightly bent, chin up. The crowd howled their approval as he cut closer, moving so fast that some ducked for cover instinctively. A yellow blur, Weston flew over thick suspension cables on the near side of the bridge, but then he dipped *beneath* them on the far side. Head-high to those standing on the deck, he aimed between vertical suspension wires. It all happened so fast, but the first sign of something gone wrong was a stomach-churning rending of metal, and a man crying out from the bridge, "Oh, no!"

Weston's parachute opened directly in Jeb's path as he emerged from beneath the bridge. Moving at more than a hundred miles an hour, Jeb swerved hard to avoid a collision and passed through a shower of debris. Confused, he wondered if people were throwing things from the bridge, but he quickly regained his composure. Any small lapse in concentration could kill him in the narrow gorge. "I don't have time to think about this right now," he told himself. "I just need to fly."

When he pitched and his canopy opened, a wave of exhilaration washed over Jeb. He guided his parachute to the canyon floor, back near the bridge, along a railroad bed, rocks crunching beneath his boots. He had completed the best flight of his life and looked for someone to hug or high-five.

All eyes were aimed upward, and Jeb whirled around in time to watch Weston's yellow canopy settle on a ledge high up on the gorge. The faces around him registered shock.

"What?!" Jeb yelled. "He hit the cliff?"

"He didn't hit the cliff," a woman explained in a shaky voice. "He hit the bridge."

Looking around in confusion, Jeb spotted a severed leg not far from where he stood. Recoiling, he touched his wingsuit and noticed it was wet. Looking down, he saw that it was drenched in a dark liquid. That's when it hit him that he was covered in Weston's blood.

IT WOULD BE a long time before Jeb came to terms emotionally with what had happened. But the facts were plainly obvious: Weston had struck the bridge with such force that he bent a metal guardrail, scattering blood, tissue, and body parts dozens of feet in every direction. He was killed instantly, thirty years old, the violence of the collision opening his parachute directly in Jeb's path.

Iiro drove to LAX to retrieve Jeb, who carried the bloodstained wingsuit in his luggage. "He's a tough cookie," Iiro recalls. "He can handle, but I could see he was shaken and stirred."

Four days later, dozens of jumpers arrived at the Malibu beach house for a memorial and paddle-out ceremony. A half-dozen surfers sat on their boards in a circle beyond the waves and scattered Weston's ashes to the water. Jeb caught a wave on the way in, clutching Weston's remaining ashes in a plastic bag. "This is your last wave, dude," he said.

DiGiovanni was there. So was Iiro, wearing a neck brace and using crutches, having been injured in a low-pull competition at the Perrine Bridge. Both men would recall a debate among those present about Weston's motive for cutting his flight so close.

"That was his playground—that dangerous area, that riskier area, that walking-on-the-edge place," Karin Sako would say.

Someone floated a suicide rumor. But Iiro, Jeb, and DiGiovanni argued otherwise. Weston had not been an experienced wingsuit pilot. "He had the comfort level of taking risks as a BASE jumper, but he tried to implement those skills in wingsuits, and it's a different sport," Iiro would say later.

"He came into wingsuits and didn't treat it with the same kind of mindset and same kind of training," Jeb would say. "He thought that, because he was so good in one area, it would transfer into wingsuits, which it doesn't."

Days passed before Jeb experienced a cathartic release of emotion. Waking one morning, he swung his feet off the bed and crunched down on a box containing Weston's ashes and that's when it hit him: He recalled plans he and Weston had made to meet in Bali for a surf trip, plans that were now beside the point.

"He realized that if you put yourself in these situations, you're going to miss all these BASE-jumping adventures," Iiro recalls. "Life ends with death. You can glamorize death, but then when you really experience it, life just goes on. That was the turning point."

That winter, Jeb did not make his annual trip to South Africa for training. He spent long hours in his room, contemplating the meaning of life, and how jumping fit in. He wondered if it was worth dying for, and how his family would feel if it had been him instead of Weston.

The answers did not come easily. Still, he would return to jumping, fulfilling a commitment on February 1, 2004, to plunge from rafters 265 feet above the field at Reliant Stadium, in Houston, for a Super Bowl crowd about to watch New England defeat Carolina, 32–29. The excitement of the game was overshadowed by Justin Timberlake's ripping Janet Jackson's blouse during a halftime dance routine, exposing her breast to millions of TV viewers. A tempest of outrage among newspaper editorials and TV pundits swirled all the way to the floor of Congress.

Reaction eventually passed from headlines, replaced by some fresh scandal, a cycle similar to that playing out in the wake of Weston's death. Once he had been the talk of the drop zone, but Jeb and others noticed that as the months went on, Weston's name was scarcely mentioned any longer. Life had marched inexorably onward, as it does.

"It's okay to die," Jeb would say later about the accommodation he made with losing someone whom he idolized, "because it's going to happen to you, so get over it. And get on with living your life, because that's what's important. Not dying. But what you do with your life while you're here."

Jeb understood that planning and executing new challenges gave his life greater meaning. And new challenges beckoned, maybe the ultimate challenge.

*I*n September 2004, eleven months after Weston died, three jumpers stared into a gaping sinkhole a half mile across, in the remote jungle highlands of the Chinese interior. One of the jumpers was Chris McDougall, the wildly funny, Mohawk-wearing Australian. The other was a nimble and fearless woman from Norway named Vibeke (*VEE-beck-uh*) Knutson, vice president of the Stavanger BASE Klubb, which manages jumps from the big walls over Lysefjorden. The third was Jeb.

Accompanied by two female interpreters from China, the trio had set out from Shanghai to this spot, seven hundred miles west, near Fengjie, a journey that required a flight, a boat ride up the Yangtze, and a van for the final few miles along winding mountain roads, inches from a sheer drop into the jungle. Their destination: Tiankeng—"Heavenly Pit"—a sinkhole with an underground river running through its lower reaches. The cave had been discovered by a BASE jumper named Paul Fortun on a scouting mission. Massive, remote, mysterious, and challenging, the cave appealed to a jumper's most basic instincts.

Jeb, Douggs, and Vibeke were determined to be the first to jump the place. They were already in China, among forty invited jumpers representing sixteen countries who would plunge thirteen hundred feet from the Jin Mao Tower into the financial district in Shanghai. The exhibition was sponsored by the Shanghai Sports Bureau and scheduled to be televised nationally.

They had not actually sought permission to jump into the cave, though. And as they geared up to clip onto the steel cable that was strung across the hole like a lone guitar string—which they would use to make their way out over the middle—security guards materialized and explained to their interpreters that jumping would require a permit. "There was no way we were going to be able to get permits there in the time we had," Douggs would acknowledge, "so we politely nodded our heads, packed up our gear and started thinking of a way to sneak in and do the jump."

Making their way to the other side of the hole, they quickly geared up, clipped onto the cable, and began making their way out, just as security arrived on the scene. "I quickly clipped onto the wire," Douggs would remember, "and managed to get just out of arm's reach, to which the guard became very pissed off."

As they shimmied along the wire, security picked up logs and began beating on the cable, vibrations violently bouncing the jumpers and echoing into the cave. Then the guards seized their interpreters roughly, persuading the jumpers to turn back, and this time leave for good. (A year later, Jeb and Douggs would return, with Fortun—and a permit—to film a documentary about their pioneering cave jump.)

Returning to Shanghai, they joined their fellow jumpers at the Jin Mao ("Golden Prosperity") Tower. At eighty-eight stories and built in a tiered pagoda style in the city's financial district, along the Yangtze, Jin Mao was a potent symbol of China's growing economic might.

The invited jumpers were the crème of the sport, including Slim, who had recovered sufficiently from his injuries to carry the banner for Australia in the event's opening ceremony, on October 6. Although he walked with a detectable limp, Slim had moved back to Australia and lived outside Sydney, working as a forester.

Seduced by the promise of wingsuits, Slim made a study of their growing use in BASE jumping, and the benefits and dangers. In an online forum, he noted: "God help you if you have line twists."

The day before the event, one dedicated to practice, Slim brought his suit up the Jin Mao Tower. Cunningham was jumping at the time. Under canopy, floating above the financial district, he recalled seeing Slim soaring in his suit. He watched as Slim's chute opened off-heading and spun into severe line twists. Kicking frantically to free his lines, Slim ran out of altitude and options. He aimed for the roof of a lower building, disappearing from the view of Cunningham, who figured his friend would wind up with a broken leg at worst.

It was not until later, back at the hotel, that many of the jumpers learned that Slim's situation had been serious. On the roof, Slim had slammed headfirst into an air-conditioning unit, cracked his helmet, and fractured his skull. He was rushed to Shanghai East hospital with head trauma. Jumpers as a group are not given to superstition, but they could not help but note that it was one year to the day since Weston had died.

The show proceeded as planned, with pomp and fanfare. Hundreds of thousands watched live in the streets, and millions more witnessed the spectacle on television as jumpers dropped a quarter-mile, the finale a dozen jumpers in the air at once, trailing colored smoke as they fell.

Two weeks later, on October 22, Slim died from his injuries at Canberra Hospital, in Australia, where he had been transferred. He was thirty-four. The deaths of Weston and Slim one year apart closed the book on an era in which they had defined avant-garde jumping. A new mode ruled by wingsuits began to take hold, and neither man survived the transition. This era would require a fresh set of skills for even the most accomplished jumpers.

Jeb, who was present at Weston's death and nearby when Slim went in, understood this as well as anyone. Back at Perris Valley Skydiving a month later, he teamed with a parachute test pilot named Luigi Cani to gather data on forward speeds, fall rates, and glide angles. Cani had come from Brazil to California to study at UCLA and turned a skydiving hobby into a profession as a parachute tester. He was small in stature, capable, and charismatic; those who met Cani noted how he instantly produced a business card. Sponsored by several companies, he is in every way the epitome of a "pro," called on to test the smallest, fastest, and highest-performance canopy designs for manufacturers.

For two days, in November 2004 he made test jumps with Jeb over the desert. Cani flew an Icarus VX-39—thirty-nine square feet of fabric, a canopy not much larger than a twin bedsheet. Fast and agile, Cani's canopy kept pace with Jeb's wingsuit, which had only half the surface area. The results of their tests were promising, and Go Fast, one of Cani's sponsors, eager to seize an opportunity for publicity, issued a press release on their findings two days before Thanksgiving:

PERRIS, CA
(NOVEMBER 23, 2004)

Pioneer B.A.S.E. jumper Jeb Corliss and Go Fast!–sponsored test pilot Luigi Cani, have paved the way for a world record landing attempt of a wing-suit, minus a parachute. Jeb and Luigi teamed up to gauge speeds and gather data to safely land Jeb's wing-suit. Testing was critical, as no one has ever survived a landing attempt without a parachute. Jeb flew in free fall donning a parachute alongside Luigi, who was at the controls of the world's smallest and fastest parachute, known as the ICARUS VX-39. The two were able to gather data using GPS systems attached to Luigi that tracked exact forward speeds, exact fall rate and glide angles needed for a safe landing. After two days of test piloting, Jeb Corliss said landing the wing-suit was possible as early as next year. "We found there is a definite and reasonable speed for a landing attempt sometime next summer. We're now developing four different types of technologies to land safely, it's very important to land with zero injuries," said Corliss after analyzing data from the test flight.

Showcasing the evolution of the sport of skydiving, Luigi Cani remarked on the uniqueness of Jeb's wing-suit project. "The testing shows the technology of the sport, nowadays we can jump a parachute that flies as fast as a person in free fall and currently we're discovering technology to land a wing-suit without a parachute," said Cani. "If Jeb lands the wing-suit without a parachute and survives, he is going to be my hero," added Cani.

Privately, though, Cani was less sanguine. "I'm afraid Jeb will be killed," he confessed. Robert Pečnik, who had made Jeb's wingsuits, remained skeptical, too. He suggested anyone thinking of landing with a wingsuit should first attempt to land a parachute face-first, an unpleasant scenario.

Others remained undeterred, including Loïc. "What we are all aiming at is flying," he said. "Natural flying. And you need to be able to take off and land, to be a little bird. It's the dream of everyone since the beginning of humans." He told the press of an idea he had for an air-brake method, wherein he'd flare his suit at the critical moment before impact, to skim either on a prepared snow slope or possibly land upright while running to a stop.

In New Zealand, a former aircraft engineer and wingsuit pilot named Chuck Berry floated an idea for landing on a snow slope with skis. In Cape Town, Maria von Egidy, a costume designer for film and television, hefted a wingsuit in her hands and began experiments with modified designs that she hoped would permit an upright landing on a flat surface.

Jeb closed ranks with acquaintances in the Hollywood stunt industry, inquiring about nets and decelerator fans. He wondered about landing in a box catcher, a low-tech airbag equivalent in which hundreds of stacked cardboard boxes compress and cushion during a high fall. *Jeb, you could die,* said the stuntmen he consulted. *Unsafe,* they said. Over and over, they dismissed his best notions as bad ideas.

Chapter 11
"HOLY CHUTE!"

Turning and turning in the widening gyre
The falcon cannot hear the falconer;
Things fall apart; the centre cannot hold
—*William Butler Yeats, "The Second Coming"*

NEW YORK, SPRING 2006

His landing ambitions stalled due to the lack of a solid theory for touching down unhurt, Jeb Corliss considered an extraordinary job offer.

Jordan Stone was a producer in Los Angeles who worked on a succession of cable TV shows that had bought much of Jeb's stunt footage. Working at *Real TV,* Stone acquired the first video Jeb sold, documenting his trip to Angel Falls. Stone called Jeb regularly in search of fresh footage. One day in 2004, he phoned with an altogether different proposition: Had Jeb ever considered working as a TV host?

Jeb hadn't, and he wasn't thrilled with the idea. But Stone explained that he had something different in mind. The host of his show would act like a fly on the wall, talking with athletes—in this case, skateboarders, snowboarders, skydivers, motorcyclists—as they dreamed up, planned, and attempted to execute never-before-seen stunts. Each episode would feature a different athlete pursuing a first in his discipline.

Stone was impressed with Jeb's performance in a documentary called *Fearless,* on the cable network OLN, which explored Jeb's life and the circumstances of Weston's death. He would later write in an e-mail what had prompted him to pursue Jeb, a novice, as a TV host: "Jeb is a larger-than-life character, and that comes thru [sic] on camera—he also has a genuine interest in other people and what motivates them . . . I knew he'd be a huge asset to my show."

The show's other producer and cohost was a former stuntman named Perry Barndt. Their show would be called *Stunt Junkies* and air on the Discovery Channel. With a salary of $10,000 per episode, all of Jeb's hard work and risk taking appeared to have finally paid off.

Right away, though, certain aspects of production chafed—reading from scripts, parroting dialogue, doing voice-overs. "All of a sudden I was a regular host," Jeb would recall. "I didn't like that very much. It really wasn't what I was designed for."

Worse, Jeb was on the other side of the microphone from the men who took the risks in each episode. The erstwhile BASE jumper was eager to return to stunts. He began working an idea over in his mind. With a group of confidants, he spent months fine-tuning a plot, which they would finally set in motion on April 27, 2006, under a bright spring New York sky.

*I*t was the kind of day on which, from the observation level on the eighty-sixth floor of the Empire State Building, visitors gained views of Manhattan's muscular grandeur—the spires and pinnacles of the city's lesser skyscrapers, New York Harbor, and the iconic bridges leading to the outer boroughs and beyond. West, across the dark waters of the Hudson, the vast promise of the American continent stretched from New Jersey's satellite cities and burgs to the barren hills on the horizon.

Jeb Corliss had been in the city a week, waiting out winds and rain for just such a day. He had admired the Empire State Building from street level while out walking. And when favorable conditions finally arrived, he entered the building's ground floor at around 3 p.m.

With his tall, lanky frame and shaved head, Jeb normally stood out in a crowd. *Stunt Junkies* meant he had a modestly famous face. But no one recognized him as he made his way through the building's lobby. To ensure no one would, he wore a $15,000 disguise consisting of a fat suit and a latex mask with a wig, fake mustache, and sunglasses, which had transformed him into an aging, overweight tourist.

Cameras in the building captured images of visitors and relayed them to command-center monitors, which security personnel scanned for anything unusual. Footage that would later figure prominently in a trial showed Jeb pass through one of the building's X-ray machines, his bulky suit stuffed into beige pants and jacket. He waddled through the lobby and up an escalator. A camera at the top captured him coming into view: first his sunglasses, followed by a blue-striped button-down shirt, and finally a disguised Jeb Corliss stepped off, duck footed, in dark shoes, moving down a corridor to a staging area. He had paid an extra $40, on top of the price of admission, to be escorted to the front of the line to ride the express elevators. He was in a hurry. Underneath his disguise he wore a parachute specially constructed with plastic parts, to ensure passage through the building's metal detectors. In his head he carried a plan to leap from the building and float into midtown Manhattan.

On the eightieth floor, Jeb disembarked one elevator car and boarded another for a ride up the final six stories to the observation level. Cameras followed his every movement, feeding video images from an Intellex surveillance system to security personnel, who by now were looking for him. Four hours earlier, an anonymous caller had phoned with a vague tip about a large man in a disguise who planned to jump from the building. Security personnel scanned the sidewalk and corridors. They looked in the lobby, scrutinizing visitors. Informed of the tip, the New York Police Department dispatched an officer to the eighty-sixth-floor observation deck, where he took a position along with several retired NYPD detectives now serving as private security at the building.

Once on the eighty-sixth floor himself, Jeb Corliss proceeded past a bank of windows to a handicap bathroom, locked the door, and quickly shed his fat suit and disguise. He pulled a black helmet with a video camera mounted on top over his mask and completed his outfit with black fingerless gloves. Measuring himself in the mirror, he looked lean and long, decked out head to toe in black. Finally Jeb inspected his rig, unlocked the bathroom door, and stepped into a souvenir shop. Wearing a black jumpsuit and rig, black boots, black kneepads, black gloves, and black helmet, he made a startling impression on tourists as he strode with purpose past postcard carousels and King Kong curios.

Moving quickly, he burst through a door to a wheelchair ramp along the southwest corner of the observation platform, in the middle of the block overlooking Thirty-third Street and the city's jagged skyline, shreds of blue sky showing through the clouds. A few feet to his right, three members of the building's plainclothes security detail had gathered to scan the crowd for the suspect described earlier by the anonymous caller. Former cops, they were large men with probing eyes and stern expressions, dressed neatly in sport coats, khakis, and slacks. They did not exactly blend in. A member of the building's security team monitoring metal detectors in the lobby had radioed them about a large man. Something about the man did not sit right with him. With their backs to the door, searching for someone meeting the description provided by the security officer in the lobby, these men did not immediately see Jeb emerge onto the observation platform and, in one motion, stand on a railing along the ramp and vault onto a ten-foot-tall security fence. The fence's vertical bars bend back toward the building at the top like a shepherd's crook. As Jeb dangled there, security— searching for an overweight man—finally spotted him.

"There he goes!" a plainclothes security officer shouted. Reaching for Jeb's legs as he swung over the bars, the man lost his balance and his eyeglasses as he toppled headfirst from a six-foot wall. In the chaos, Jeb slid down the outside of the fence and settled onto a four-inch ledge, 1,044 feet above an early-rush-hour streetscape. Three hundred tourists were gathered on the other side of the bars. Some screamed. Others pointed cameras and began taking pictures. A baby wailed in the background. The commotion summoned the uniformed police officer, who sprinted through the gift shop.

For two years, Jeb had carefully prepared and plotted what would happen next, just as he had studied and probed weaknesses in the building's security setup. A tiered wedding-cake design makes the building more than fifty feet wider at the base of each side than at the top. To avoid the building's outcroppings during his jump, Jeb would need to maneuver to a section where a channel runs down the side. There he would be able to leap safely clear to the street.

He had studied vehicle patterns on Fifth Avenue and learned that traffic lights up and down the strip turned green simultaneously. He would time his jump so that vehicles on Fifth Avenue, at the intersection with Thirty-fourth Street, would be halted at a red light, allowing him to avoid a dangerous landing amid moving traffic. By his calculations, the whole stunt would be over in a matter of seconds. He would leap, deploy his parachute, and land at a predetermined spot in the street below. Afterwards, he would quickly gather his parachute, climb into a hailed cab, and disappear in Manhattan's teeming early-rush-hour traffic. On the observation level he would leave behind only memories, a few images in the cameras of startled tourists, and his disguise.

Legal research had convinced him that parachuting from the Empire State Building broke no specific laws. Still, that did not mean the building's owners would welcome him, and indeed, once security spotted Jeb, they moved quickly. Before he made his way to a safe takeoff spot, they reached through the safety bars and grabbed him around the legs. Two men grabbed him by his parachute harness and held tight.

Jeb had prepared for this possibility, too. He'd concocted a script, one that had been used by Thor Alex Kappfjell seven years earlier, when he had jumped the Empire State Building during his Manhattan spree. Pleading with security to let go, Jeb explained that he could lose his balance and drop to his death.

"What you're doing right now can kill me," he said.

"I will fall and die if you don't let me go. Let me go!" he repeated.

Guards briefly discussed releasing him. "Hell, no!" one shouted. No one would jump from the Empire State Building that day, he said. Then he called for backup.

The NYPD officer posted on the observation level lent his handcuffs to a retired police detective working for the building's private security detail, named Tim Donohue. Donohue locked Jeb Corliss to the suicide bars. Then the officer called in a 10-13, "Officer needs assistance," and a 10-85, "Additional units needed," on his police radio.

Caught, Jeb changed tack, his priority shifting to self-preservation. If his parachute opened while he was handcuffed to the bars, a gust could rip his arms from his body. He conveyed those concerns with increasing desperation. "If my parachute opens, my arms will be severed from my body and I will *die*," he said. "Please take my parachute. My arms will be ripped from my body and I will *fall*!"

"What did you say?"

"If my parachute opens while I'm handcuffed, my arms will be severed and I will fall and die."

The officer pulled out a knife and handed it to Donohue to cut the straps securing the parachute. Next they removed the rig and helmet and passed them over the bars, pieces of latex mask peeling from Jeb's face.

Uniformed police swarmed the deck and set up a large net to cordon off the hundreds of curious tourists.

"Remove the handcuffs and I'll climb back over," Jeb offered. Police weren't convinced he wouldn't try to escape, and without a parachute, he could fall and die. After some discussion, they employed the nets used to cordon off the observation level, wrapping them around Jeb to secure him in place as they unscrewed a small section of the suicide fence. At 3:40 p.m., police pulled him back onto the deck and placed him under arrest. He and his ambition of parachuting from the Empire State Building were busted.

In an interrogation room at the Midtown South precinct, on Thirty-fifth Street between Eighth and Ninth Avenues, Jeb met with two detectives, who read him his Miranda rights. Providing details of his plans, Jeb explained that he was an experienced BASE jumper with more than a thousand jumps. He said he had been plotting his Empire State Building stunt for years, developing plastic parts for his parachute to bypass metal detectors in the building's lobby. He had paid $15,000 for the fat suit from a supplier for Hollywood films. He had timed traffic lights to avoid landing among moving cars. His stunt would have been "very safe," he said, with little possibility for injury to pedestrians. The mood in the room was relaxed. One of the cops, a Detective Whelan, would testify later that he found Jeb "likable" and "professional." Nevertheless, Jeb was charged with first-degree reckless endangerment, a felony. He was taken for the night to the Tombs, the Manhattan Detention Complex downtown on White Street, a clearinghouse for anyone arrested in the city. There, Jeb was placed in a cell with half a dozen other inmates. "To be put in a cell with a bunch of scary, gnarly people—it was disturbing," he would remember. "It was not the kind of place I would normally hang out."

In the morning, Jeb posted $3,000 bail and stepped into a city that was not entirely prepared to treat him as a conquering hero. A girlfriend was waiting, and as a photographer snapped their picture, Jeb stuck out his tongue. The tabloids pilloried him on their front pages, the *Post* calling him a "Jumping Jerk" and the *Daily News* countering with "HOLY CHUTE! Dopey daredevil nabbed trying to dive off Empire State Building."

News coverage mentioned that Jeb had leaped from the Palace Hotel. As he headed uptown in a cab to collect his belongings, Jeb prepared for an angry reception and possible eviction. Once in the lobby, though, he was surprised when staff turned and began applauding.

Not everyone was in a mood for celebration. In the aftermath of his arrest, Discovery fired Jeb from *Stunt Junkies* and issued a public statement expressing disappointment "at his serious lack of judgment and his reckless behavior." The office of Manhattan district attorney Robert Morgenthau prepared to put evidence before a grand jury to indict Jeb on felony reckless endangerment charges.

A fierce legal battle lay ahead. His very freedom at stake, Jeb hired Mel Sachs, a flamboyant figure in New York courtrooms who had represented Mike Tyson, Lil' Kim, David Copperfield, Derek Jeter, and comedian Jackie Mason. Sachs wore bow ties, rimless eyeglasses, and three-piece bespoke double-breasted suits with watch pockets occupied by a gold timepiece. An amateur magician, he sometimes used the watch to demonstrate sleight of hand to jurors, making the point that things were not always as they seemed—that eyewitness testimony could be flawed. Comfortable in front of cameras, Sachs appeared as a legal analyst on shows for Bill

O'Reilly, Sean Hannity, Larry King, and Greta Van Susteren. Journalists and clients visiting his office found a framed sign on the wall reading HAVE FAITH IN GOD AND MEL SACHS.

Jeb had few, if any, advocates among BASE jumpers. "He did the Eiffel Tower and then he did New York, the Empire State Building, and put that up," Helliwell would say about video footage of Jeb's stunts. "It was like *Oh God, Jeb, you don't need to make yourself famous by burning all these objects.*"

"He was coming really close to what we used to call a glory hound," DiGiovanni would say. "There's other BASE jumpers in New York and other BASE jumpers jumping all the time in New York. He made it tough on those guys. What happened to the next guy who went to court? I don't know if Jeb ever thought of that. There's a lot of guys who were down on him because of that. To a lot of guys at that time, that wasn't what BASE was about. You go out and you jump. You love it. You don't do it to make yourself famous."

The following summer, Jeb returned to Switzerland. Wrung out emotionally, stepping from a cliff was like stepping from a curb. A doctor diagnosed adrenal fatigue, a condition similar to the battle fatigue experienced by soldiers returning from combat.

His problems paled, though, compared with those of others around him. In Switzerland, Karina was critically injured while flying a wingsuit when her parachute lines snarled in a tension knot and she collided with a rock at sixty miles an hour, snapping her legs like matchsticks, sustaining more than twenty open fractures in her femurs and knees. She lost seven pints of blood before a rescue helicopter whisked her to a hospital. She regained consciousness after two days. Doctors explained that she was lucky to be alive. They said she would likely never walk again. When Jeb arrived at Karina's bedside, he told her that the accident had probably saved her life.

"How's that possible?" she asked.

Jeb said that, given the direction Karina was headed in the sport, she probably would have eventually been killed if she were to continue.

Back in New York, ten days after Karina's accident, on August 30, 2006,

Mel Sachs died from complications related to pancreatic cancer. With Jeb's legal defense in disarray heading into grand jury testimony, the district attorney's office pressed him to plead guilty and bring a swift end to the case. Instead he hired Mark Jay Heller, a flamboyant and controversial figure in New York courtrooms who had once represented "Son of Sam" David Berkowitz. Impish, with arresting blue eyes and slicked-back hair, Heller had been suspended from practicing law for five years during the 1990s after a disciplinary committee charged him with deceit, puffery, abusive treatment of clients, fee gouging, neglect, and willful failure to return unearned retainers to his clients. The panel accused Heller of being a "menace to the public" and "shockingly cavalier and abusive." He admitted to professional misconduct, but a decade later he had been reinstated and was seeking high-profile clients. Jeb qualified. When a grand jury handed down an indictment on October 7, Heller's client was facing felony reckless endangerment and the possibility of seven years in prison.

Weeks later, at State Supreme Court in Manhattan for a hearing, Heller told Justice Michael R. Ambrecht in a brusque New York accent that his client had a right to risk his own life, and that he had made more than one thousand jumps around the world without injuring anyone else. He added that there was no law against jumping off a building in the state anyway. Then Heller said that it was the *officers* who showed depraved indifference to Mr. Corliss's life by handcuffing him to the suicide bars. "If the parachute opens," he said, "the thrust of it would separate him from his limbs." Afterwards, Jeb emphasized for reporters: "This is completely absurd that people are coming down on me this way, because my life is *mine*."

A week later, Heller pursued a motion for dismissal of the charges, arguing that Jeb could not be guilty of reckless endangerment because his client hadn't actually jumped, and anyway, he had a constitutional right to jump. "This gentleman, I maintain, is an artist and has freedom of expression," Heller told the court. "His art is not with pen or music; his art is with his body movement."

It was an inspired defense, but it would be months before they knew if it was enough to win Jeb his freedom.

*I*n London, Gary continued his own flirtation with the limits of the law. With the city dark before dawn on November 28, 2006, he splashed into the frigid waters of the Thames in central London wearing a dry suit and clutching a dry bag containing his parachute. He wore a wool beanie on his head and wet-suit gloves. Beneath his dry suit he had a radio and a knife.

During the previous two weeks he had visited Jubilee Gardens, along the river, ten times to gaze at the London Eye, the 443-foot iconic Ferris wheel, a city landmark looming across the Thames from Parliament, Big Ben, and Westminster Abbey. He studied and probed the security setup. Each time he returned, Gary wore different clothes so he wouldn't be recognized, sometimes donning a cap or glasses or growing a beard. He wandered into a restricted area and observed how security reacted. He talked to the guards and learned that a fresh crew swapped over for a new shift at 7 a.m. "I knew that at five or six o'clock they were probably at their lowest ebb. That was probably a good time for me to strike."

For six years, since the structure had been built in observance of the millennium, Gary had fantasized about jumping the London Eye. He had aborted plans several times due to concerns about the tide or winds, but on this day all conditions lined up favorably. He entered the water around 4 a.m. about a quarter of a mile downriver at Festival Pier, and rode an incoming tide beneath the Hungerford Bridge. As he floated in the dark, cold water, the shadow of Westminster Bridge loomed ahead.

It took Gary forty minutes to bob up on the tide to London Eye Pier, beneath the big wheel. An accomplice watched from shore as Gary arrived and signaled two other men to begin a staged fight, which attracted the attention of eight security guards. That was when Gary got the signal, a voice crackling over static on his radio to make his move. He climbed out of the water and sprinted to the wheel, launching onto a spiral staircase that led into the wheel's drive mechanism. Once there he cut open his dry suit. He was wearing a dinner jacket and tie beneath, and a harness, which he fastened to the rim of the wheel, hanging on for a ride up. It was 4:40 a.m.

At ground level a cleaning crew had arrived, working on each car, rotating the wheel to bring the next one into position, and inadvertently giving Gary a ride up.

Clutching a walkie-talkie, Vivienne waited with her children, Lydia and Kali, in the frigid darkness at a deserted Jubilee Gardens, monitoring Gary's progress. "We couldn't draw attention to him," Vivienne says. "His stunt friends were distracting security. We weren't watching and looking up. We had to be quiet about it."

Hours passed, and finally at the top, four hundred feet above the city at daybreak, Gary cut free from his dry suit and prepared his parachute. Sunrise came at 7:40 that day and Gary watched warm light wash over the waking city. "The visuals for me were amazing," he says. He waved to the people on the ground to indicate he was jumping soon. A photographer he had hired stood by to capture the moment. And at 7:45 Gary launched. "He gave us the go-ahead, in terms of *It's going to start,* on the walkie-talkie," Vivienne recalls. "But then it was looking up and watching, really. We just see him go, hoping the parachute deploys properly and he lands safely."

The jump came off so smoothly that Gary went undetected as he landed in the grass of Jubilee Gardens, behind a long row of plane trees, bark peeling and leaves golden in the autumn air. "The security guards never even knew he jumped the wheel," says Vivienne, who, along with the kids, gave Gary a hug. After posing for photos, Gary strolled off in his dinner wear, looking like James Bond, in search of a place to grab breakfast with his family.

He would sell photos of the stunt to the *Daily Mail* and tell the paper: "It's something I've always wanted to do. I'm just attracted to the thrill of jumping off dramatic structures. It's a sheer adrenaline rush.

"I certainly wasn't trying to expose any security concerns. If anything I wanted to highlight what a wonderful attraction the London Eye is."

Security did not learn of the stunt until a *Mail* reporter called for comment. A spokesman for Scotland Yard said it had no complaint regarding the incident and would not be investigating.

Gary had gotten away clean. But if he thought that notoriety from his jump at the wheel would act as a catalyst to securing support for a landing attempt with a wingsuit, he was mistaken. "Straightaway I thought, *Someone is going to pay for that, because this is the Holy Grail*," Gary says, recalling his views about a landing. "Imagine jumping and not deploying a parachute. Wingsuits is a young sport, and I was really excited."

But the offers weren't there. Although he had earned money and a small measure of renown as a BASE jumper, skydiving and wingsuit flying never paid Gary's bills. Tending to his family, Gary stuck mainly to stunts in TV and the movies. "I just didn't pursue it," he says about landing. "I was still maintaining a public presence with BASE jumping, but I wasn't doing anything in the wingsuit world."

Not yet anyway.

Three, two, one . . . liftoff: Each summer, hundreds of BASE jumpers and wingsuit pilots from around the world gather in the Bernese Alps, in Switzerland, lured to the Lauterbrunnen Valley by sheer, two-thousand-foot cliffs. Here, in July 2011, American wingsuit pilots Joby Ogwyn and Brian Drake prepare to fly from High Nose, one of the more popular exit points. Drake died in April 2014 following a wingsuit accident. He was thirty-three.

The jagged course of the the Crack cuts along Hinderrugg, a 7,500-foot mountain in eastern Switzerland's Churfirsten range. By 2011, wingsuit pilots had begun redefining skill and daring in their sport by flying through the Crack. Here, Andreas Gubser is waiting to photograph a flight by California stuntman Jeb Corliss.

Close Encounter: On the morning of July 16, 2011, Jeb Corliss, wearing a wingsuit and parachute, launches from the Sputnik exit on Hinderrugg, starting a sequence that would make him internationally famous when video footage went viral. One mile below, just above the Crack (sequence at right and below), Jeb homes in on balloons held by accomplice Christian Gubser for a heart-stopping stunt that recalled William Tell. Christian dives for safety just as Jeb blasts overhead at 123 miles per hour and continues flying down the Crack. "It's *so* close," a shaken Christian would say.

A stuntman for TV and film and a former British paratrooper, Gary Connery conceived of landing a wingsuit without a parachute as a way to fulfill his desire "to be the best at something."

Gary had already jumped from the Eiffel Tower and Nelson's Column in Trafalgar Square. But in a caper worthy of James Bond, Gary climbed the London Eye undetected on November 28, 2006, while wearing a tuxedo and a parachute, and launched 440 feet from the Ferris wheel just after daybreak, making a clean getaway.

In September 2011, eight wingsuit pilots from around the world arrived in a remote region of central China to participate in a historic wingsuit exhibition at Tianmen Mountain, culminating in an attempt by Jeb Corliss to fly through a natural arch in the mountain, a first for wingsuits. Geared-up (left to right) Chris "Douggs" McDougall, Joby Ogwyn, and Jeff Nebelkopf relax before a practice flight from a platform perched 990 feet up on the mountainside.

Once in flight, the pilots traveled a course above rugged cloudy terrain, where a road "like a strand of wet spaghetti" wends to the arch called Heaven's Gate (translation: Tianmen), which gives the mountain its name.

Wingsuit pilots Matt Gerdes and Roberta Mancino demonstrate a smoke canister for the Chinese media. Attached to the pilots' ankles, the smoke would cast a bright trail through the sky and make the fliers easier to track from the ground. Complications with a smoke canister, though, would nearly lead to catastrophe on Jeb's first attempt to fly through the arch.

The Eye of a Needle: On his second attempt, this time without smoke, Jeb soars through Tianmen Shan and makes history as thousands watch live from the mountain. Afterward he tells reporters: "The next real project I want to do is to land a wingsuit without deploying a parachute. That's a goal that I've been working on for six years. And I will do it."

With Lion's Head and the south Atlantic lapping at the coast in the background, Jeff launches from Table Mountain in January 2012. Flying camera, Jeff captured footage of Jeb's increasingly daring flights from the air. Their growing confidence and comfort on the mountain would lead to tragedy for Jeb.

Joby and Jeb hike toward the cable car station following another successful flight from Table Mountain in Cape Town, South Africa, carrying their stash bags. In keeping with the ethics of BASE, they *leave no trace*.

In a scene that resembled an old-fashioned barn raising, on May 23, 2012, hundreds of volunteers built a landing area of cardboard boxes in a field at Mill End Farm, about twenty-five miles outside London, in Buckinghamshire.

That afternoon, Gary would leap from a helicopter 2,400 feet up and, on his first attempt, flare his specially built suit in the final moments to bleed off speed, hitting the empty boxes at 70 miles an hour. A few tense minutes later, having achieved a first in human flight, he strolled from the box rig without a stitch out of place, his wife, Vivienne, and cameras waiting to greet him.

A chance meeting with wingsuit designer Tony Uragallo in Norway in the summer of 2011 led Gary to collaborate on a wingsuit design called the Rebel that would allow characteristics of slow, but stable flight—crucial for a landing attempt.

Mark Sutton (right), a former British Army officer, acted as Gary's wingman, helping plan and execute the landing project. Here, following a trial jump from Andrew Harvey's helicopter, they walk through a pasture at Mill End Farm. A year later, Mark would be killed in a wingsuit accident.

Chapter 12

THE WINGSUIT LANDING PROJECT

Fortune favors the bold.

—*Virgil*

RIO DE JANEIRO, APRIL 24, 2007

In January 2007, Judge Ambrecht threw out the indictment, saying he was moved by Jeb Corliss's preparation and the care he had taken not to cause injury, to either himself or others. He cited the fact that Jeb had worn a parachute and studied traffic-light patterns at Fifth Avenue and Thirty-fourth Street in order to land when all the cars were stopped. In an eight-page decision, he wrote: "Before this court is a professional BASE jumper, attempting to jump off of the Empire State Building with appropriate safety equipment. To hold that defendant's conduct rises to this level of blameworthiness is manifestly unjust and contrary to prevailing law."

To commemorate his victory, Jeb climbed out a window at Heller's office, onto a ledge nine stories above the sidewalk, for a photographer for the *New York Times*. Clad in his black coat, a black knit cap pulled low to his shades to guard against the winter chill, he stood high above New York's streets, looking serious, but triumphant.

But in the *Times* and other papers the following day, legal experts, police, and a spokeswoman for the district attorney's office expressed outrage and dismay at the court's decision. They wondered if the court really wanted the Empire State Building and other landmarks to become magnets for jumpers. And District Attorney Robert Morgenthau's office mulled options for an appeal.

In the meantime, the owners of the Empire State Building had sued Jeb for $12 million for "endangering customers, employees, tenants, visitors, and the building's reputation."

*T*o pry Jeb's mind from the coming legal showdown, Jeb's friend Luigi Cani, who had been so instrumental with wingsuit testing in preparation for landing, coaxed his friend to Rio de Janeiro. Luigi wanted help with a project promoting efforts to have *Christ the Redeemer* (*Cristo Redentor*), the iconic seven-hundred-ton statue of reinforced concrete and soapstone rising from the half-mile-high granite dome of Corcovado— named one of the New Seven Wonders of the World. Standing 125 feet tall, arms outstretched north and south in cruciform, *Christ the Redeemer* offers residents of Rio's rich and poor sectors—the latter living in the infamous *favelas*—a familiar benediction upon stepping out each morning.

Three days shy of the first anniversary of the Empire State Building episode, Jeb and Luigi rode in a red helicopter clattering a half mile above Rio's breathtaking scenery. Beyond the green mountains, hillside slums, and high-rise complexes, the coastline sweeps all the way to Sugar Loaf, a thirteen-hundred-foot hunk of rock like a canine tooth in the mouth of Guanabara Bay. The view beyond the city took in islands and peninsulas breaching the blue Atlantic like the spine of some great sea monster. Stepping beneath the whirring blades and onto the skids they launched for Corcovado, buzzing the big statue and thrilling throngs of tourists gathered on the pedestal.

Back on the ground, they discussed getting closer to the statue. Jeb planned to fly near enough to dip beneath an outstretched arm eighty feet off the deck. On the skids, Jeb blocked out the arresting scenery and homed in on the statue's arm, then slashed beneath.

When it was his turn, Luigi aimed for the upper portion of the statue, closing within fifty feet of the shoulder with an ease that surprised him.

Soaking in the reaction of the spectators below, he lost his bearings for a moment and, moving at more than a hundred miles an hour, suddenly found the mountain fast approaching his face. Fear in his throat, Luigi figured he was going in, a splash of blue sky and lush vegetation his last sight. But a survival instinct kicked in, and an evasive maneuver left him brushing the bushes that, like a beard, cover the face of the craggy mountain. Green blurred beneath Luigi's chin, fabric from his wingsuit snagging and snapping off branches like the vibrating arm on an electric hedge trimmer. What happened next was not the result of conscious thought. Operating on years of fine-tuned muscle memory, Luigi reflexively tracked away from the mountain and over a rain forest. With altitude between him and the forest, Luigi reached back and pulled his parachute handle. Lines stretching, the canopy opened, slowing everything down—except Luigi's heartbeat. His body gorged with cortisol and adrenaline, his fine motor skills abandoned him. With his hands palsied from fright, he recalls, "I couldn't control my parachute handles."

When Luigi landed unhurt, an inspection of his wingsuit revealed bits of bushes, twigs, and leaves clinging to the nylon fabric. He had become the first to survive contact with the ground while flying a wingsuit. It was a stunning achievement, and he received a round of congratulations. But Luigi was badly shaken and simply grateful to be alive.

Jeb, though, was profoundly impressed and inspired. A vision for landing took shape in his mind. The statue's scale and height, a half mile above the city, had allowed them to line up their flight paths from the helicopter. If Jeb built a massive marker—say, of balloons—he would have something to line up on while jumping from a helicopter a great distance away. Another realization was that the statue's perch, two thousand feet above the city, had also permitted them to soar by with sufficient time and altitude remaining to deploy their chutes before landing. The margin was so great that Luigi had even made contact and lost control and still had plenty of altitude to correct and get his parachute performing. Parachutes are reliably effective at an altitude of two hundred feet or greater. Once below 150 feet with a wingsuit, you would be taking your chances. A pilot at that altitude would be more or less committed to landing: he would either make it or die trying. But if a landing area were hundreds of feet high, a pilot could approach and then, if not lined up properly, bail out and pitch his chute at the last moment. In other words, he would not be locked in. He would have a crucial out.

Taken together, on the flight back to California from Brazil, Jeb figured he finally had a blueprint for landing.

*A*n ocean away in Gap, a city of 38,000 in the French Alps, Loïc had, after flying down the mountain over Verbier in such dramatic and celebrated fashion five years earlier, docked on the wing of an airborne glider while flying his wingsuit. Setting his wingsuit down on terra firma was another matter altogether. "I'm not really pursuing right now," he said about a wingsuit landing. "But the idea is interesting. I think it's doable."

Loïc believed that a skilled pilot could land on a snow slope, though he acknowledged that forward speed could pose a problem. Even slowing to seventy-five miles an hour "is quite fast to land headfirst on snow," he explained with a laugh. "A *big* try! The basic idea is getting parallel to the snow so we don't have a vertical speed at all, so we don't have a shock when we touch the snow, then touch and slide. You can try it now, and you can stand out of it now with the technique I have right now. But I don't really feel like taking this risk, because I think it's a little stupid and not really interesting because you might do it well one time and try another time and crash and die. It will be interesting to do if it's controlled and not just a try."

Eight thousand miles to the south of Loïc, in Bo-Kaap, Cape Town's charming Muslim quarter, where a shrill call to prayer punctures the afternoon from the minaret of a mosque, Maria von Egidy was in search of a pilot willing to test her design ideas. The world's unlikeliest wingsuit designer, von Egidy had never been skydiving. But she became obsessed with human flight from the moment she set eyes on a wingsuit, when a pilot approached about sewing a pocket on his suit to hold a GPS device. "Because it's such an unusual-looking thing, I was fascinated by it," she would remember.

She had fashioned a career from creating costumes for the make-believe of movies and TV. Yet a wingsuit conveyed the power of flight for *real*. "Human flight is such an ancient dream," she says. "Everybody's got that dream. It's something so archetypal and inside of us all."

With the eye of a seamstress, she fixed what she believed were design flaws, cranking out prototypes on a sewing machine, which were tested by a rangy South African pilot named Julian Boulle. They created a suit called the GS1, incorporating fresh design elements, such as a wing that stretched from wrist to ankle, for more surface area. They brought the suit to market under the brand name Jii-Wings in 2005. The suit received good reviews, but they didn't sell many.

In the meantime, von Egidy had a vision of a suit that wouldn't require a parachute—a suit that would contain properties necessary for landing. She had drawings and sought investors for the $400,000 she would need for prototypes and testing. After a falling-out with Boulle, she needed a test pilot, and she approached Jeb. "He's a believer, and I think that's really important," she would say. "You have to believe it can be done."

Jeb was skeptical, though; not of landing but of von Egidy's method. "She makes great wingsuits," he said. "She's nice, but her ideas on landing are not reality—no way I would go for her plan."

W hich plan was best, and created optimal conditions for a successful landing, continued to be a matter of debate and deliberation. One person who weighed in on the discussion was Jean Potvin, a physics Ph.D. and professor of physics and calculus at St. Louis University. For thirteen years Potvin had performed parachute-inflation research for the U.S. Army, a field of study he continued at the Parks College Parachute Research Group, at St. Louis University. A skydiver himself, Potvin had made more than 2,500 jumps, though none with a wingsuit. "All of this is technically all possible," he said in a pleasant Quebecois timbre when asked about landing without a parachute. "The thing I'm not sure is, what's your margins in terms of safety or likelihood to crash?"

Potvin thought of wingsuits in terms of airplanes, which have ailerons, rudders on the wings that rely on deflection to allow a plane to turn. The slower a plane flies, the more deflection is required to turn. Faster-moving planes require less deflection, but there's a trade-off in precision. "When you go fast, your inputs have to be much smaller and metered more accurately," Potvin explained. It was the same with wingsuits. Screaming along at seventy miles an hour or more, even a slight movement would be exaggerated. Any slipup at such speeds, while flying close to the ground or a landing apparatus, would mean hitting the deck hard.

Still, Potvin believed a landing could be performed, and that to do so would require a flare. The key to a flare is glide, which means increasing lift to cover a lot more ground for every foot of descent. Airplanes and birds both flare on landing. Although weighing several hundred thousand pounds, a commercial airliner comes in and performs a flare to increase lift and drag, swooping almost parallel to the ground and touching down first on its rear landing gear, adroitly reducing what could potentially be a catastrophic impact. Mimicking the action of a bird's feathers, aircraft flare by altering their wings using flaps along the trailing edge, resulting in less downward and forward speed and an uneventful landing.

Parachutes flare on landing, too. "Ram-air canopies have a basically 3:1," Potvin said about glide slope. "For every foot of descent, they cover three feet forward. For your landing, what you need to do is have a flat glide slope."

Even under a parachute, hitting the ground at forty miles an hour would be a painful endeavor. So a parachutist flying a ram-air canopy flares, say, a dozen feet off the deck, by pulling down on toggles that alter the shape of the canopy, converting forward speed into temporary lift. It's an act that relies on timing and precise action.

Wingsuits, though, due to their design and small surface area, do not allow for much of a flare. To flare a wingsuit sufficiently for landing on flat ground would require either radically modifying the suit or training a pilot to execute a near-impossible maneuver moments before impact. "If you land on a horizontal surface, you need to be able to flare your landing," Potvin said. "That is, to increase the glide tremendously so you're almost moving parallel to the ground so that your descent rate is very small."

But there's one other way to move parallel to the ground: land on a decline. "Imagine you're falling at a 1:1 glide ratio," he explained. "If you have a slope that's 1:1 or a little less than that, you're going to hit the ground—relative to the ground—at small speed. And that makes the whole thing possible."

Nordic ski jumpers land this way by soaring great distances through the air at a 1:1 glide ratio and landing on a slope that is 1:1. An added benefit of landing like a ski jumper: "By a slope covered with snow, there you improve your odds," Potvin noted with a chuckle. "If indeed you crash and burn, at least the snow is going to save your ass."

Yet Potvin was careful not to laugh at anyone who dreamed of landing, or call them crazy. He had a friend and colleague named Roy Haggard who ran a small research-and-development firm near the drop zone in Lake Elsinore, California. For years Haggard had talked about a device he called "the Luge," based on the principles of the icy chute, which would make it possible to jump from an aircraft and land without a parachute.

Approaching his sixth decade on earth, Haggard was known for not suffering fools, and if he claimed he could jump out of an aircraft and land without a parachute, then people who knew him were at least willing to listen. A skydiver himself, and a gruff autodidactic aircraft engineer, Haggard built his first hang glider at fifteen and qualified to fly it in a national competition. After completing high school, he skipped college and instead began designing gliders for a leading manufacturer. He founded Vertigo from a garage with partner Glen Brown. The operation had grown to about fifty employees working on projects for NASA and the U.S. military, building decelerators for space vehicles reentering the atmosphere. High-tech stuff, anyway. Vertigo employees included champion hang glider pilots, mountaineers, skydivers, helicopter and fixed-wing pilots, and world-class sailors. The company ethic espoused "a keen desire to continually explore new boundaries."

Still, with a family to support, and limited time and money to dedicate to a pet project, Haggard had reluctantly put the Luge operation on the back burner; which was why he was eager to help when Jeb came along to his facility, on the fringe of Skylark Airport, looking for assistance with what he was calling the Wingsuit Landing Project. Given their esoteric interests and shared geography in the Perris-Elsinore area, it was perhaps inevitable the two would cross paths. In Haggard, Jeb had found a kindred spirit, an uncompromising figure driven by innovation and achievement.

"Is it possible?" snapped Haggard when asked about landing a wingsuit. "Yeah . . . anything is possible. It just requires time, money, and innovation."

Haggard described an apparatus similar to a huge vertical skateboard ramp. "You would have no real impact," he said. "You would simply slide at 120 miles per hour like World Grand Prix motorcyclists" when they fall. "The human body can handle pretty high accelerations."

If Jeb raised the needed money, Haggard would help design and build a runway. They estimated the cost would be $3 million. At least $1 million would be needed for the landing apparatus alone. They would be using high-tech materials enabling Jeb to touch down face-first at terminal velocity and, as he would say, "stand up and do it again." The remaining $2 million would cover production costs to create a televised spectacle to pay for everything. Jeb looked for funding where he always found it—in the entertainment industry. "For enough money," he said, putting the price tag in perspective, "you could go to the moon."

The plan called for Jeb to wear a wingsuit and an exoskeleton neck brace, jump from an aircraft one thousand feet up, and fly as slowly as possible, with a glide of, say, 3:1, lining up with massive tethered balloons creating a grid in the sky, according to ideas acquired at the Christ statue in Rio. "This is my Everest," he said with brio. He hoped to line up his attempt in the next year, because, as with the push to first scale Everest, he was aware others wanted to beat him and grab the glory. He heard rumors of groups in Russia and New Zealand working toward the same goal, and he could not discount the possibility that first some "psychopath person would land on a snow slope."

"Is there some crazy person out there who might beat me because he's willing to do something more dangerous than me?" Jeb said. "Yes, but I'm not that guy."

Concerned that a competitor might steal his plans, Jeb remained circumspect about revealing details or designs of his landing. With the technology extant, Haggard gauged whether other engineers around the world might be making progress in developing their own wingsuit-landing mechanisms. With prestige and pride at stake, Haggard said, "Everybody wants to be the first one to do it."

Well, almost everybody. By 2008 Loïc was out of the running. While soaring at low altitude under a parachute down a mountain in New Zealand—a practice known as speed-flying—just before Christmas 2007, he had broken his back in a crash. Recovering from surgery to his L5 vertebra months later, it was unclear to what extent he would be available to resume flying. But after spending time in bed at home, around his wife and two young children, whom he tucked in each night with a *"Mon cheri,"* Loïc had a change of heart and was no longer interested in landing.

"For me it's not worth it," he confessed. "The idea of landing—you will have no return point. This means you need to land or you're going to die. I don't want to put myself in a position where I have no out. If I can do it with an out and safely, I will be really happy to do it. Until this moment, for me it's not going to change my life. It's not going to make it so much better, and it might make it much worse. It's a cool thing, but it's not that important."

Chapter 13
THE TRIAL

> That immaculate manliness we feel within our-
> selves, so far within us, that it remains intact
> though all the outer character seem gone; bleeds
> with keenest anguish at the undraped spectacle
> of a valor-ruined man.
>
> —*Herman Melville*, Moby-Dick

About the time Loïc got injured, the media sank its teeth into the wing-suit landing story. In New York for court appearances, Jeb took the opportunity to make the rounds among the city's media outlets. On December 10, 2007, a story about the quest to land a wingsuit appeared on page 1 of the *New York Times*. Soon Jeb landed on *Today*, where he was interviewed by Matt Lauer, and *The Colbert Report*, where he told Stephen Colbert about his goal of jumping from an aircraft without deploying a parachute.

"Um . . ." Colbert said, chuckling. "I guarantee you, you will eventually *land* on the ground without deploying a parachute."

"The thing is, doing it *again*," Jeb said.

"Oh, doing it twice," Colbert cracked. "And that *is* the trick."

Jeb described how he needed money to build a runway.

"Is it like two miles of bathroom tile with a little bit of wet soap on it so you can just slide in on a belly landing?" Colbert asked, urging Jeb to generate excitement by wearing a red-white-and-blue wingsuit and bring glory to America.

When Jeb said he only wears black, Colbert eyeballed him for a second.

"Is that because . . ." he said, adopting a tone of profound concern, "you're sad inside?"

All joking aside, Jeb had reason to be down. His legal problems only continued to grow more complicated. On January 15, 2008, he filed a countersuit against the Empire State Building Company for $30 million, citing its employees for defaming his character, unlawfully imprisoning him on the observation level, and causing emotional distress and lost income. He announced the suit during a press conference on the steps of the neo-Hellenic State Supreme Court building downtown, Heller at his side. He issued reporters a video of events on the eighty-sixth floor and said the whole episode might have been averted had the Empire State Building bothered with adequate security measures, measures that would have prevented someone like him from getting to the ledge at all. "Very small tweaks in their security will make it impossible to jump off that building," he told the *Times*. "I would be more than happy to come in there and show them how to do that." How representatives from the Empire State Building felt about his offer, they never made clear, but they did not avail themselves of Jeb's services.

The countersuit was a strategy designed to push back against police and prosecutors. Video footage from Jeb's helmet cam had been seized when he was arrested but went missing from a police evidence room. All of which took on greater urgency when, in March, a state supreme court appellate division panel unanimously reinstated the indictment—not for felony reckless endangerment this time, but for *second degree* reckless endangerment, a misdemeanor punishable by up to one year in jail.

Worse for Jeb, political sentiment in the city would soon turn hard against stunts after two men scaled the new fifty-two-story New York Times tower, on Eighth Avenue, on June 5.

The first was Alain Robert, the so-called French Spider-Man, famous for scaling skyscrapers all over the world. Robert had no difficulty scrambling up ceramic blinds on the Times Building's exterior and unfurling a bright green banner that read GLOBAL WARMING KILLS MORE PEOPLE THAN 9/11 EVERY WEEK. Waiting cops arrested him on the roof at about 12:22 p.m. Barely had they trundled Robert off to a precinct when a copycat scaled the West Fortieth side of the building, wearing a T-shirt reading MALARIA NO MORE and a huge grin.

Mayor Michael Bloomberg had seen enough, and in September he signed into law the bill introduced by Councilman Peter Vallone, banning climbing, hanging, jumping, or swinging from city structures. Violators would be punished by up to a year in jail and a $1,000 fine. "We don't want New York City to become a Disneyland for daredevils," said Vallone, summing up prevailing sentiment.

*T*hat was the mood of the authorities on October 1, 2008, a bright, crisp autumn morning, when a yellow cab eased to a stop on East Fifty-first Street in front of the New York Palace Hotel, brakes whining. The rear driver's-side door swung open and Jeb unfolded his long legs and stepped into the thrum of the city. His head shaved clean like a monk's, eyes hidden behind mirrored sunglasses, he threaded a crowd of cars with loping strides and planted himself on the sidewalk near the hotel's uniformed doormen, who greeted him. They knew the thirty-two-year-old stuntman from California had twice parachuted from the fiftieth floor of the hotel.

Jeb would have been difficult to overlook, clad as he was all in black, from his combat boots to his cotton pants to a hooded wool sweater, topped with a sleek ankle-length leather trench coat constructed from the skin of cows, stingrays, and a rare species of frog, all stitched together to create embossed images of demons and flames fanning out over the back and sleeves. Shiny silver buttons shaped like skulls ran in a studded line up the front of the coat. This would be Jeb's uniform during the coming trial.

Jeb had just come from a hearing at criminal court downtown, where he was facing reckless endangerment charges and a prosecutor who wanted to put him in prison for a year. Clomping defiantly into the courtroom, accompanied by his lawyers, cruising past citizens caught up in their own criminal-justice-system dramas, he had arrived in Judge Thomas Farber's courtroom, a windowless cube with high ceilings, bright fluorescent light, and blond wood. Heller made a motion to dismiss the charge, based on the missing video evidence. But the judge was not swayed and announced that a trial would begin the next month.

Jeb's mind was already elsewhere while standing on the sidewalk outside the Palace Hotel, though. He scanned the black-tinted facade of the building, paying particular attention to the ramparts. He calculated that they were about as tall as the landing structure he planned to construct, the one that would borrow from the principles of Nordic ski jumping.

That morning, in a far-ranging conversation with a journalist, Jeb had talked about his plans for landing. Between bites of breakfast at a diner a couple of blocks from the hotel, he explained how he had once been suicidal but that BASE jumping had been the agent of his salvation. "In my journey for death," he said, a Zen koan delivered in a California surfer's voice, "I found my life."

"Every time I wake up in the morning, I wake up with a smile on my face," he said. "Even on days like today, when I have to go to court and deal with this crap, I'm still here, and worst-case scenario is always dead. I had a lot of really cool friends that are dead. Being dead was really uncool for them, because they had to stop experiencing this thing called life."

He brought up the most recent Batman movie, *The Dark Knight,* expressing admiration for the incorruptible Joker character played by Heath Ledger. Jeb's parents had offered him $1 million to not attempt a wingsuit landing, and he had been insulted that anyone would assume he could be so crass. "I'm like, 'I don't want *money,*'" he explained. "I have no desire for money. My life isn't about the acquisition of things. That's why I don't own things—because I don't care about things."

A vibrating phone would eventually bring this particular jeremiad to an end. The call concerned an assignation later that day with television executives eager to talk about his wingsuit-landing plans. They would possibly be willing to fund the project—at least they were willing to hear his pitch—and he needed to return to the hotel to prepare. He swept from the restaurant, black leather coat billowing behind, filling the doorway like a stage curtain coming down on a dramatic act.

THE TRIAL WAS A show of sorts. It began on Friday, November 14, at the Criminal Courts Building, on Centre Street across from the Tombs. After more than two years of hearings and motions and legal wrangling, Jeb's freedom was in the hands of a New York jury, nine people screened and hand-selected in a city in which acts involving landmark structures post-9/11 result in highly charged and politically symbolic reaction. The jurors had seen two iconic buildings destroyed during the terrorist attacks, office workers desperately jumping to their own deaths, and during the course of the trial they would hear how more than thirty suicides had flung themselves from the Empire State Building since it opened in 1931. That was the subtext into which Jeb Corliss waded on a bright autumn morning.

Perhaps the mood would have been different if Jeb had succeeded. He might have joined city lore, like Philippe Petit, who walked a tightrope spanning the World Trade Center towers in 1974, an event depicted in the critically acclaimed film *Man on Wire* in 2008; or Owen Quinn, who jumped from one of the Twin Towers with a chute in 1975 to highlight the plight of the homeless; or Thor Alex Kappfjell, the oil worker from Norway who, during a six-month span in 1998 and 1999, mocked Mayor Giuliani as he parachuted from the Chrysler Building, the Empire State Building, and the South Tower of the World Trade Center. But in the interceding years, the zeitgeist had changed, and so had city laws.

The trial would last nearly a month, and the jury would hear a Harvard University meteorologist testify to the impossibility of predicting wind speeds and directions in the swirling currents around skyscrapers. Prosecutor Mark Crooks would cite the defendant's Howick Falls jump, where Jeb wound up with gruesome injuries when he miscalculated, and as the trial wore on, a professor of physics from New York University, an expert in projectile motion, would take the stand to explain how before he had a chance to get ready or deploy his parachute, a ten-mile-per-hour wind gust could have carried Mr. Corliss right over the final fifty-five-foot tiered wedding-cake section on the sixth-floor level of the Empire State Building, all the way on down to Thirty-third Street, to a thick current of pedestrians and vehicular traffic.

Flanked by his lawyers at a table, Jeb listened attentively, occasionally whispering in the ear of Heller's assistant Peter Toumbekis. Concerning all the hypothetical scenarios put forth, he commented wearily during a recess: "I could land on a unicorn. A fairy could have landed in front of me."

Following court each day, in the cool darkness below Canal Street, Jeb would step into a cab for a ride uptown, and he surely saw the lighted ramparts of the Empire State Building glowing above the city.

On Monday, December 1, Jeb took the stand to explain how he'd made more than a thousand safe jumps in the United States, Japan, Russia, France, and Malaysia. "I'm not doing anything wrong," he said. "And I don't think there's anything wrong with what I do. Some people choose to use elevator systems, stairwells . . . I use the parachute system."

But he did admit to the prosecutor that even if he had landed precisely, his deflating parachute might have gift-wrapped the windshield of a moving car and blocked a driver's view. It took the jury a day and a half of deliberations following closing arguments Tuesday to find Jeb guilty.

HE RETURNED to New York for sentencing on January 22, 2009. Seated on a bench outside the courtroom, between Toumbekis and Gigi, waiting for bailiffs to signal the start of proceedings, Jeb listened as Toumbekis explained how events would unfold. If given jail time, did Jeb want to begin serving a sentence immediately or come back at a later date?

Jeb did not hesitate. He wanted to begin immediately.

Toumbekis explained that in that case, Jeb would be led from the courtroom in handcuffs by bailiffs. They would strip him of his shoelaces as a precaution so he could not hang himself out on Rikers Island.

"Oh, Jebbie," Gigi sighed.

Inside the courtroom, two jurors who had convicted Jeb a month earlier asked the judge that he be spared prison. Prosecutor Mark Crooks nevertheless asked for the maximum sentence. "Defendant routinely went to countless media outlets . . ." he said, "repeatedly lambasted the people of the State of New York . . . He would go back to the Empire State Building, try it again . . ." Crooks noted that Jeb had to see "tourists, strollers . . ." Jeb, he said, had shown no remorse, and he pointed out how nine fire trucks and four ambulances had responded to his Empire State Building escapade, diverting valuable city resources.

Hands clasped, head bowed, Jeb sat like the very picture of Caravaggio's Penitent Magdalene. Heller called his client contrite. "Mr. Corliss is in complete acceptance of responsibility for his actions . . . He's not defiant. He's certainly not happy about it. But he accepts it."

Heller rattled off concessions his client was willing to offer, from issuing a public service announcement in which he would discourage anyone from BASE jumping in New York City to lecturing youth and BASE jumpers. Hearing this, Jeb suddenly buried his face in his hands. After all the hassling, posturing, and lawyering, he had thrown himself on the mercy of the court in a bid for leniency. Given an opportunity to address the court, he declined.

Judge Farber said, "It is clear to me that defendant's actions were reckless actions . . . Selfish actions designed to benefit himself." The judge described the pressure he was under to mete out the harshest punishment. Representatives from the Empire State Building had sent *four* copies of a six-page letter asking for the maximum sentence. The president of the Real Estate Board of New York asked for the maximum, as did New York Police Commissioner Raymond Kelly. During a dozen years as a judge, Farber had never been contacted by a police officer—and certainly not the commissioner—regarding sentencing. "From some of the letters I received, you would have thought the defendant tried to commit a terrorist act," he said.

Farber allowed that Jeb's statements to the media were "bizarre" and "absurd." But he noted that jurors had asked that he not be jailed. He called Jeb a role model for courage, not recklessness, noting that he himself rode a motorcycle. He finished by saying that after careful consideration, he'd concluded that jail time was "simply not warranted in this case."

Noting that the defendant had no prior criminal record and had merely been convicted of a misdemeanor, Farber gave Jeb three years of probation and a hundred hours of community service.

"It's truly terrifying," Jeb told the press afterwards about his feelings sitting in the dock. Reporters pursued Gigi into an elevator and outside to a waiting car for comment, but she shooed them away.

Still, the prints would have the final word, as they do. A headline in the *New York Post* the following day read "Chute-for-Brains Jumper Ducks Jail."

Chapter 14

PAINT IT BLACK

*T*hrough the trial, Jeb had kept it together with help from Roberta Mancino, a model from Italy who had appeared in the pages of *Vogue* and *Playboy*. A pixie with large brown eyes, she was a champion skydiver, a black belt in kickboxing, and a scuba diver who had been underwater with sharks—as unlikely and beguiling a combination of traits as those of a unicorn or mermaid.

Although he had been facing prison, Jeb had continued to make future plans. In the interest of resuming his career, he had sent Roberta a business proposal concerning an animal conservation show he was pitching to producers. He wanted a female cohost, and Roberta possessed all the prerequisites. She was beautiful, fearless, and athletic. She lived in Arizona, where she trained as a competitive skydiver, yet she had never heard of Jeb.

Asking around the drop zone about him, she found that opinion was mixed. "'How stupid is that to go and jump the Empire State Building when you know the security is going to be . . .'" she recalled some saying. She wondered if Jeb were perhaps crazy. Yet his skills as a jumper were beyond dispute. Some said all the carping about him amounted to professional jealousy because of the coveted commercial work he won.

When the trial was over and Jeb was a free man, Roberta agreed to come to L.A. to meet in person for the first time, provided Jeb would teach her to BASE jump. Of course, he said yes.

The animal conservation show never did get off the ground, the producers having become furious that Jeb had violated their mutual pledge to keep their appreciation for Roberta strictly platonic. "Fuck you, guys," Jeb had told them. "What can I say? I'm in love."

JEB FULFILLED HIS COMMUNITY service at a clothing store where proceeds benefit HIV charities, and brought Roberta to the Perrine Bridge, in Idaho, for BASE training. He cautioned her to proceed only if prepared to give her life for the experience. "'Only do it if you love it,'" she recalled him saying. "'Don't do it to show off to other people, or for TV.'"

Jeb himself, however, was back on TV. A camera crew had followed him through the trial and sentencing for a British TV documentary to air on Channel 4, called "The Human Bird." For the climax, Jeb jumped from a chopper and flew his wingsuit along the jagged dragon's back of the Matterhorn. Yet not all was good in Jeb's world as scenes in the documentary made plain. Fitzmorris and Gigi were on the outs.

In the Lauterbrunnen Valley with Roberta, he coached her to track from an exit called Yellow Ocean, an ocher-streaked cliff fourteen hundred feet above the valley floor. By October 22, Jeb and Roberta were in Kuala Lumpur, Malaysia, at the KL Tower International Jump, a festival where about seventy plunged from a thousand feet up an antenna. There, they were invited to jump the fifty-five-story Menara Telekom tower, an office building known as the Shark Fin for its distinctive profile. It was Roberta's first building, a chance for the crucial B and completion of the BASE cycle. On a scorching-hot equatorial morning, she launched and opened without a hitch. Jeb followed, bending a gainer and plummeting fast down the face of the building. From the ground, Roberta counted four seconds until Jeb pitched, black parachute blooming off-heading, lines twisting into spaghetti. Without time to correct, the parachute swung into the building, Jeb's left hip striking the glass with a resounding boom. Canopy still intact, he managed to turn from the building, and disappeared from view behind a stand of trees.

Roberta took off running and found a cluster of people gathered around where Jeb had crashed into a concrete retaining wall. Shouts for "Medical!"

crackled on radios. His face a mask of pain, Jeb laughed at the sight of Roberta. "My love, are you okay?" she sobbed.

"Yeah, yeah," he replied through clenched teeth. He had broken his left hip and foot.

Back in the States, wheelchair bound, Jeb returned to Venice Beach. With Barry Fitzmorris and Gigi bound for divorce, mother and son had moved from Malibu down the coast. It was not beachfront, but it was hardly hardscrabble, either.

Still, friends noted that it was as if the prince had been banished from the palace. Long sheltered by family money and a lifestyle of privilege, his new circumstances chastened Jeb somewhat. He was experiencing, he said, "how normal people have to live."

"You're just a person," Iiro would recall his friend realizing. "Jeb can do amazing things, but you're just a person like everyone else."

Jeb adjusted, decorating his place in Venice with black carpet, black bedsheets, a black sectional sofa, and black knickknacks, including plates printed with black skulls beneath the enamel. Roberta prevailed against painting the walls black, explaining that the rooms would feel claustrophobic. She also coaxed Jeb out more socially, although she could not convince him to dance. Mostly he sat in a dark corner of L.A. clubs, wearing earbuds and playing *Angry Birds* on his iPhone.

Back home late some nights he would express frustration concerning the Wingsuit Landing Project, how sponsors and TV executives had failed to support his vision. Roberta warned about the dangers, but Jeb was not swayed, and in those moments Roberta understood that she, and anything else in Jeb's life, would simply have to settle for being number two.

*A*s 2008 gave way to 2009, wingsuits were gaining increasing prominence as footage of pilots rocketing along big walls and into valleys across Europe thrilled viewers online and went viral.

In February, the Golden Knights, the U.S. Army's Parachute Team, pulled a world record flight above Yuma Proving Ground, in Arizona, flying from more than thirty thousand feet. A month later, the *Sunday Times*, the national newspaper in the UK, published a feature about BASE, focusing on a phlegmatic train driver in Paris named Hervé le Gallou. He had made more than a thousand jumps, launching from the Eiffel Tower perhaps more than anyone. He was one of the first off the Burj, in Dubai, the tallest building in the world, stretching 155 stories toward the desert sun. Le Gallou's dream, one he'd had from childhood, was to fly like a bird, which he predicted he would fulfill soon by landing a wingsuit without a parachute.

Later in 2009, a thirty-seven-year-old American named Dean Potter would pull off a record wingsuit BASE flight. Jumping from eighty-eight hundred feet up on the North Face of the Eiger, in Switzerland, he stayed aloft for two minutes and fifty seconds. Known as the Dark Wizard for his brooding intensity, Potter was a world-renowned free climber who stood six-five and weighed 190 pounds, and spawned Paul Bunyanesque stories about incredible feats and eccentricities, which all happened to be true. He once dwelled in a cave. He walked barefoot in winter around his home in California's Sierra Nevada to toughen up his feet. In 2003, Potter made a BASE jump into Mexico's twelve-hundred-foot-deep Cave of Swallows. His parachute opened into line twists, and he wound up colliding with a dangling rope that jumpers used to pull themselves back to the surface. The result was that his parachute collapsed, but Potter had the presence of mind to grab the rope and, dangling two hundred feet off the deck, slid safely to the bottom.

Potter would popularize slacklining over a yawning chasm while wearing only a BASE rig on his back. If he lost balance, he would fall away from the rope and pitch his parachute.

Given his reputation, Potter's announcement that he wanted to land without a parachute was taken seriously. "It's not crazy to think we can fly," he had said during an interview in Austria, "because we're already doing it. And we can *land*. . . . Now my ultimate goal, or thing that drives me, and I dream of night after night and in every waking moment, is to do just that: to fly my human body and land it on the perfect snow slope."

Still, Jeb was the most prominent exponent of wingsuit flight. He pitched TV executives his landing project, opening with video of a record ski jump by Matti Hautamäki, of Finland, as he traveled 235 meters (771 feet) through the air, nearly the length of a long city block in Manhattan, before setting down smoothly eight seconds later on snow. "He's doing the exact same thing we're doing," Jeb would say. Next he would play footage of Loïc buzzing the skiers above Verbier. Finally, he showed video of motorcycle racers going over on asphalt at 150 miles per hour, sliding in their leathers and standing up without a scratch. "You put these three things together," Jeb intoned, "you're doing something no one has ever done before . . . It is every bit as big a deal as summiting Everest for the first time."

Jeb's idea was to attach his runway to a building—say, the six-hundred-foot Wynn Las Vegas, on the Strip. The landing apparatus would attach to the building via two twenty-foot towers at the corners of the roof, spaced twenty feet apart, like football goalposts. Cables would run from the top of the towers to twenty-foot towers located below on the resort's golf course. These congruent lines would narrow to shoulder width as they descended at a forty-five-degree angle. Stretched between them would be fabric, followed by a flat run extending two thousand feet to allow Jeb to bleed off speed. Dampeners similar to the suspension springs used on off-road motorbikes would prevent Jeb from being bounced off the landing as he touched down at terminal speed.

"It's a very simple concept," Jeb would say in summation, animation of his landing playing in the background for potential patrons to see, a cartoon Jeb Corliss looking as though he were flying and landing on a massive waterslide. "Everything is going to be completely controlled," he would reassure nervous executives. "The variables have been eliminated."

ONE VARIABLE they would have to contend with, though, was Jeb himself. Although a dynamo during prepared remarks, he had a tendency to veer into discomfiting tangents during ad-libs.

When he and his Wingsuit Landing Project were profiled in *Smithsonian, Popular Mechanics,* and *Men's Journal,* Jeb at times betrayed a tone-deaf quality with some comments that he would come to regret. One producer he worked with said Jeb doesn't fear your judgment and that frees him to be himself. Yes, he was himself, but sometimes he didn't know when to stop talking.

"I guess that I come off like a douchebag to some people," he complained after a profile appeared in May 2010, in which other jumpers sneered at his frequent use of the first person. "I guess that my personality is a bit abrasive, and some people take it as me being a self-centered conceited douche. I see it and say, *Yeah, I guess I could see how someone could perceive my personality that way.* I guess if someone writes an article that paints me like that, I don't know if I can really argue with that."

In interviews, he had a habit of invoking the Columbine High School massacre to explain his own simmering rage in school. "This makes me look like a fucking psychopath," he said afterwards. "When you read it, the feeling you get is you have just read about an absolutely dangerous crazy person [who] would take out half the planet if it would get whatever he needed to get done, and it also paints me as this total media whore that's just about publicity and will do anything to get on camera." For the record, he added: "I'm not a psychopath, and I don't want to go on a mass murdering spree, and I never did want to go on a mass murdering spree."

Later, though, he would tell another journalist: "When the Columbine thing happened, it was so absolutely clear what happened to these kids. And if I had been in school for another year or two, there's a very good chance I would have been one of those guys. I was on the verge. I was on the verge of going through my school and taking people out."

Expressing kinship with school assassins was one thing. It certainly did not help Jeb's case when the producer assisting him through the process of pitching his wingsuit landing to TV executives, an industry veteran who had worked on *Survivor,* a man named Bruce Beresford-Redman, became the focus of a Mexican investigation into his wife's murder at a Cancún resort in April 2010. (Arrested in Los Angeles by U.S. marshals the following November, Beresford-Redman was extradited to Mexico to face charges in the killing; as of this writing the case was still in the courts.)

The most unambiguous setback, though, came when Vertigo Inc. was sold to a military defense contractor from Ohio called Hunter Defense

Technologies. The result: Haggard was no longer free to work on outside projects, including a wingsuit landing. Jeb needed a new partner.

He was searching in April 2010, when he showed up to speak at a TEDx conference at the University of Southern California. Perched on a high chair on a round red carpet bathed in a cone of light, he explained innovations in his sport, specifically proximity flying, which, he said, "is the apex, where everything goes right now because it is the closest a human being can come to being that bird, stepping off a telephone pole and flying. That's what we do—we fly."

The moderator asked where Jeb was going next. "I'm going to be jumping from an aircraft, and I'm going to be landing on the ground without deploying a parachute, at over 120 miles an hour, and then standing up and doing it again," he said. "We've been spending the last seven years working with NASA engineers and really smart people to make that happen."

Moderator: "Maybe Nick can help." Nick was Dr. Nicholas Patrick, a Cambridge- and MIT-educated astronaut who was also speaking at the conference.

"Maybe he can," Jeb said.

Afterwards, the two men talked. "It's not like going to the moon," Jeb would admit. "I'm not going to pretend it's as big as that. It's not going to the moon and it's not curing cancer. But I do believe it's every bit as important as summiting Everest."

*I*t was hardly going any better for Gary Connery in late 2010. He had been making the rounds, too, trying to interest TV in his landing plans, and mostly they thought he was nuts. "I knew back in 2003, with my calculations, I knew I wasn't going to be able to afford 250 grand," Gary says. "It was a huge structure with cranes and everything else. I hadn't told anyone, because nobody would take me seriously. I had approached people and asked them to fund the training, because that would make a great show—to see how you would go through the process of doing this."

He had been working with a production company on a proposal to pick up a series of world-record and world's-first stunts, culminating in landing a wingsuit without a parachute. "What I was finding," he says, "was that it was a real struggle to get people to part with their money for me to go off and do what are, in their minds, some crazy, bonkers stunts."

As Jeb Corliss and others talked publicly about their plans, Gary remained in the background, biding time. "So I just sort of kept all my ideas to myself," he says, "and of course I wasn't a name in the sport anyway."

A break finally came when Vivienne made an introduction with some live event and television producers in the UK. The producers heard Gary's proposal for landing and decided to back him. They paid for parachutes and wingsuits. Workers on the production side were hired, and Gary set aside time for training. In July 2010 he spent five days at the drop zone in Empuriabrava, Spain, getting reacquainted with the latest modern suits during test flights, working on basic performance, from consistent turns to dives and recovery. "They put some money towards it," Vivienne would say. "The project was moving ahead. The money had been spent, and it hit us out of the blue." A few days before Gary was scheduled to get on a plane to begin training in the States, he got a phone call from the producers, telling him the project was canceled. There was no more money.

"Very disappointed," Vivienne says of Gary's mood. "But this project had been on and off for many years."

It was around this time, in September 2010, that something else unexpected happened: Vivienne left. In the days and weeks and months that followed, Gary would have occasion to reflect on his life. Falling down stairs, staging fights, and performing high falls had all been done to support his family. He seldom loved the work, and never the paperwork. He had sacrificed his ambitions. At last, he vowed, this would be *his* time. He had worked hard for others; now it would be time to do something for Gary: He would land a wingsuit. His reasons were personal. He had always wanted to be the best at *something*. He had fallen short of his ambitions as a kayaker and skier. He was forty. His window of opportunity was closing. Life had carried him down a path to skydiving, BASE jumping, and wingsuits and although his actions might not alter the way others flew wingsuits, possibly he would gain recognition from his peers. Maybe some would marvel. Gary would have to leave it up to others to decide if what he was planning had any relevance for them.

Although unsure precisely how he would pull it off, Gary reckoned that those details could be worked out along the way. Money would not hold him back. He would self-fund if necessary. He scarcely mentioned his ambition to anyone outside of close friends. He tended to keep plans close to the vest anyway. Besides, he had not been an active pilot among the close-knit worldwide wingsuit community, and he would not be an obvious candidate to attempt a landing. He needed help, though, and providence would provide it in Italy and Zephyrhills, a small town in central Florida.

Chapter 15
A FLYING PHILISTINE

> You've got to jump off cliffs all the time and
> build your wings on the way down.
>
> —*Ray Bradbury*

ZEPHYRHILLS, FLORIDA

In the central part of the Sunshine State, the flat, marshy topography of
the Florida coast gives way to green rolling hills, where cumulonimbus
clouds throw thick shadows on beef cattle, bent at the neck, grazing near
stately oaks dripping gray with Spanish moss. This is a rural place, conservative by temperament, and not an obvious incubator of innovative ideas
and products. Yet at the corner of Sky Dive Lane and Air Time Avenue, in
a square building, bleached by the sun, an aviation laboratory cranking
out wingsuits would radically alter human flight.

The building was headquarters for TonySuits Inc., the largest wingsuit
manufacturer in North America, a factory filled with fabric spools of reds,
silver, grays, copper, blues (sky, navy, royal), purples, greens (from forest to
lime), black, white, yellow, pink, and gold. Inside, workers snatched spools
and trimmed lengths of color to be placed on cutting-machine tables.
Computer coordinates mapping out size and shape cut fabric, then fed it
under sewing machine needles thrumming with thread. The hum of ma-
chinery, the movement, and the people talking all lend the factory floor a
distinct life and rhythm.

But the liveliest and most colorful aspect of the operation occupies a
separate room toward the back, where the eponymous Tony, Tony Uragallo,
owner and chief designer, can be found most days hunched monastically at

a Juki sewing machine, surrounded by scraps of bright nylon fabric strewn across the floor, the Beatles straining from nearby speakers.

On the verge of turning sixty in 2011, he looked his age. He had a paunch, thinning white hair, and skin freckled by exposure to the Florida sun. His bright blue eyes, though, were lively, flickering with fresh ideas that arrived as suddenly and intensely as the thunderclaps that sweep across central Florida. "I'm not organized," he would readily admit in a bright cockney accent, describing his methods. "I just start picking up bits and sewing. I found that on the floor. Pick up any fabric you can find."

In an idiosyncratic sport, he was considered an eccentric. And although he did not embrace the scientific method, Tony was keen to adopt the latest technology. The sports he served with his business were suddenly flooded with technology. Pilots had begun wearing goggles equipped with GPS, depicting speed and altitude in real time on an LCD in the lower right corner. Another GPS device, called a FlySight, created specifically for wing-suiting, provides instant in-flight feedback by beeping into headphones when you reach a designated glide ratio. On the ground, flight data can be downloaded to a laptop to analyze altitude, forward speed, vertical speed, and distance traveled. Linked up with Google Earth satellite data, it even allows users to plot their flight path.

Tony adopted the developments, but he also relied on his instincts. This caused competitors to call him a Philistine, he said. He was an unlikely designer anyway.

As a young man, Tony had worked as a bricklayer on cold, wet job sites while living at his parents' flat in east London. Weekends he passed in the pub with his mates. He had picked up skydiving in the army and continued after resuming civilian life.

A big part of skydiving calls for sewing skills, needed to build and repair parachutes and jumpsuits, and Tony started fooling around on his mum's machine. One weekend at the drop zone, he spotted a guy from Arizona wearing a white jumpsuit with a rainbow design. Tony didn't have money to buy one, so he set out to make one. He biked across London with a quiver of fabric as his raw materials. Listening to rock 'n' roll while sitting in a warm, dry flat at a sewing machine beat the hell out of the backbreaking labor of bricklaying at the mercy of the elements, and Tony got a notion to start a business catering to skydivers. His father was aghast when Tony asked him for a loan. *Men don't sew for a living,* he said. This was 1976.

Undaunted, Tony continued making jumpsuits for sale, slowly building his brand. When he traveled to Florida for a skydiving competition, the sunshine and warm weather convinced him to bolt from rainy old England. "They said, 'Don't go to America, there's too much competition,'" he recalls. "There *was* a lot of competition, and I was the foreigner. They *did* reject me for the longest time, and I got a lot of shit from the establishment."

Again he stuck it out, capturing the notice of the market and eventually becoming the number-one jumpsuit maker. By the 1990s, he had the contract for the French national skydive team, and it was a Tony design that Patrick de Gayardon had modified to fashion his original wingsuit, the very template for the modern suit.

But a decade would pass before Tony made his own wingsuits in 2006. A wingsuit pilot from Boston named Jeff Nebelkopf, who had a background in design and illustration but had never sewed, proposed that they partner up. "Jeff was the wingsuiter," Tony says. "I wasn't. He helped me out starting off."

The man in the field, Jeff traveled to drop zones, offering wingsuit flying lessons to skydivers, taking orders for new suits. Orders rolled in, and soon Tony turned to wingsuits full time, igniting a passion for flying his suits around fat clouds over Florida.

Tony's approach was to build a suit, then run a few hundred feet down the road to Skydive City, one of the busier drops zones in the state, where he would hop on a load for a test. Flight characteristics fresh in his mind, he would hightail it back to the shop for more modifications. "I'm a trial-and-error dude, not a mathematician," he admits. "I just make prototypes. Sometimes, before I've even finished that one, I've got another idea that I should try . . . I think that's why I'm successful: because I make a lot of prototypes. After it's been released, I may change it along the way. I'm famous for changing after it's been released."

It was hard to argue with his results. He would win wingsuit BASE competitions for flight distance and speed against men half his age. "This *old* man!" he would say, in mock outrage, echoing his competitors. "This *fat old* man?!"

By 2010, Tony was on to a design breakthrough for a suit that featured more surface area than its predecessors, and resulted in superior glide. To some minds, the larger suits left a lot to be desired in terms of aesthetics. European manufacturers and pilots compared the relatively square silhouette and thick profile of his suits to inflatable mattresses or a dog's bed.

Still, resistance to Tony's suits began to break down when it became clear how well they flew. Soon, pilots sought out Tony, eager to get their hands on one of his creations.

M ark Sutton was a former officer in the British Army who served with the Gurkha Rifles, fierce Nepalese soldiers whose motto is "Better to die than live a coward." He had begun skydiving, not with the military, but at a civilian drop zone while stationed in Hong Kong. In 2005, he graduated to a BASE-jumping course at Kjerag, in Norway, and went on to take a wingsuit training course with Loïc's Fly Your Body organization, in Gap, where the prevailing ethic placed a premium on the skills of the pilot above the characteristics of the suit, a philosophy in antipathy to the inflatable mattresses Tony would turn out.

In the summer of 2010, Mark arrived in Lauterbrunnen with two American wingsuit pilots, Andy West and Barry Holubeck. They had come to jump from the Eiger, which West had famously done with Dean Potter eleven months earlier, opening the highest exit on the mountain, for which they created the portmanteau "Heiger." That summer, when Mark arrived, Tony happened to be passing through the valley, and he and Mark happened to meet at the Horner, the pub where BASE jumpers tend to congregate. At the time, Mark owned a small, safe beginner's suit, and Tony explained that if he was serious about flying he would need to acquire an X-bird, Tony's latest creation and already rumored to be the most advanced model on the market. "It was a big step up for me at the time,"

Mark would recall. "So I said, 'I have to go and see this thing.' I ended up placing an order and flying over to Zephyrhills to pick this suit up."

Mark worked in finance for some of the world's largest banks, as an interest-rates derivatives trader. He possessed an analytical mind and wanted to know how the suit worked. *What was it that made it better?* Arriving in Florida in November to take possession of his custom X-bird, he learned that Tony had developed yet another prototype, which provided superior stability. "It's hard to explain, but when you jump it, you know this is the one you want to be in," Mark remembered. "Suddenly you've been turned into this natural pilot, as opposed to the other ones, which you really have to fly. So even though I've just spent a fortune on this new suit, we started playing about with this prototype, which is called Old Navy."

With Jeff Nebelkopf and Tony, Mark jumped Old Navy at the drop zone down the road from Tony's factory. "This suit was blowing everybody out of the sky," he says. "Out of enthusiasm I said, 'Build me this suit!'"

Every few months, Mark returned to Zephyrhills. And every few months he encountered a slightly altered, improved design. Learning to sew, he took the suit apart, made alterations, and pieced it together again. "Knowing how to sew is one of those skills that might be embarrassing in the pub," he would say, "but if it gets me a suit I'm impressed with, I'm okay with it." Meanwhile, Tony, in typical fashion, modified Old Navy until it was no longer recognizable, thus creating a new model he called Apache X.

Despite claims to the contrary, Tony actually knew something about science, specifically Bernoulli's principle—Bernoulli being Swiss scientist Daniel Bernoulli, who in the eighteenth century published groundbreaking findings on fluid dynamics. "Speed gives you lift," Tony would say, explaining that an airfoil, or wing, is flat on the bottom but curved on top, and when air hits the airfoil's leading edge, some of the air travels over the curved top of the wing. This air, moving faster, creates low pressure, which in turn leads to lift, and voilà: Bernoulli's principle in action.

Other wingsuit manufacturers knew about these principles and likewise created their own supersize high-speed models. These high-performance suits were not meant for greenhorns, which Jeff likened to putting the keys to a Ferrari in the hands of a teenager. "When you put a beginner in a big suit, they're going to give it everything it has, and the suit is going to take them for a ride," he says. "Hopefully they can deploy their parachute in time."

Even experienced pilots found that high-performance suits were more than they bargained for at first. Jeb ordered an Apache, which was rumored to deliver a staggering 3:1 glide ratio.

The new suit from Tony arrived in the mail one day at Perris Valley. Jeb pulled the big black Apache from its packaging and slipped his long limbs inside. He would recall what happened on his first test flight: "I jumped out of the airplane and, dude, I was out of control," he says. "I couldn't control the suit at all. All of a sudden I would be going left and all of a sudden I would be going right. All of a sudden the suit would do a 360 . . . I'm like, *Uh-oh*."

Each subsequent jump resulted in another wild ride. Yet GPS data revealed glide ratios of 2.8:1, 3:1, sometimes 3.2:1. They were fleeting, but still the possibilities were tantalizing. Finally, on his fourth jump, Jeb pitched in full flight and swung into severe line twists, requiring a nasty cutaway to his reserve. "The suit was terrifying," he says. "It was the scariest wingsuit I've ever flown in my entire life. It's getting the glide ratio I need, but I can't control the damn thing."

He believed the suit was two inches too long. He couldn't point his toe and alter his control surfaces. Tony insisted the suit was the right size, but finally relented under Jeb's unwavering argument. When Tony returned the suit, two inches duly trimmed, everything clicked. "It's perfectly stable," Jeb recalls, with typical understatement, "perfectly solid. Dude, I sustained like a 3.4-to-1 glide ratio. My flight was like a four-minute skydive. It was the craziest wingsuit flight I've ever flown in my entire life."

He tested the Apache on the big walls of Europe. In the Lauterbrunnen Valley, he flirted with 3:1 glide angles, nearly matching those of his parachute. He dipped a wing midflight into the cascade of Spissbach waterfall. On Hinderrugg, above Walenstadt, he buzzed deep into the Crack. "Once I finally got the hang of that suit, holy, man! I was doing things I could never have imagined doing," he says. "The precision—I was coming so close to the ground and still had a margin to pull up and fly away."

This was significant. Although Jeb hadn't yet found funding to organize a wingsuit-landing attempt, he had lined up major sponsorship for a multi-million-dollar spectacle in China, which would amount to a monumental first for wingsuits if he pulled it off. In the autumn of 2011, Jeb would attempt to fly an Apache through a hole in the side of a mountain.

Chapter 16

BOXES AND BOXES

HENLEY-ON-THAMES, ENGLAND

When Vivienne returned, ending a six-month separation, she and Gary moved out of Windsor, where they had been living, about fifteen miles west to Henley, a town on the upper Thames in Oxfordshire and host to the famous Henley Royal Regatta every July. They leased a storefront on Thameside, across from where antique wooden cruisers tied up at moorings, and Vivienne opened a Chocolate Theatre Café, named after a place operated by a friend in Windsor. The Henley location was well chosen for a café, with plenty of local and tourist traffic, and inside, it was a lively spot punctuated by the steam-shriek of espresso. Customers ordered from big glass cases containing sweet confections, and a menu of soup and sandwiches. Plate-glass windows overlooked a serene stretch of the Thames upriver from the stone arches of Henley Bridge, where oars push sculls against a current patrolled by white swans.

Wending over the bridge on his Honda sport bike, on his forty-minute ride to work in London, Gary would fantasize about landing a wingsuit. He hoped the notoriety would free him from a life as a wage earner, working as a stunt coordinator at TV studios.

Vivienne was busy running a restaurant and could not spare time to help much with managing Gary's wingsuit ambitions. It was on him to seek sponsorship and manage training, which he did by going abroad in order to improve his limited wingsuit skills.

BY 2011 Gary had made perhaps forty wingsuit jumps, a fraction of the number held by many of the leading pilots, some of whom had thousands. Seeking more experience, Gary traveled to Italy that spring.

Mark Sutton was in Italy that season, too, for the same reason. Closing in on one hundred wingsuit flights, he suddenly had the leisure to dedicate to flying. The meltdown of world financial markets in 2008 had led Mark to a series of positions with various banks where he assisted with setting up emerging-market derivatives-trading operations. Burned out by long hours and stress, and having savings banked to support himself for a while, he took time off to travel, arriving in Arco with his girlfriend for what he said would be a romantic holiday. The fact he just happened to have his wingsuit along in his luggage and there was a large cliff at Brento were bonuses. Each morning, when the weather is right, jumpers gather at a parking lot outside a café renowned for its coffee. Mark was waiting to arrange rides to the trailhead when he spotted Gary. "He's quite a striking character, so you tend to see him straightaway," Mark would recall. "He was in boardshorts, and he has his earring. He's a colorful character. My girlfriend recognized him first."

Gary and Mark hit it off immediately. They are both British, and Gary was a stuntman, which Mark hoped to be someday. Plus they had a similar assessment of acceptable risk.

"We sort of clicked, really," Mark would recall. "BASE jumpers are a hinky group. I won't jump with people I don't feel comfortable with. They have to have the same approach, the same approach to safety. They have to be competent. There are people who want to push it a bit further, which is totally cool. I stay away from those people to keep it safe. Gary had a method to his approach, though he learned how to wingsuit quite recently."

At the end of their time together in Italy, they agreed to meet in June in Voss, a small city in western Norway, about a hundred miles north of Stavanger. Every year, the city hosts Extremsportveko (Extreme Sports Week), featuring, among other sports, skydiving, BASE jumping, skateboarding, kayaking, and a wingsuit distance competition. While there, Gary made an introduction that would alter his life. "Come meet Tony," Mark said one day.

"I didn't know that Tony was Tony Uragallo of TonySuits at the time," Gary recalls. "It was only during discussion that I realized this is Tony of TonySuits. I was flying an X-bird at the time."

Mark was already flying an Apache, which he had assisted with developing at Tony's Zephyrhills shop. "You need one of these," Mark told Gary. "You need to have an Apache suit."

Gary placed an order with Tony, who continued traveling through Europe that summer to Switzerland.

In August Mark and Gary met Tony at a drop zone in Cornwall. Tony had just returned from the Crack.

It was the end of the summer of 2011, a time when Jeb Corliss was beginning to get recognized back on the streets of Venice, California. The tall man with the bare scalp and baleful wardrobe had always drawn long stares from citizens, but now many knew who he was, and they rushed forward to request autographs and to have their photos taken with the star of "Grinding the Crack," a three-and-a-half-minute video created by Gian Autenrieth that Jeb had uploaded to his YouTube channel that August. Set to the song *"Sail,"* by AWOLNATION—*"Maybe I'm a different breed, maybe I'm not listening, so blame it on my ADD, baby"*—the video, showing Jeb nearly decapitating Christian Gubser as he dove out of the way, balloons scattering, went viral, with more than a million views by the end of the month, on its way to more than twenty-five million. At the end of the sequence, Jeb removed his helmet and beamed while speaking directly into the camera. "Well, I came extremely close on that one," he said with a laugh. "Yes, I did." The song, the editing, the sequence showing a heart-stopping brush with disaster, Jeb's pure joy . . . everything combined to create unforgettable footage. Yes, viral video in the age of Gangnam Style!

The hubbub did not escape the notice of Gary and Mark. "Jeb Corliss had just done it over the summertime," Mark said about the Crack. "We had seen the videos, and Tony had just been out there, so we asked him where it was. Gary and I said, 'We have to go to do this.'"

They arrived in September, driving along Route 3 through the valley to Walenstadt, where they pitched a tent at a campground along the Walensee. To Mark's mind, the place was paradisiacal. "It is just beautiful, stunning, gorgeous, with a lake in the background and this incredible feature, and you've got access while you're there. They've got cable cars."

Taking the cable car from Unterwasser to the summit, they saw spires of mountains stretching south toward Italy. Neither man had made a proximity flight before, but from Sputnik they found it surprisingly easy to swoop at stands of trees, and into the Crack. "We started to fly to and through this," Mark remembered. "This is the first time we had been able to fly to a point consistently and in control."

Without a man holding balloons at the mouth of the Crack, they did not flirt with ground. They were conservative. But after several days of flying, an idea rattled around Gary's head.

Nursing beers at a lakeside restaurant one evening after a day of jumping, a white moon trail shimmering on the dark water, Gary suddenly turned to Mark. "We were hanging out in the evenings and stuff," Mark remembered, "and he started to tell me about this project he had in mind, and it wasn't really specific. He said, 'Look, you've got to keep it a secret, but this is what I'm looking to do. I'm going to be the first guy to land a wingsuit.' He's saying, 'I know I can do this.' I'm quite skeptical, but I wanted to listen to a well-put argument. 'Oh, fine, give me the spiel. If this is some maverick bullshit, I'm not really interested. But you're a professional stuntman, so I recognize that.' That's when he explained the concept. He's well known for doing high falls, and the high falls used cardboard boxes to land. I've never heard of this before. I'm familiar with an airbag, but I've never heard of cardboard boxes. He explained you put all these cardboard boxes, and you can jump off a building and it will break your fall. He explained that he had done some wingsuiting quite some time ago—he realized he could fly well enough and at the same sort of speed you jump off a building at, and the two cross over. At which point I started taking him seriously."

When they returned home, Mark started investigating the physics behind falling and landing. "I looked it up. Guys can make 150-foot falls into cardboard boxes, at which point they're traveling about sixty to seventy miles an hour, and they're quite safe. You can jump motorcycles into it and it decelerates the motorcycle or body or whatever, where no injuries occur. We were finding, with wingsuits we had, we could fly them slowly in relative terms, but with a lot of control, and they were stable. In my mind, you had these two circles that had always been separate," Mark said, about this emergent Venn diagram. "You had the maximum speed somebody could jump off something and survive. And you had the wingsuits, which fly really fast, and there's a big gap between the two. The way Gary described it, what if these two circles had come together and merged, and the high speeds some of these guys had jumped from a building were seventy miles an hour and the slowest speeds that somebody could fly a wingsuit were about sixty-five miles per hour? There was this little sliver where the two circles crossed over where what he was proposing was possible. I thought, *Well, I've had the summer; do I go back to the city and a job and the rest of it? Or—this is a world's first! This is the Holy Grail of skydiving—to jump out of a plane and land without a parachute.* It has happened, actually, in the war, and falling into a large pine forest and snow, but they have managed to survive—that's been unintentional, and they all got injured in some way. This is the first time anyone was proposing deliberately and intentionally to jump out of an aircraft and not use a parachute to land. For me it was too exciting. I've got to give it a go."

Mark made an offer to Gary. "Look," he said, "I'll self-fund myself and I'll be your project manager and film it."

The two of them worked well as a team. They possessed complementary skill sets. Gary had the honed instincts of a stuntman. Mark was more methodical, behaving like the trained financial analyst he was, hewing to established procedures. Together they believed they could pull it off.

With a partner at last, Gary returned home to Henley and Vivienne. She was overworked at the café, but in time Vivienne would become the backbone of logistical operations, but for the moment Gary was forced to handle much of the preparation and planning himself.

A decade earlier, following his first wingsuit flight, he had calculated that a landing on a large structure with cranes and other apparatuses would set him back $250,000—money he simply didn't have. He had failed to persuade others to commit during his many meetings and proposals with potential sponsors and TV producers. Determined not to allow financing to foil his plans, Gary resolved to pay his own way, if necessary by borrowing whatever it took to cover costs, from training to supplies to execution. "I budgeted it all out as cheaply as possible," he says, "decided how many boxes I would need, started doing all sorts of calculations— calculations I'd made in the past—and got it down to 18,600 boxes of varying size, and really set a date, early April, because my training I'd mapped out finished late March." The boxes alone would cost £20,000—about $32,000. There would be additional costs for travel to train, during which time he would also have to take off from work, which meant he wasn't earning money. And he would need to pay for wingsuit development and flight time.

When Gary worried, it concerned money and variables beyond his control. He wondered, *What might others be up to?* "I knew there was a race on and suits were developing and the Apache had just launched—that was one of the TonySuits," he recalls. "It was getting easier and easier to fly slower and slower. I said, *If I don't do this for me now and if I don't fund this, someone else, somewhere around the world, is going to achieve it, and every morning I will get up, look myself in the mirror, and kick myself in the bollocks and destroy myself, and the rest of my life, for not having got off my ass and achieved it.* That was really my driving force: the fact that I knew I had to achieve this now if I was to be the one to achieve it before anybody else."

Again, he told only a small circle of friends and collaborators of his plans. "I'm under the radar, because I'm not that experienced," he would say. "I hadn't told anyone, because nobody would take me seriously."

He hadn't yet told Tony, either, who was busy in Zephyrhills finishing an Apache Gary had ordered. Gary was eager to get his hands on the completed wingsuit so that he could test it—flying slowly without stalling, and experimenting with altering his body position to achieve greater accuracy. Such choreography would need to be honed to perfection. While waiting for his new suit, Gary's concern that another pilot would beat him to landing only grew when he saw news coming out of China.

Chapter 17

DRAGONS AT HEAVEN'S GATE

ZHANGJIAJIE, CHINA, SEPTEMBER 24, 2011

In a humid corner of Hunan Province, in central China, some five hundred miles from Shanghai and about eight hundred miles from Beijing, Zhangjiajie (population 1.5 million) straddles a winding river in a broad valley. Archaeologists say people have been living here for ten thousand years, in the shadow of 4,982-foot Tianmen Shan (Heaven's Gate Mountain), a feature that had a hold on their collective imagination. In an amphitheater at the foot of the mountain, local folklore takes the form of a musical production telling of a realm ruled by magic and fairies.

Along with mystery, bees and black butterflies inhabit the dense forests along the lower slope, and variable weather dominates along the craggy upper reaches of the mountain, where it may be hot and moist as dog's breath one moment and wrapped in cool fingers of fog the next. It's hard to shake the feeling that there may be other forces at work, a fact Buddhists appreciated when erecting an elaborate shrine above a natural wonder some 4,200 feet above sea level that's said to be a portal to the afterlife. This arch, leading from one side of the mountain to the other, is the celebrated Heaven's Gate, which Jeb planned to fly through.

Resembling a keyhole, the so-called gate rises 360 magisterial feet, yawns 96 feet wide, and stretches 260 feet straight through the mountain, spacious enough for the Statue of Liberty to stride through, torch raised high. It is large enough for a small plane to fly through, which happened in 1999 as part of a stunt.

Nobody had ever piloted a wingsuit through, however, and that was the purpose of what, in clunky translation, was called "Red Bull Wingsuit Flying Through." From a publicity standpoint, it was the largest stunt ever for wingsuits and BASE jumping.

Iiro, the former magician and Jeb's longtime friend, had quit jumping following a series of injuries and reinvented himself as a producer. He and a Beijing-based partner named Frank Yang were putting on the China event for Red Bull. With a $2 million budget, three hundred support staff, and a TV broadcast to tens of millions in China, the scope and profile of the event would leave them under enormous pressure and working long into the night.

To increase the odds that everything would go off without a hitch, Jeb had invited some of the most talented and accomplished wingsuit practitioners. There was Joby, the high-altitude climber and TV veteran, and Douggs, the libertine and exuberant Australian with tattoo murals and facial piercings. A jumper named Stephan Mueller, who lived and worked in Shanghai and had organized the event at the Jin Mao Tower, had come for logistical assistance, but would not perform. Jeff Nebelkopf, Tony's business partner, would come to fly camera. He had three video cameras mounted on a helmet flat as a mortarboard, along with a still camera activated by a remote device clenched between his teeth, which he chomped down on midflight to activate the shutter. Roberta Mancino would be there, too. Although they were no longer a couple, she had trained under Jeb for two years, and he knew she could handle the workload. Then there was Barry Holubeck, a former head skydiving instructor at Perris Valley, who had made more than fourteen thousand skydives and countless BASE jumps, including several with Mark Sutton. A certified senior rigger, Barry could pack a parachute in ten minutes, about a third of the time it took most. Jokke (pronounced *yocky*) Sommer, a small, bird-thin hotshot from Norway, had fast made a reputation for flying closer to objects than just about anybody. Finally there was Matt Gerdes, a former professional skier from California who'd moved to France and had written a very good and comprehensive reference, *The Great Book of BASE*. "He's probably the best wingsuit pilot in the world, period," Jeb had said.

In the spirit of their host country, the pilots had assigned one another dragon nicknames. Thus, Mancino was Dragon Lady. Douggs was Puff the Magic Dragon. Joby they called White Dragon. Jeb was, of course, Black Dragon. Jeff Nebelkopf became Dragon Eye, for his many camera lenses. Matt Gerdes was Disgruntled Dragon, for his acerbic commentary—to wit: "Wingsuit BASE jumpers are for the most part narcissistic to a fault and cagey." Barry Holubeck and Jokke would receive no sobriquets, because, as Jeb would say with a laugh, "They aren't cool enough for dragon names."

EACH PILOT had a role to perform as part of a series of stunts that would take place in three phases.

In Zhangjiajie, a modern cable car station built in 2005 offered visitors a leisurely thirty-minute ride on cars strung like patio lanterns for five miles up the mountain. The cable car did not lead to Heaven's Gate, but the hole came into view about halfway up, an oval of light against the dark mountain, positioned on a saddleback ridge between two peaks.

The first phase of the event called for Matt and Barry to leap from a cable car about three-quarters up the mountain, from an altitude of several hundred feet above the forest. They would fly along the terrain, darting around pinnacles and outcroppings before pitching their chutes and drifting down to a narrow bridge—one of the few straight sections along a winding road on the mountain, surrounded by wild forests.

Another group of pilots would continue to the top of the cable car line and hike a short distance through the woods to a platform built from scaffolding and plywood on the edge of a 990-foot cliff. They were responsible for the second phase, which would commence when Roberta, Joby, Jeff, Douggs, and Jokke launched and flew down a mountain drainage, opening their chutes to land along the bridge and meet up with Barry and Matt.

The roadway they all landed on wound upward through ninety-nine nauseating switchbacks, threatening any inattentive driver with a plunge into the thickets of Tianmen National Forest. The road led to a different part of the mountain than the cable car, culminating at a parking area, the stepping-off point to 999 steep steps carved from stone, the final path up to the gaping mouth of the gate, through which could be seen a generous view of sky on the far side of the mountain. It was in that sky that the third and final phase of the event would begin. A helicopter would line up over the back side of the mountain and Jeb would exit with his suit and attempt to fly through the hole, as if threading a needle. Of all the pilots, only Jeb would have an attempt to fly through the gate.

The same natural forces of erosion that had created the gate had formed the back side of the mountain into almost a funnel shape. From the vantage point of the chopper, the upper portion of the gate resembled a land bridge, creating a narrow opening that Jeb would need to fly into. On either side, rock walls extended hundreds of feet. Below, the slope was covered in thick trees. "There's nothing but death on that side of the mountain," Jeb explained early in the week at practice while considering contingency plans. "I can't land on the back side of the mountain."

The front side of the mountain presented its own dangers. Once through, Jeb would need to maintain his glide over the stairs and cruise down the slope before opening his chute and joining his accomplices at the bridge several miles below. That is, if everything went according to plan.

The fact that he was going to fly through a hole in a mountain, an act whose outcome was uncertain, was all starting to seem *real* to Jeb once he arrived in China. "Once you commit, there's no escape," he would admit. "Normally you have an out. This one, there's no bailing."

In Zhangjiajie, the pilots were put up at an opulent hotel with decor inspired in equal measure by Vegas and Versailles. The lobby featured miles of marble tile. A multitiered fountain rippled with water shrouded by fog produced by a machine like the kind they use at rock concerts. When Douggs arrived from Australia, Jeb was sitting in a wing chair in the cavernous lobby. They had not seen one another since Switzerland, before "Grinding the Crack" had broken big. In the meantime, Jeb's growing fame had meant propositions from all manner of women—one kind, anyway.

"You married?" Douggs called out as he ambled up.

Jeb grinned. "Yeah." He had changed his marital status on Facebook in honor of one particular woman he had been corresponding with online.

"Congratulations!"

"I'm a strange dude. We haven't met yet."

"That's fucking perfect! Australians wouldn't think that's weird."

Not everyone was in agreement. To some of Jeb's friends, the woman had presented herself as too perfect: a model, a mixed martial arts master, and independently wealthy. Iiro called her "Santa Claus," a figment of Jeb's imagination. Iiro believed it was a case of catfishing; he believed the stress of the coming jump had clouded Jeb's judgment.

Certainly there were other signs of strain. "I'm okay with dying," Jeb had said from his hotel room in Beijing. "If I die on this project, I'm okay." A few minutes later, he confessed: "Now, I kind of don't *want* to die. I want to meet and spend time with this person." He talked of fate, a notion he normally dismissed as superstitious nonsense.

The tense, uncertain anticipation of a project building for more than a year would affect everyone differently. Iiro had nearly slugged Jeb in the dark of the cabin on their flight over the Pacific when Jeb woke him from a deep sleep for what turned out to be some trifling question on their customs and immigration cards.

Unpredictable weather conditions added stress. As did Chinese bureaucrats—known in the vernacular as "Little Devils"—who, feeling their power, attempted to hold up any number of essential approvals required to proceed with the show.

A pack of reporters hovered around Jeb and the other pilots, filming their every move, firing questions. Each night, Jeb was obliged to dine with yet another round of dignitaries. During dinner, one asked Gigi, who had accompanied her son on the trip, if she prayed before Jeb's jumps. "I don't believe in God," she replied. "I believe in him."

Joby had arrived in Zhangjiajie hammered by jet lag and, after a sleepless night, felt nauseated. Splashing water on his face in a bathroom at a cable car station before his first scouting mission at the mountain, he was asked how he was feeling. "Nervous," he said.

He would have reason to be. On a practice jump from the platform, Joby opened his parachute and wound up off target, hung in the trees by his canopy, dangling more than a hundred feet over a precipice. Unhurt, he was snared like a fly in a spiderweb, necessitating a rescue that required hours to free his chute, which was ruined, shredded by thorns, forcing him to resort to his only backup.

Joby would remain nervous two days later following final practice flights that went off without a hitch. Unfamiliar conditions would put everyone off balance.

During practice that week, clouds had moved around the platform, and with a media contingent watching expectantly a few feet away, Jeb had tilted his head back, closed his eyes, and breathed deeply. "I was just centering myself because I was scared," he explained. "You're always kind of a little bit scared. You've got a variable you're not used to dealing with, which is fog. The fog is just moving around your line. Just breathe. There's no thinking. It's not about thinking. It's just about calming. Your brain starts to think too much, and you start overthinking. It's about trying to shut that down and try to relax. It's sometimes difficult. It's not always easy to relax."

The platform construction did not inspire relaxation. Some of the materials employed included dead branches from trees and baling wire, to create a barrier so no hapless journalist or PR flack tumbled off the side while staring at the spectacle. It required distraction to not imagine the whole creaky setup crashing free and plunging into the jungle in a loud pile of junk. All week, journalists had lain on their stomachs, peering over the edge as Jeb inched the toes of his black hiking boots to the edge of the platform and commenced a one-minute countdown. Pushing free, he vanished into a cloud without a sound, shrieks of joy and terror issuing from those watching. Few in China—a country without access to YouTube, and cut off from Western images—had ever seen such a thing. Moved by the sight, one photographer lifted his hip Western-style black Buddy Holly frames, and dabbed at his eyes. "I cry," he said, incredulous. "I *cry*?!"

On Friday, less than twenty-four hours before the live event they had all been building toward for months, Joby and Jeb and several other pilots bounced along in a chartered bus from the mountain to the hotel. Emotions remained high, and Joby had something to get off his chest. "Not bad," he said, describing one of his practice flights earlier. "Not evil. But a spirit . . ." He paused. "Felt like a gargoyle was on my back, pushing on me. It wasn't bad feelings at all, but something telling you it's here."

None of the other pilots said anything right away, but their silence was pregnant with skepticism. Finally someone asked Jeb what *he* thought about Joby's premonitions.

"Are you on *crack*?" he said, practically exploding. "Are you on heroin!? Have you been smoking weed?! We are all highly trained, and we're going to make it happen. And you live and die by your own actions." He turned to gaze out the window again, the bus dead silent except for a mouse squeak of rotten springs. Outside, the setting sun painted the sky salmon. The weather was as good as it had been all week, rain and fog having cleared. "Okay," Jeb said finally, calmly, still staring out the window at clear skies, "maybe there is fate."

*B*y midmorning on the appointed day, Saturday, September 24, a large crowd had assembled, crawling up the mountainside in cars and cramped diesel buses. Thousands of people had come to watch the show, hunkering down on the stone steps leading to the gate with picnics and playing cards. Below, a carnival atmosphere prevailed at the base of the stairs, with kiosks hawking gewgaws and a blue hot air balloon adorned with the Red Bull logo drifting lazily from a tether, carrying aloft a fresh batch of visitors with each blast of fire.

From there you could practically see all the way down to Zhangjiajie and the cable car station, where, in a conference room upstairs, eight wingsuit pilots listened to a final briefing from Iiro and Frank Yang. Iiro had delivered a similar message at the hotel three nights earlier, after everyone arrived. "You are the best athletes in the world," he had said. He warned them away from discussing politics with the media and against flying too close to the cable car. "We have to have a perfect safety record," he had said.

"Do it at seventy percent rather than ninety-five." He was talking about pushing their limitations.

Across the conference room, stern-faced Chinese apparatchiks in gray suits inspected the pilots. If Jeb appeared preternaturally calm to officials, it was because, unknown to them, shortly after seven that morning, he had flown through the hole during a practice jump from a helicopter. The mountain virtually empty at that hour and the other pilots at the hotel sleeping, he simply went for it during what was intended to be merely practice. Landing along the mountain road afterwards, he'd shouted, "I've got this!" Still, he would need to nail it again, this time in front of millions on TV. Inside, emotions began to stir.

The others were dealing in their own way. As they sat on a couch together, Douggs turned to Jokke Sommer and whispered, "I've got sweaty palms."

"Why?"

"Nerves," Douggs whispered, rubbing his hands together and grinning. "Nerves and fun!"

BRIEFING COMPLETE, the pilots filed into cable cars and were carried over rooftops, past a railyard, out of the city, and into the foothills, where farmers till fields and barefoot women under coolie hats wash laundry on rocks along a stream. Occasionally the peasants looked up at the procession with brown-gummed grins, eyes saddlebagged, squinting into stratocumulus clouds giving way to a descending haze. The weather, perfect hours earlier during practice, was changing.

Halfway up the mountain, there was a cable car station where passengers could disembark along the road. That's where Jeb got off and settled in a room upstairs at the station that had been set aside for him. Normally used by truckers catching some shut-eye on their routes, it was lined with metal bunk beds. In this spartan space, cardboard wedged over the windows to block out light, were Iiro and his parents, Gigi, Frank Yang, a filmmaker and jumper from South Africa named Nic Good who goes by "Moose," a talented and avante-garde photographer friend of Iiro's named Kristian, and a cameraman from GoPro headquarters, in Half Moon Bay, California, who called to mind Dennis Hopper's manic photographer in *Apocalypse Now*. His name was Jordan, but everyone called him GoPro Joe. A Chinese fixer eager to provide a taste of home to the Americans had fetched Kentucky Fried Chicken. Unable to swallow more than a few bites, a nervous Jeb twice trotted off to use the bathroom. As the minutes ticked by, the room took on the tense atmosphere of a trainer's room before a big prizefight.

They were waiting for word of the other pilots who had continued on the cable cars to the top. From there, Douggs, Roberta, Joby, Jokke, and Jeff hiked toward the platform on the edge of the 990-foot cliff. Matt and Barry, meanwhile, hopped another cable car and headed *down* the mountain, as they had practiced all week, to begin the first phase of the pageant. Five minutes on, passing over a familiar gorge, they alerted their interpreter to halt the cable car. Hundreds of feet above slopes carpeted in trees they opened the doors from the inside and dropped rocks to gauge their height— six seconds to a solid ledge, eight with a good push on exit. They were between five hundred and eight hundred feet above impact.

As they geared up and scouted their line, the radio crackled in Chinese to commence a one-minute countdown. At ten seconds, Barry activated a smoke canister on Matt's ankle, and Matt and his blue suit vanished out the door, Barry right behind. "We flew through this little spire together and flew along the right side of the trees and opened and landed together," Barry recalls.

They landed on the road, where a bridge crosses a narrow gorge. "You only have a couple places to land, and it's all concrete," Barry says. "Everything else is trees, and it's gnarly, thick, bad trees. It's going to be soft on the landing, but getting out is not going to be easy. If you have some type of injury, there's no rescue. They don't have a chopper on site to highline you out. A broken leg could mean that you're going to die."

UP ON THE PLATFORM, a fifteen-by-twenty-foot plywood structure, Douggs, Roberta, Joby, Jokke, and Jeff geared up and looked over the edge to a sheer nine-second rock drop to the treetops, preparing for the event's second phase. From there, the road looked like a strand of wet spaghetti on its way toward Zhangjiajie.

On the day of the actual show, Joby, like the road, was twisted in knots, dealing with his own churning emotions as he stood on the platform. Afraid of heights, he was a mountaineer whose worst phobia was always falling. As a jumper, in those moments before exit, he would sometimes think about his wife and their peaceful life at home in Santa Barbara. He tried not to think about his close call earlier in the week, when he had wound up in the trees. "I could have been dead," he would admit. "I *should* have been dead. That was light the way I got off."

Douggs and Jokke, though, were scheduled to go first. Activating smoke canisters, they stepped forward on the wooden platform, counted down, and took off. Jokke headed straight for a section of road twelve hundred feet below, where three switchbacks pile up in what, to some, resembles a coiled snake. But Jokke saw a triple cheeseburger, and dubbed the feature "Triple Cheese," which he dove at, moving more than 120 miles per hour in his red-and-blue Phoenix-Fly suit, roaring right over spectators as Douggs swung wide into safer airspace, both men disappearing down the valley in the direction of the landing area.

Minutes later, Joby, Roberta, and Jeff followed Douggs's line. At the landing, everyone gathered their canopies and piled into a bus headed up the mountain to watch Jeb, who had ridden down to get ready at a parking lot that served as a helipad. The final phase of the event was about to begin.

ONLY BARRY REMAINED on the bridge. He had no radio to communicate with the rest of the group, but he knew Jeb was on his way when he heard rotors thudding down the valley. Looking up, he could not see the chopper through a thick haze that had settled over the mountain.

From the helicopter, Jeb could scarcely see the ground. All afternoon, a cloud ceiling had descended, and they needed to move quickly before haze closed out the entire flight path. Once they reached a point 2.5 kilometers from the hole, on the back side of the mountain, Jeb removed his headset and pulled on helmet and goggles. Zipping the sleeves on his suit, he crouched in the open door, boots resting on smooth rivets running along the threshold. Fingers folded over the ends of his wings, his long body bent at the knees and elbows, he resembled a giant wasp.

He was alone in the back of the chopper except for a woman, possibly a government minder or a Red Bull employee—he didn't know. They did not exchange more than a glance. The pilot, who called himself Harrison, in the manner of many English-speaking Chinese who adopt American names, had brought the aircraft forward and was holding steady at 1,640 vertical feet from the rear of the cave. Machine noise made talk impossible, so he and Jeb used a system of hand signals they'd worked out earlier: If Jeb pointed his left thumb left, Harrison would swing the chopper five degrees in that direction. Thumb right correlated with a five-degree shift to the right.

Eyes on the cave, Jeb waited for an exit position that wouldn't place him too close and require a steep, dangerous dive. He also didn't want to be too far away.

A small pinnacle above the cave served as a focal point as the chopper swayed in the wind. Jeb held his hand flat to indicate that Harrison should maintain position. He reached down to activate the smoke canister on his ankle, and as the device sputtered to life, he turned his attention to the cave again. In the time it had taken to light the canister, the chopper had moved and they were no longer lined up.

The cabin began to fill with red smoke. Jeb's mind raced: The smoke could foul visibility for Harrison, or the heat from the canister could start a fire. He needed to go, and in a panic, Jeb bailed out. He was unstable, tumbling for a moment before his wings inflated and he corrected. Scanning for a visual on the cave, he realized instantly that his altitude, distance, and glide were all off. He was too far away and would come in too low. He would not make the cave. Jeb pitched, parachute opening cleanly, and he assessed his options. Everywhere he saw rocks and trees below. He thought about attempting to fly his canopy around the mountain, but he was uncertain about what he would find there. The cave itself was crowded with people; it would be too risky to attempt a landing inside. He thought about dying on the mountain.

Finally he spotted a scree field, where a jumble of rocks slashed a gray scar in the forest. Aiming, he steered 266 square feet of white fabric adorned with the Red Bull logo toward the scree. It was his only hope.

Barry knew something was wrong when he heard the clatter of the chopper returning to the landing area, near the amphitheater, but there was no sign of Jeb, not the cracking sound from his canopy opening in the haze above. When rescue personnel stationed nearby suddenly took off in a van up the mountain, Barry's suspicions were confirmed. They—all of them—were in an emergency situation.

As minutes passed, Barry worried. Finally he approached a woman wearing a white shirt and carrying a radio. "I know Jeb didn't make it through," he said. "Where do I need to be? Do you need to get me to my people? Do I need to stay put?"

The woman hustled him aboard a bus, and they headed up the mountain. He did not know it, but meantime rescuers and a doctor sprinted down the steep stairs that run along the back side of the mountain in the direction of where Jeb's canopy disappeared in the forest. Reaching a platform overlooking the scree and jungle, rescuers spotted Jeb a few hundred feet below on the rocks.

A doctor called out, "You all right, Jeb?"

"I'm fine," he yelled back, sounding annoyed, helmet and wingsuit off.

Rescuers scrambling down the rocks soon reached him and attempted to strap a harness on Jeb so they could assist him in climbing up the steep jumble of rocks.

"I don't have time," he said, pushing past them, aware that his window to jump was closing as the cloud cover descended. Wingsuit draped over his shoulder, helmet in hand, he picked his way up the rocks. Drenched in sweat, covered in white dust from the rocks, Jeb huffed for breath as he reached the platform and started for the stairs. A pack of rescuers, handlers, minders, interpreters, and medical personnel followed. His feet stepped in a steady one-two cadence. It was a long, strenuous climb, his face red, temples spiderwebbed with veins. Perspiration ran down the bridge of his nose. He appeared on the verge of a stroke.

"Jeb!" a woman called from behind. "Jeb?!"

He turned and spotted one of the interpreters, a college student who went by the "American" name Monica. "Will you jump again?" she yelled.

"Yes!" he said, sounding weary but resolute. Hunched over, catching his breath, Jeb straightened up after a minute and continued. As he passed through the cave he picked up an escort of soldiers. He brushed past Joby, Matt, Jeff, and Jokke, who were startled to see him. They had just arrived and missed his first jump entirely. They didn't know he had made an attempt yet. They assumed he would be down the mountain, preparing to take off. Jeb didn't stop to explain. He pushed through a confused crowd down the stairs.

Iiro met him with a car at the base of the steps. That's when, as he prepared to climb in, Jeb noticed his wingsuit was missing. He scanned frantically, and a sea of expectant faces stared back. That's when something inside Jeb cracked, and a black, boiling rage spilled out. Everything he had worked for came undone because of a fuck-up as unlikely as misplacing his suit.

Douggs, recognizing what had happened, plunged into the crowd and minutes later emerged, waving Jeb's wingsuit over his head. He had found it with the doctor, who in the confusion had been holding it for safekeeping.

The driver floored the car down the mountain, through hairpin turns, in the direction of the chopper. Jeb was nauseated when he staggered out at the helipad, where Barry was waiting to grab Jeb's parachute, which happened to be full of rocks and weighed about seventy pounds. "I've got to inspect this," he said. "It's not like I can whip out a pack job."

Jeb didn't need the chute right away. He had another rig ready to go. But in the event that he would require a third attempt, he needed Barry to re-pack his original rig, just in case.

Jeb assured Barry there was nothing wrong with the chute. But Barry could not be certain. Pulling the parachute from the bag, he removed the rocks and began inspecting the canopy and the lines. If a third attempt was required, he would need time to pack the parachute properly, and time was a commodity they didn't have.

Pulling on his wingsuit and helmet, spare rig in hand, an impatient Jeb hopped into the chopper and urged Harrison to go. But they had to wait for clearance from the authorities. When it came at last, the rotors wound to life, stirring a storm of dust and whipsawing small trees in the wash. Rising slowly above the parking lot, they roared off into the haze.

The clouds had settled under seven thousand feet, and Jeb would need to exit closer to the cave, especially with visibility poor. He could no longer see clear through the cave to the other side. But spotting the pinnacle di-rectly above the gate, which he had used as a reference earlier, Jeb crouched in the open doorway again, guiding Harrison to line the copter up.

*I*nside the cave, the chopper's racket echoed off the walls, and Jokke gazed into pewter skies, at a black speck. Joby, Matt, and Jeff stood nearby on a ledge thirty feet off the floor of the cave, eyes fixed on the chopper. The crowd below them roared when Jeb plummeted, a black dot beneath the silhouette of the machine, forming an exclamation point. Carving an S-turn—heading left, then right, before bending left again, he bled off altitude. Leveling off, Jeb aimed for the opening. His flight analyt-ics would later reveal that he entered the cave sixty feet off the deck, at 110 miles an hour, gliding steady at 1.5:1. His black suit vanished in the shadow of the cave for an instant before bursting into the light on the other side, speed peaking at 120 miles per hour as he flared over the stairs, glide flat-tening to 3.2:1 with the crowd cheering, arms waving in his wake.

Dropping away down the slope, Jeb faded in the distance and disappeared altogether. "My heart keeps going like this," Joby said in the aftermath, tapping his chest. "I knew he could do it. I knew he *would* do it. I don't know that I've ever been so nervous for someone else doing something . . . I can't wait to get down there and give him a big hug and tell him—"

"Epic shit!" Jokke interjected. "Epic stuff, man!"

Jeff called out to the crowd below, *"Black Draguuuuuun!!!"* The other pilots joined, and they held the note, and the crowd roared in reply. Monica the interpreter was among them, tears running down her cheeks. "I'm nervous for him," she explained between sobs. "It was the most exciting moment for me."

SAPPED OF ENERGY, Jeb flew on, legs shaking, toes curling, his suit vibrating. He needed to get on the ground fast. Darting beneath a cable car, he dumped high, slowing everything down as he swung lazily beneath his canopy in a pendulum motion. Lining up for landing on the bridge, he hoped not to hit trees or snap his legs on the roadway. Trembling, his brain on fire, he touched down at a slight trot.

Afterward, he was whisked to a press conference. Surrounded by pots of colorful flowers and women in traditional Han dress standing at attention, members of the media and dignitaries mingled, and bouquet in hand, a laurel around his neck, a smile on his face, Jeb's bare head still sticky with sweat, he smiled contentedly, the very picture of poise. "I really enjoy wingsuit flying, because it's the closest thing I've ever come to feeling like a bird and actually flying," he told a Chinese reporter. "It gives me the ability to fly great distances very close to trees, people, everything. And the wingsuit made this jump possible. Without a wingsuit, you would not be able to jump out of a helicopter, fly through a mountain, fly down the mountain, and open a parachute. It makes impossible things possible. And that's what I like to do—I like to try to do things that are impossible, and the wingsuit is making me capable of doing things that weren't possible ten years ago."

What's your next goal? the reporter asked.

"The next real project I want to do is to land a wingsuit without deploying a parachute. That's a goal that I've been working on for six years. And I will do it." It would take time, he explained, adding, "It's expensive."

Pausing, Jeb stared into the distance as if turning some thought over in his mind. The reporter waited expectantly. But no words came, just the most beatific expression, and Jeb just laughed, a pure laugh.

Part Three

LANDING

Chapter 18

A MEETING OF
THE MINDS

Four days after Tianmen Shan, on a flight from Zhangjiajie back to Beijing, Matt, the Disgruntled Dragon, read a novel while the other pilots peered at POV footage from the mountains that week, playing on their laptop screens. Equipoise between a thoughtful, restrained quality and sharp candor makes Matt unique among his fellow pilots. When he put down his book to weigh in over the jet's roar on the subject of landing a wingsuit without a parachute, he spoke of Jeb's connections in entertainment and his single-minded pursuit in pulling off such a large production in a fringe sport. If anyone could figure out how to land a wingsuit, Matt said, it would be Jeb.

Matt had ideas for how it could be done. He suggested pulling on a motorcycle helmet and a neck brace and landing in deep powder snow in, say, Grand Targhee Resort, in Wyoming's Teton Range. It would require a forecast calling for a nice isothermal band, with powder snow piling up ten feet or so. And it would require selecting the right slope, with the proper pitch, and friends to dig him out afterwards. But it was doable.

"Every single wingsuiter here has their vertical descent rate and forward speed down to a survivable number," he said about a landing attempt. "Deep snow, for sure. Everyone here can get their vertical descent in the twenties and forward speed under sixty or eighty miles an hour. It's not that fast."

Still, there were good reasons for caution. "I would never want to risk my neck," he said. "There's no amount of money that would convince me to risk paralysis. It's survivable. If you did it once, you may not want to do it again."

Back on the ground in Beijing, Barry picked up the subject, essentially arriving at the same conclusion. Seated in the back of a taxicab crawling the superhighways and eight-lane byways of smog-bound Beijing, returning to the Radisson hotel where the pilots were put up, he said, "Each year the pilots get better, and the technology last year really stepped up." And yet, he believed, any landing would require a next-generation suit—not to mention a set of steel balls. "The commitment that it's going to take as a pilot to go past that point of no return—that's the biggest question. The speeds are there. The downward speed is there. Getting rid of some of the forward speed: that's the issue. In order to produce that slow descent rate, the forward speed is quite high. Some of what the technology in the wingsuit is giving us . . ." He paused for the right words. "If someone winds up in a bad situation, we're getting into the realms of what's survivable."

After the cabdriver was paid, Barry stood on a sidewalk outside the hotel, the Chinese capital covered in smog, skyscrapers vanishing in the clouds like Jack's beanstalk. Barry got down to the nub of the matter. "Repeatedly landing a suit with current technology?" he asked. "No." Then, characterizing the idea of touching down on a slope, any slope, as something less than a true landing, he said: "If you say land a wingsuit, what I would think is level ground, and they're going to fly in and they're going to land."

Seven time zones and half a world away in Henley, Gary Connery had something similar in mind.

Jeb's flight through Tianmen Shan was viewed, they said, by tens of millions on Chinese TV. The stunt certainly made news around the world. Jeb would sit for interviews on *Today* and *Good Morning America*. Newspapers picked up the story, word spreading further through social media and on BASE and skydiving message boards.

When Gary heard, he knew one thing for certain: soon enough some-one would fork over the money Jeb needed to build his landing apparatus, and then it would be game over, Gary. Grabbing his X-bird, Gary headed straight for Devon, in the West Country, and jumped out on load after load at a drop zone at Dunkeswell, his mind turning the whole time. When he returned, Gary knew what he had to do. He made a vow to clear his sched-ule of all work commitments so that he could dedicate all of his time to preparing for a landing. He'd had several false starts, but this was a prom-ise to himself he intended to finally keep.

Gary would be judicious about taking on additional jobs. With several commitments to fulfill, he spent October working, socking away his earn-ings for what would be a lean several months when his and Vivienne's sav-ings would be required to float them, when they might need to dip into debt for added expenses related to all the travel and training necessary for landing.

Come November, having tied up loose ends with stunt work, Gary boarded a flight for Florida, joining Mark Sutton in Zephyrhills, where the Apache that Gary had commissioned from Tony was finally finished, and ready for testing. Over several days, Gary made five jumps in the Apache, flying over the flat Florida landscape.

"As soon as I went out in the aircraft, the difference from the X-bird I had been flying to the Apache, it was incredible," he recalls about the in-creased control at a range of speeds. "I thought right then and there, *This is the one.*"

Tony, though, would continue research and development, producing new iterations of each suit, making small alterations and tweaks to im-prove performance. Gary's suit was merely another prototype, something to build on, merely a suggestion to Tony's restless mind.

Tony had not been working with the idea in mind of building an Apache suited for landing. He still did not know Gary's intentions. Gary had tried to tell him over the summer, but Tony, in his distracted way, did not pick up on the bread crumbs Gary laid. And Gary did not push the matter fur-ther. He did not know Tony well enough to be certain how he would react. At any rate, Tony could not be seen encouraging customers to attempt landing with his wingsuits or he would risk losing everything in a wrong-ful death suit.

When Gary finally returned home to family and work, Mark and Tony remained, hunched over sewing machines in Tony's workshop, spools of colored thread lining the shelves, Beatles harmonies in the background. Altered suits in hand, they would head off down Sky Dive Lane to the drop zone and scramble aboard a plane rumbling along the runway into the air for another round of testing, flinging themselves over the miniature world below. Returning to the factory, flight data fresh in their minds, they tweaked their suits in the shop, fashioning new prototypes, which they took turns inflating in Tony's office using a leaf blower he kept on hand for just such a purpose. With air blasting into the vents, their wings would inflate, causing their arms to rise forty-five degrees at their sides. Standing there in cruciform, they took the measure of the latest flying creations they had made.

In Henley, Gary seldom told anyone of his plans, except for a few confi-dants. He hardly knew anyone in town. But at the café, Vivienne got acquainted with the locals, meeting new people daily, making friends and connections. One of those who stopped in for coffee and a bite to eat was Chris Wright, a Henley resident whose friends, two brothers named Nick and Giles English, had recently founded Bremont, a British luxury watch company with headquarters in a modern building outside town. Aware that Gary sought sponsorship to help pay for his landing plans, Wright phoned up Nick English.

"'You've got to meet this chap,'" Nick remembers Wright telling him. "'He's going to do this wingsuity thing.'" Nick did not know much about wingsuits, but Wright deflected any questions. "I can't tell you more," he said. "It's worth meeting up for a cup of coffee."

Nick and Giles had a background in aviation, having learned to fly from their father, Euan, an aeronautical engineer and RAF pilot. Nick was fly-ing with his father in a World War Two–era Harvard on March 4, 1995, when they crashed. Euan was killed, and Nick broke more than thirty bones. Nick returned to the cockpit as soon as he healed, and the tragedy was a catalyst for the English brothers to alter their lives. They left careers working in finance in the City to start their own business with Bremont.

The company's founding philosophy encouraged adventure, and they sponsored mountain climbers and pilots. Curious about Gary, they agreed to an assignation at the café on a cold winter day to meet.

Gary made quite an impression, wearing his customary bright clothing, earring sparkling in his left lobe like the twinkle in his eye. Nick noticed right away a vital energy barely held in leash. "When you first meet Gary, you think he could be a crazy person, with his wired-up energy," Nick says.

But it was Gary's confidence and the way he told of his experience as a stuntman that made a crucial difference and put the English brothers at ease.

Gary explained how he had jumped from heights into boxes while working for TV and major films. He had been knocked down by cars without getting hurt, rumbling over hoods and roofs. He had performed dozens of high falls from several stories up, leaping from buildings into prepared cardboard boxes. A wingsuit landing would mean hitting the boxes at sixty to seventy miles an hour, speeds he had achieved leaping from a nine-story building and walking away unhurt. Gary explained how, if not on target, he would simply deploy a parachute at two to three hundred feet above the ground, a critical provision for Nick and Giles. "It would have been a different thing for us if he said 'I want to do this without a parachute strapped to my back just in case,'" Nick says. "That would have been a suicide bit."

Mark created a video presentation on his laptop showing what he and Gary had done so far with their suits, describing the dynamics and displaying their GPS records. He explained the physics of a flight and landing in as convincing a fashion as possible. "It just takes a big mental leap," Mark would say later. "They are pilots, and they get the dynamics and the physics."

Vivienne listened to all of the talk. For years, she and Gary had attempted to secure support from the likes of Red Bull, Coca-Cola, and Virgin. But the big players could be forgiven for fearing that if things went wrong, their brand would be stained by failure. Bremont, though, was small. Nick and Giles were aviators. They were from Henley. Finally, they turned to Vivienne and asked if she had confidence in Gary's ability to pull off the stunt. Without a hint of doubt, Vivienne told them that Gary could land a wingsuit every day of the week. "That gave us a huge load of confidence," Nick says.

"It was more a meeting of minds," Mark would recall. "They're really great guys." Everyone was about the same age, standing on either side of forty. They all had a background in aviation somehow. "It was just a chat," Mark said.

Exiting the café with his brother, Nick was certain Gary would attempt a landing with or without the support of Bremont. But he and Giles wanted to support him.

It did not happen right away, but in the end a deal was brokered in which Gary would act as an ambassador for Bremont. The watchmaker, in turn, would kick in £5,000 (about $8,000) toward the cost of boxes. Estimates for all expenses, from porta-loos to paying to rent the land where he would build his box rig to helicopter rental and catering for the production team, were expected to reach £30,000, or $48,000, money Gary and Vivienne would pay from their own pocket. Bremont sweetened the deal by making available its marketing and PR staff, which began gearing up a promotional apparatus for an April landing.

Financing in place, Gary could focus on flying and landing. He ramped up his training for an attempt that was only three months away.

Chapter 19
TOUCH-AND-GO

Ambition is so powerful a passion in the human breast that however high we reach, we are never satisfied.

—*Niccolò Machiavelli*

CAPE TOWN, SOUTH AFRICA, JANUARY 16, 2012

Jeb Corliss had spent Christmas in California and New Year's Eve in Singapore, where he launched from the observation platform at the Marina Bay Sands hotel as part of a BASE-jumping exhibition. It had been a long time since he performed acrobatics, but he pulled an elegant gainer as guests gaped from the infinity pool on the roof.

The future, though, would be in wingsuits. They were beginning to appear in TV commercials, conveying the coveted traits of speed and innovation so crucial to selling cars and high-speed Internet service. In this emerging realm, Jeb Corliss, star of "Grinding the Crack" and his cave flight in China, was the biggest name of them all.

From Singapore he went straight to South Africa to train for his most advanced wingsuit stunt yet, which would bring him one step closer to landing: In the spring, Jeb planned to brush briefly against a snowy slope while in full flight, an act he was calling the "Touch-and-Go."

He would practice in South Africa. Two producers, Tim Walker and Spencer Wilking, and reporter Jon Frankel from HBO's *Real Sports with Bryant Gumbel* had agreed to meet Jeb in Cape Town to film his training at Table Mountain, a place where Jeb had been afraid to fly following a mishap ten years earlier in which he had nearly gone in, narrowly missing boulders the size of minibuses during a hard landing. That episode had led Jeb to swear off wingsuits for a spell. But with a modern suit and more advanced skills, Jeb prepared to test himself and the mountain again.

He had begun planning during the summer, after witnessing video of pilots soaring down Table Mountain. Julian Boulle vouched that suits and skills had advanced sufficiently that Jeb could jump there again safely. Jeb had high hopes for his return to Cape Town. "If it turns out to be a good wingsuit flight," he announced, "it's going to become my wintertime training zone."

Jeb and Joby had rented a two-bedroom apartment in St. James, a seaside colonial enclave with a view of a turbulent False Bay and the long, gray finger of the Cape of Good Hope pointing toward Antarctica. Iiro had come down, too, and was assisting Moose with editing documentary footage of the flight through Tianmen Shan. Kristian, the fashion and wildlife photographer, had rented a compound for the season above Camps Bay, Cape Town's answer to the Riviera, and the scene there called to mind Jay Gatsby's West Egg manse. Fashion models, playboys, photographers, trust funders, and athletes drifted through the big rooms and out back by the pool, biding time till the next shoot or party. Jeff Nebelkopf and Frank Yang would arrive, too, and nearly make the reunion from China complete.

The scene at Moose's provided a counterpoint. He lived in Scarborough, on a hill above the Atlantic with his charming wife and their beautiful children, a place where seals surfaced in kelp beds offshore and a wild baboon territory spread in the hills along the Cape of Good Hope. Under a night sky smeared with stars, the steady crash of surf mixed with conversation, music, and the ice clink of cocktails on the veranda one night when Julian Boulle turned up. He was living out of a van in some remote territory, still recovering from the leg he'd broken in Lauterbrunnen six months earlier. His signature dreadlocks were shorn, but his laconic humor remained. "I heave friends who've linded wingsuits," he said in a thick Afrikaans drawl, adding: "They're ool dead."

That night Jeb crashed on the couch not long after Moose's kids went to bed. Curling up, shoes placed neatly on the floor nearby, he fell fast asleep during the dinner party.

Maybe he dreamed of the mountain, a 300-million-year-old block of granite and sandstone, the defining feature of Cape Town, responsible for much of the city's weather, including a curious phenomenon the locals call the "Tablecloth" when thermal columns from the Cape Flats create clouds that shroud the peak, and a scouring wind rushes through the city and out to sea.

The Bushmen who occupied the lee of the mountain when the Dutch arrived told of a god who had draped an animal pelt over the mountain to quench a fire. When the Dutch subjugated the San, they applied their own logic, describing a pirate puffing a pipe in a duel with the devil. Modern citizens understood the circumstances as part of a meteorological cycle, resulting in wind funneling into the superheated city at up to eighty miles an hour, a bad time to be flying a wingsuit from the mountain.

So, waiting for the weather to change, Jeb and Joby and the HBO crew—including a local cameraman named Chris and a soundman named Kenny—trooped around town, shooting B-roll and interviews till the wind died down.

*F*rom the cable car up the mountain there's a breathtaking view of skyscrapers and the warped roof of Cape Town Stadium, the breakers beyond—clawing the long sands of Table Bay—and the tawny hump of signal hill, capped by Lion's Head, another queer fin of rock lending the city its unique character.

On a clear, calm morning, Jeb and Joby rode up to inspect a ledge they had selected for their exit, a thirty-foot scramble below a platform where tourists took in the ample view. The ledge, filled with lichen-flecked boulders, yellow wildflowers, and stubborn vegetation, was a six-second rock drop.

Taking in the view, Jeb geared up on the ledge. On his first attempt, he hurtled along the mountain over Tafelberg Road, opened his canopy, and drifted to a landing area at a field on the verge of a residential neighborhood called Higgovale. "That was awesome!" he shouted. "It felt a lot more dangerous last time."

Joby had no trouble on his flight either. Linking up at the landing area, they made their way back up Tafelberg Road to the cable car station, passing through knots of tourists. Somewhere in the crowd, a teenage boy with an American accent suddenly rushed up to his father. "I just saw a guy go off on a wingsuit!" he said, catching his breath. "My heart was pounding!"

"Where?"

"Up at the top . . ." Then the boy caught sight of Jeb and Joby strolling past, stash bags slung over their shoulders. "Mom!" the kid called. "There they are!"

Even without his parachute, on the mountain, at the mall, and in restaurants, people recognized Jeb. They requested autographs or asked for a photo. The "Grinding the Crack" footage and coverage of Tianmen Shan had made him famous. Encounters with fans puzzled Jeb, but he also drew energy from them. His mood improved from the fact that he had been flying ratios of 2.5:1 consistently. "I'm not scared of Table Mountain," he boasted to HBO. "Table Mountain has now become my playground."

Hiking a hot, dusty trail out from the landing area after one particular flight with Jeff and Joby, they all stopped to rest. Shading the display on Jeff's camera, Jeb watched footage of his flight minutes earlier. "That's right, bitches!" he called out upon seeing his image sweep past a boulder perched on a ledge. "I *love* that feeling. I'm going to touch down. I'm like . . . I could *kick* that rock right there."

"I would try it on snow first," Joby said, frowning.

All week, Jeb had talked of a touch-and-go, the next step in proximity flight, which would possibly pave the way for landing without any multimillion-dollar landing apparatus. Come March, somewhere in the Alps or possibly Alaska, he said he would soar along a slope, drag his feet in deep snow, and continue flying.

"It's the next step for what we're doing, for sure," he said. "This idea of flying close to things and touching things—this will be the first touching things."

First, Jeb had to finish the shoot with HBO. By Friday, January 13, the HBO team had returned to the States, but before departing, someone, he said, had remarked while viewing footage from that week that he thought Jeb would have cruised closer to the mountain. It was an innocent comment, not calculated, but the words stuck in Jeb's head. He had been ten feet off the deck. *Closer?* he thought. *Closer?!* Well, if they wanted him *closer,* he would deliver a guaranteed showstopper.

A final flight sequence remained to be shot. Delayed for days by rain, Jeb used the additional time to cook up something special. He e-mailed photos of the mountain to Moose, with instructions on where to set up equipment and cameras.

On Saturday, January 14, Jeb packed his rig on the floor of the living room at his and Joby's apartment, Marilyn Manson panting through a rendition of the Eurythmics' "Sweet Dreams" in the background. The flight was all set for Monday and there was nothing to do but wait. The plan was in place.

By Sunday night, sitting around the apartment with Joby and Frank, sifting through e-mail, Jeb might have been thinking of Table Mountain, but his mind had traveled several months forward, fixing on the touch-and-go. Joby had worried about Jeb's state of mind. Ever since hitting it big with "Grinding the Crack," he seemed more grandiose than usual.

"I could drag my legs across the rocks on the mountain if I wanted to," Jeb announced that night before the final shoot. "If I get below the knee," he added about the depth of snow during a touch-and-go, "then I hit the ground. I don't think I survive that uninjured." He weighed the consequences further. "If I land, I'll get hurt. I don't want to get hurt. I think there's a good chance I'll live, but I think I'll be broke up for a while."

In the morning, Joby woke to sounds of Jeb in the kitchen. Jeb had insisted they rise at 6 a.m. to be out the door and on the road by 7:30. Looking at the clock, Joby saw they were already running late.

"You ready?" Jeb asked, an edge to his voice. "You *ready?!*"

"Yeah," Joby drawled.

Gathering gear, they hurried out the door and into a rented white Toyota 4x4 pickup, making their way through the big, swinging security gate at the complex, into a bright sunny morning, turning left onto Main Road, the sea exploding with white foam on the rocks out the windshield. Surfers stroked into rollers at Muizenberg Beach, and warm, salty air rushed through the open windows of the truck as they passed barefoot black boys, heels kicking up golden dust along the roadway.

On the M3 they were halted by Monday-morning rush-hour traffic. Already late to meet their team on the mountain, Jeb sat in the passenger's seat, head ticktocking in agitation with the passing seconds. Their route from St. James to Table Mountain skirted the mountains of the Cape Peninsula, through city streets, climbing Kloof Nek to Tafelberg Road. It usually took a good thirty minutes, but now they were stuck and Jeb fiddled with his phone. At 8:05, a text message popped up: "You at cable car yet?"

"No," he typed, "we are in traffic."

Moose and two trusted friends were already on the mountain. Moose had risen at 5 a.m., and he and his helpers had lugged their gear from a parking space on Tafelberg Road up the flanks of Table Mountain, carrying two metallic party balloons, one silver and the other black. It was not easy following Jeb's instructions in the half-light of morning, but they eventually located a particular ledge, a giant fist of granite, knuckled with boulders. By the time they arrived the sun had emerged, and they were sweaty and exhausted. Temperatures that day would reach ninety, and the heat was already carrying a zing.

Mopping his forehead with his T-shirt, Moose stared down the mountain toward the city, where joggers and dog walkers traversed dusty trails in Table Mountain National Park. He did not know it, but down near the landing area, Maria von Egidy was walking back to her car. Having heard of Jeb's plans to fly, she had come out in hopes of watching and possibly discussing plans for landing. She still hoped they could collaborate. But with Jeb running late, she needed to head into work for the day.

It would be nearly 8:30 by the time Jeb and Joby tooled up Tafelberg Road in the white pickup. At the cable car station, Jeff and his girlfriend,

Taya Weiss, one of the rare female pilots, were waiting to buy tickets for the ride up. Jeb was in a sour mood from the combination of traffic, heat, pressure to perform, and the knowledge that Moose was waiting with his mates on a ledge, frying like strips of bacon. By the time he neared the exit point, it was 9 a.m., and the observation platform was crowded with tourists and members of Kristian's menagerie at Camps Bay, anticipating a show.

Iiro and his pop singer girlfriend, C.C., were there, along with Frank Yang and the camera and soundmen, tasked by HBO to capture the exit while Moose handled the money shot.

More than a thousand feet below, the sun's rays exploded off the metallic balloons as if they were mirrors. Moose had developed serious misgivings about the balloons by now. Dancing in the wind on eight-foot strings, they continually snagged on rocks. Complicating matters, he and Jeb had forgotten walkie-talkies, and their attempts to communicate by cell phone kept getting interrupted by dropped signals.

When they finally connected, Jeb asked Moose how the ledge looked.

"I don't feel good about it," Moose said. He worried that if Jeb lined up on a balloon that was snagged on a rock, he would come in too low.

Jeb said the balloons were critical—not only as targets but as props for the shot. Eager to deliver a showstopper to HBO, he planned a close flyby, similar to the stunt he had performed at the Crack, and he was not going to allow a little wind to alter those plans.

"Dude," Moose pleaded. "I'm not happy with them. I want to take them down."

Jeb insisted they stay, promising to give the balloons a wide berth if the wind was a factor during his flight. How he meant to make such an assessment at more than one hundred miles an hour, he did not explain, but after hanging up with Moose, he, Joby, and Jeff began pulling on their suits and helmets as tourists stared at the spectacle from above. With six cameras stacked on his helmet and thick black sunglasses shading his eyes, Jeff appeared more machine than man.

Joby prepared to go first. Calling his wife for a few private words, he tucked the phone in a pocket and zipped his suit.

Exhaling loudly, he jumped without preliminaries, the fabric of his red suit fluttering faintly until air filled the vents and his wings pressurized, causing his trajectory to turn more horizontal. He shot like an arrow at the ledge, where the black balloon danced drunkenly in the wind. Roaring past Moose and his companions, Joby missed the leading edge of the ledge by about four feet, vortices trailing from his suit pulling hard at the balloon, like a dog on a leash refusing to heel. His heart pounding, Joby pulled high and came in hard under canopy—not at their landing area, but along the walking trail higher on the mountain. Shaken, but unhurt, he began stowing his gear in a stash bag for the return trip back to the cable car station.

At the exit, Jeb phoned Moose, spitting curses when the connection was lost yet again. When he finally got Moose on the line, Jeb announced that he and Jeff were going off in a minute. With the crowd watching expectantly from above, the toes of his black boots dangled over the ledge. Jeb had two POV cameras attached to his helmet, one on his belly, and yet another near an ankle. Jeff and his lenses lined up to Jeb's right, ensuring complete coverage.

"You all right?" Jeff asked.

"Okay," said Jeb, voice calm. Then, after a moment, "Three, two, one . . . See ya!"

The pair went off in tandem, opening their wings with a *whoosh* and racing in the direction of the ledge. From above it was difficult to track them. Jeb's black suit and Jeff's blue one both blended with the mottled rock as they shot away from the spectators. How close Jeb came to the ledge no one could say. But a terrific boom that everyone assumed to be one of the balloons exploding testified to his precision in nailing his target.

Joby knew better. Something strange had happened that he could see more clearly from below. He heard the booming sound, too, but saw Jeb veer hard to Joby's right. He watched Jeff abandon his flight path and pitch high. An instant later, Joby saw Jeb's black chute bloom dangerously low and collide with a cliff.

Joby dug in his pocket for a walkie-talkie. "I think he just crashed into a rock wall," he barked, in a voice strained with panic. "He hit *bad*. Right fuckin' now! Y'all come down!"

At the exit, Taya heard the message on her walkie-talkie. "On the way down now," she replied in a quavering voice.

A moment later, Joby, a little delirious, discovered that he was *unpacking* the parachute he had just placed in his stash bag. Snapping to his senses, he began quickly to stuff the chute back in before pausing. *I can't believe this happened . . . I can't believe this happened . . . I can't . . . There was no reason to hurry. Jeb was dead.*

On the ledge, Iiro was on the phone with Moose. "We have to leave as soon as possible," he said in calm tones. "He had a pretty bad flight. At least that's what it looks like from the bottom. All right, so we'll start organizing and we'll start making our way down. If you try to get to him fast, I don't know how badly he's hurt, but I think—"

"Joby says it's bad!" Taya interrupted.

"Joby says it's bad, so it might be chopper time . . . All right, bye!"

Moose did not take the news well. With his eye pressed to the viewfinder of his camera, he had watched as Jeb whizzed past at a hundred miles per hour, and he assumed the thunderous boom came from a balloon. But looking over, he could see the black balloon bobbing a few feet off the rock, string snagged in a fissure. The sight left Moose nauseated. His inattention had caused Jeb to clip the ledge and tumble over. He had killed Jeb.

Grabbing a bottle of water, Moose bounded down the slope. At the bottom of the ledge he found no trace. Scanning for black fabric, he leaped rocks, worrying over what horrors he might find. He wanted to stop and go no farther, but an internal voice urged him to press on. It was Jeb, after all. Carrying on, he finally spotted Jeb's black parachute in the distance, in a rumpled heap at the base of a cliff and ran for it.

When he arrived, three hikers were already standing around, having watched the parachute drop out of the sky. "I hope there's not a person in there," an American woman in the group had said. They had found Jeb injured, lying in a clump of bushes, and helped him remove his helmet and gave him sips of water.

Moose was shocked to find Jeb talking and quickly called for a chopper from mountain rescue dispatch. He knew the protocol. He had worked there as a rescuer before starting a family.

Jeb was pallid and in obvious pain, although the extent of his injuries was unclear. You'll probably want to film this, he whispered to a relieved Moose.

Jeff and Iiro arrived next, shocked to find Jeb alive. Jeff had landed on Tafelberg Road, among moving traffic. Ditching his gear, he sprinted up the mountain, nearly collapsing from heat and exhaustion, cajoling a bottle of water from a hiker he encountered along the way. Iiro had stared out the window of the cable car on its descent, scanning for Jeb's remains and composing in his head how he would break it to Gigi that her son was gone. At the scene, he, Moose, and Jeff took turns tending to Jeb, giving him sips of water and using his canopy as a shield from the sun.

"I just want to sleep," Jeb croaked.

"That's probably not a good idea, buddy," Jeff said.

The chopper came clattering up the mountain, a red bird, hovering feet from the cliff as rescuers and their equipment descended forty-foot lines to a trail. Jeb had been especially lucky—not only had he narrowly missed striking the cliff, but he landed on the only vegetation in an area filled with rocks. He was adjacent to the Contour Trail, which would only make rescue easier.

The rotor wash caused Jeb's canopy to flap furiously, exposing his cadaverous skin to the sun. "Jeb, Jeb, Jeb, Jeb!" Jeff shouted, over the noise. Sweaty, Adam's apple bulging, a few awkward seconds passed before Jeb turned his head slightly, indicating that he was still hanging on.

Rescuers cut him out of his wingsuit, revealing a gaping hole in his right shin, muscle spilling out of a football-shaped wound. His thigh, marbled with hematomas, had swelled to twice its normal size. There was one good sign: Jeb could feel his injured legs. "The pain is incredibly *painful!*" he howled as rescuers bandaged his wound.

"You're gonna be famous, kid," Jeff announced as the cameras rolled. By that time, the trail was crowded. The cameraman, the soundman, and various people wielding phones and professional-grade cameras darted between rescuers as they loaded Jeb onto a litter. The trail had turned into a circus. "You're stepping on my fucking hand!" he screamed at one point.

Moments later, someone else spilled water on him. "Oh, that's too *cold*," he gasped, chuckling. "Jesus Christ!" Finally stable, an IV in his arm, swaddled in blankets and strapped into a harness, Jeb was hoisted up above the crowd by ropes to the clattering chopper and flown to the parking lot at the cable car station.

There he was bundled into an ambulance. Joby piled in for the ride to Christiaan Barnard Memorial Hospital, where a white-bearded emergency room doctor, having heard the report of a wingsuit accident on the mountain, asked, "You know a guy named Corliss?"

"Yeah, I do know him really well," Jeb said. "I am that guy."

There would be more surprises. X-rays revealed that Jeb had broken both ankles. The right one would require pins. His left knee sustained ligament damage. And beneath the gaping wound on his right shin was a broken fibula. But doctors said he would make a complete recovery.

Having expected to lose both his legs, Jeb absorbed the bright prognosis just as the hospital's marketing director, a woman named Michelle Norris, entered the room. Word of his crash was out, already on social media. TV satellite trucks were lined up outside. Reporters were prowling the waiting room, eager for comment. Would Jeb be willing to make a statement?

"Just tell them I feel better than I've ever felt," he said.

SO THAT WAS what appeared in the papers the following day, Tuesday, January 17. The *Cape Times,* an English language daily, made the biggest play, with a banner headline splashed across the front page, top of the fold: "Jump That Went Wrong." A six-column color photo showed Jeb and Jeff taking off from the ledge.

Inside, the *Cape Times* quoted Merle Collins, spokeswoman for Table Mountain National Park. Authorities were considering fining Jeb and pursuing criminal charges for jumping without a permit. "He was absolutely not allowed to jump," Collins told the paper. "It is worrying to me, because people may think they can do this now without permits."

Iiro worked to minimize the damage. In an e-mail to authorities, he explained that there had been a misunderstanding over permits, and in any case Jeb and his insurance company would bear the costs for rescue and medical treatment.

The press refused to let the story peter out. Reporters posing as friends sneaked into the ICU to talk to Jeb. Moose was hounded because he had called in the chopper rescue. He hid out at home and refused to answer his phone.

The increased attention was not welcome among BASE-jumping and wingsuit enthusiasts in South Africa, who worried that they would be under scrutiny and no longer permitted to jump. Julian Boulle explained how hardfisted jumpers from Johannesburg had vowed to come down and teach Jeb a painful lesson.

The fallout from the crash affected everyone in different ways. Succumbing to stress and exhaustion, Moose had been practically carried off the mountain by friends, like a wounded soldier. At the car they dumped a five-liter bottle of water on his head to revive him.

Later in the week, still dodging the press while Jeb remained in the ICU, Moose invited the others to screen footage of Jeb's crash at his home. Iiro whipped up lasagna for dinner. There was wine, vodka, and whiskey. Everyone watched from Moose's cramped office as Jeb, in slow motion, clipped a rock just below the knee and cartwheeled over the ledge. It didn't seem possible that he should survive.

"Let's just enjoy him," Joby said, toasting to Jeb's recovery, "because a person like that won't be around long."

Moose sat in a chair on the deck outside, cradling a cup of Cape red. "Danger is," he said, summing up his feelings, "you become an extraordinary person. Jeb is rapidly becoming or already is extraordinary. He's unique. He's extremely skilled and has an amazing perspective on this sort of thing. So he shoves himself into a position of esteem or uniqueness. The danger is getting addicted to the dream of being unique or being up there on this pedestal and keeping yourself up there. He's on his own little mission. He doesn't give a fuck. One way or another, he's going to get there . . ."

Moose mentioned how he had talked to one of the doctors at the hospital, a man Moose knew personally, who had put pins in Jeb's legs during surgery. The doctor recalled, just as Jeb was about to go under from anesthetic, the patient's last words: "I know I can land it."

*I*n the ICU, Jeb's legs were covered in white plaster, from the knees to where his long toes, black with bruises, peeked out. He was surrounded by beeps and alarms, monitoring vital signs, and strange tongues from fellow patients, reminding him that he was in Africa. His bed was surrounded by flowers, stuffed animals, and balloons. More than two hundred e-mail messages swelled his inbox, from friends and fans inquiring about his well-being.

Lying alone in bed afforded him time to think. He hadn't expected to impact the mountain—and didn't know he had until he was tumbling through the air. Years of acrobatic training activated at the level of muscle memory allowed him, after flipping and rolling five times, to get belly down again, like a falling cat locating its feet. It was only then that conscious thought intruded. His sense of time slowed, and he began to think. *Had he done so much damage that his situation was hopeless? Was it worth the effort of opening a parachute? Maybe he should just let it go . . . Maybe he could survive this hit the way he had survived all the others. Maybe it was not that bad. It was now or never . . . Pull now!*

The lines of his parachute twisted, and two seconds later, Jeb crunched down on a bush, only feet from the face of the cliff. It was as if he had fallen out of a barn loft and landed, out of sheer luck, in a haystack.

He would jump again, a decision the doctors could not understand. "My biggest fear is dying of old age," he explained. "I fear that more than anything—getting cancer, HIV, dying of disease."

He was accustomed to people not understanding his reasoning, and he did not fear their judgment. "They're so worried the other monkeys are going to make fun of them," he said about social opprobrium, "or the other monkeys are going to reject them. Hell, I was rejected at birth. I've been rejected my whole life. I got over that a long time ago. I stopped trying to make the other little monkeys happy when I was a kid. I don't care what the monkeys think. I only care what I think. I know what I'm doing. I'm okay with it. I'm okay with taking risk and making the decisions I do. And I'm okay with dying. None of that bothers me. I know that it's going to happen. I'm going to fight to make it not happen, but when it does, it does."

Three days after his accident, on January 19, Jeb was out of the ICU. He had been hidden away on the hospital's maternity ward to keep him from curious reporters. A station nurse appraised all visitors with skepticism before allowing anyone into his private room, one with an expansive view of Table Mountain.

Michelle Norris arrived that afternoon. More than a hundred media outlets had requested comment, she said. "The best comment you can give," Jeb said, "I want to thank the hospital and staff for taking such good care of me, and the rescue crew and Table Mountain for being such wonderful people."

"I'll say you're not speaking to the media and not doing interviews," she said. Such a bland statement would not fly with a hungry press horde. Norris knew that.

"Say Jeb is lazy and he just wants to rest. But that I'm very grateful to everyone involved in all this, and I hope it wasn't too much of a negative impact on their lives."

After a moment, Jeb had another idea. "You might say, 'Hey, for a couple million dollars I've got some footage to show, too, for the right amount of money.'" Laughing, he added, "I'm a whore. I'm a very *expensive* whore."

Jeb had reason to be in a jolly mood. It looked as if authorities at Table Mountain would not pursue charges. His only complaints concerned grooming. His hair had grown long enough to cover his scalp. "It already looks like a hippie's," he said.

His most vexing condition, though, concerned his inability to use the bathroom. "It's worse than being a baby, when you're not aware of it— you're a grown man!" he thundered. "It sucks ass!"

He did not intend to remain helpless for long, though. He had future plans. "My next goal?" he intoned. "Get my ass into a wheelchair."

Chapter 20
"THE REBEL"

Halfway around the globe, in another hemisphere, Gary took a seat with Tony inside the dark, air-conditioned dining room of a Ruby Tuesday's overlooking U.S. Route 301. Surrounded by the salad bar and booths packed with lunchtime patrons, Tony had something on his mind other than what to order.

Gary had come to Zephyrhills for two weeks to fly the Apache, and he had brought a FlySight GPS to track his speed and glide ratio. It was a busy time. Gary would make more than forty-five jumps—sometimes more than three per day—rattling up the runway at Skydive City, breathing the thick fuel smell in the cramped fuselage, knees hunched to his chest in close quarters with the rest of the load. Each jump, he focused on a new wrinkle. Sometimes he tried to maximize glide. Other times he experimented with turning. There were times when he experimented with holding his hands differently to gauge the effect on flight performance. Afterwards he studied the data on a laptop in Tony's shop.

The results, as far as Tony was concerned, were not impressive. This bothered him. Every wingsuit pilot in the world was preoccupied with flying faster and farther, maxing out. That was the measure of his skill. And here was this stuntman, a smart man, obviously athletic, whom he really liked. Yet he could not get it right.

Sitting at a table along a bank of windows at the restaurant, thinking of some fillip to performance, Tony offered poor Gary tips on how to fly faster. Gary stopped him short, though. "I actually want to go slow," he said.

Tony stared in disbelief. Nobody wanted to go slow.

Gary explained that he had found a couple of lines he hoped to fly. Carrying too much speed through a turn would mean he wouldn't make a crucial corner, which would be catastrophic. "It's a BASE jump," he said, as if that settled it. "Valley stuff."

Tony's bright blue eyes hung half lidded, so heavy were they with skepticism. "You can't bullshit me, mate," he said, summoning a no-nonsense cockney he usually held somewhere in reserve. "I think you want to *land* this thing."

Gary's earring and eyes twinkled back at Tony. The jig was up, and there was no point pretending otherwise. "Yeah, actually, you're right," Gary said finally. "I want to land this thing."

Tony wasn't upset. He was inspired. He suggested making a suit that would fly slowly and began sketching designs on a napkin. Tony had a challenge before him, and he liked challenges. "The whole idea was to go slower," he would recall. "All my life is trying to go as fast as I can. All wingsuiters want speed. So now I'm doing the opposite."

Back at the shop, they fired up the cutting machine, trimming fabric to size. Tony hunched over his sewing machine, feeding fabric beneath the needle. He had other reasons for wanting to make a slower suit. A niche discipline among skydivers had sprouted up that involved flying wingsuits together with high-performance parachutes in formations; Jeb and Luigi Cani had been among the first years earlier while performing testing to determine possibilities for landing. Since then the practice, called extreme relative work, or XRW, had grown into a full-blown discipline, and these suits needed to be flown slowly, too. There were commercial opportunities for such a creation, which Tony attacked using Bernoulli's principle, fashioning a fat wing by increasing the distance between the top skin and bottom skin when inflated. Over more lunches of chimichangas at Los Chicos, a Mexican joint in Zephyrhills, he and Gary hashed out a design that would deliver aerodynamic lift, stability, and slow flight. It was a task easier said than done, and the first prototypes were unstable. Gary noticed during testing that they felt "twitchy." They did not improve on the Apache. They did not even fly slower.

WITH TIME RUNNING SHORT for an April landing attempt, Gary returned to the UK with his Apache. He linked up with Mark, and the two of them headed to Italy and the Dolomites. It was January and they knew midwinter was a bad time to be in the mountains, but they were desperate to get low-altitude experience with the Apache, which they could get only by BASE jumping. Gary had never made a BASE jump with his Apache before, and at Monte Brento he and Mark planned to fly as slowly as possible from the four-thousand-foot cliff, which would simulate the experience of exiting a helicopter at low altitude.

The resulting GPS and other flight data concerning flight paths, fall rates, altitude, and the time required for their canopies to open would be compiled and used to demonstrate to officials from the UK's Civilian Aviation Authority that they possessed the skill to land safely—"that said we were professional and not a bunch of nutters," Mark said. All of which would help make their case for permission to use a helicopter for a landing attempt.

As they had feared, the conditions at Brento did not cooperate. The temperature was five degrees Fahrenheit. The mountain was so snowbound that the road was impassable, forcing them to hike the entire way on the first day, a journey of several hours. "We knew everything was against us," Mark would recall. "The mountains in winter are full of snow. It was completely the wrong time to be out there training, but we had no choice, because everything on the Web or in the press was effectively that Jeb Corliss is going to land the suit. If he had managed to land, who cares about number two?"

They were at Brento when the news came that Jeb had struck Table Mountain. "With Jeb going in, all sorts of chat surfaced" that others would attempt a landing soon, Mark would recall. "There was a guy who had been flying on a lake north somewhere with jets, and he was trying to take one off. There was chat somewhere in South Africa, but it was all rumor control."

Weather conditions in Brento permitted Gary to make only four jumps. The flights hadn't gone as well as he'd hoped, and he had spent his fast-dwindling savings to travel to Brento. He was worried.

While still in Italy, he and Mark received an e-mail message from Tony. "Tony says he's cracked it," Mark would recall. "He sent us an e-mail saying, 'Boys, I've got this amazing suit. It falls so slow—it's brilliant, stable.'"

For five days, e-mail traffic hummed between Italy and Florida. "We're going, 'Right?'" Mark recalled. "'Do we completely change our plans? Is it as good as he says? Do we go to the States and get a completely new suit, or do we stay where we are?'"

They decided to take Tony's word for it and headed to Zephyrhills. The suit Tony had created turned out not as brilliant as advertised. It needed refinements. "It was all hands on the deck," Mark said. "I was sewing. Gary was sewing. Tony was madly sewing. In about thirty-six hours, we managed to make these suits. We did a couple of jumps in them and flew back to the UK—and they were brilliant."

The new suit flew slower, with increased stability over the Apache. Gary gave hard inputs. *Check.* He leaned hard, dipped an arm and leg to turn. *Check.* He was like a driver testing the brakes, steering, and acceleration on a sports car. He flared hard. *Check.* In the Apache, a hard flare had sent him skittering out of control; not so with the new suit.

The numbers on his flight analytics fell within the ranges he had been seeking for landing. He managed to slow descent to twenty-two miles an hour, the equivalent of high-performance parachutes, while moving forward at sixty miles an hour. This speed was comparable to a 140-foot-high fall, a feat Gary had already done successfully. He knew the world record high fall into boxes was 220 feet. A sixty-mile-an-hour landing, at a 2.7 glide slope, on the other hand, he believed would be a walk in the park.

Tony had made a suit that not only could fly as fast as an Apache but could cruise relatively slowly without sacrificing stability. "More efficient," he would say, summing up his new creation, "like a machine." He called it the Rebel, because it violated all the rules concerning performance.

By now they were deep into February. With the Rebel in hand and an April deadline looming, Gary convened with his partners at Bremont. At last everyone was ready to unveil their plans for a landing attempt.

*T*he press release would appear on the Bremont website on March 1:

"The Bremont Wingman"
Bremont Watch Company Supports Stunt Man Gary Connery
in Setting a New World Record
March 2012

Bremont Watch Company is delighted to be supporting Henley based stunt man Gary Connery in preparation for his biggest stunt yet. In April 2012 Gary plans to make a new world record in being the first man ever to jump out of a helicopter with a wingsuit and land without deploying a parachute. April 2012 will see Gary Connery realise a lifelong ambition of jumping from a helicopter 2,400ft above the height of the box rig over Ridge Wood to the ENE of Henley on Thames. Gary will drop for 3 seconds before his suit starts to fly, he will then accelerate to approximately 80mph. He will get into his tried and tested best glide position where the speed will decrease to 60 mph forward speed with a 22 mph vertical descent rate. The flight to the box rig will be 1.4 km and as Gary approaches the box rig approximately 200ft away, he shall begin to flare bringing the speeds down to 50 mph forward and 15 mph vertical. The whole flight should last in the region of 50 seconds and will come to an end with Gary landing on a box rig.

Having lived a life of adventure in many different ways such a pursuit was of natural interest to Gary and he has since become a pioneer in the field. Gary is now ready to take this to the next level and cement this fact in the world record books— with some stiff competition out there Gary is determined to be the one to set this record.

THE PRESS RELEASE went on to describe Gary's biography and background, including his stints as a competitive kayaker and skier and in the army— omitting the part about going AWOL. It told of his career on the Stunt Register, his more than fifty high falls, mainly into cardboard boxes, and his 100 percent safety record. The document described his jumps from Nelson's Column and the London Eye, among others. An accompanying photo showed Gary wearing a wingsuit, standing on the stone balustrade of Henley Bridge in the Vitruvian Man pose.

This would be Gary's grand introduction, because hardly anyone in the wingsuit realm had ever heard of him. In the ensuing rush for information, the BASE and skydiving message boards buzzed. *Gary who?* His anonymity, in combination with an April landing date, left some to wonder whether the release wasn't some elaborate put-on, perhaps an April Fools' prank. Everyone also wanted to know what Jeb thought.

*A*s it happened, on March 1, the very day Gary's press release appeared, viewers of *Conan* on TBS watched Jeb appear through the curtains on a set on a Warner lot in Burbank, California. Head freshly shorn and gleaming under the stage lights, he was clad in black pants, black T-shirt, and black hoodie and leaning on metal crutches, a four-legged creature clomping across a buffed floor. Given his difficulty walking, flying seemed a distant and unlikely possibility.

It had been less than six weeks since his accident and he was recovering at his sister's house, in Palm Springs, attending physical therapy sessions and talking to producers from TV networks around the world who were eager—especially now that *Real Sports* had aired its segment, in February—to buy footage from Table Mountain. Fan mail and Facebook posts piled up, testifying to a range of powerful reactions to not only his near death but his unconventional life philosophy. One missive from an Army cavalry scout and infantryman who had done two tours in Iraq typified some of the responses. In his message, the combat veteran wrote of his detachment from haunting memories and how Jeb's zest for life had reminded him of the person he used to be. One of the particular phrases he used that resonated with Jeb concerned the belief that Jeb was living a life worth dying for. The message concluded by thanking Jeb for reminding him what it was like to be alive again and for conveying the hope and strength this combat-scarred vet needed to continue living.

On the set of *Conan*, the host also evinced genuine concern for his guest, who had appeared on the show six months earlier, before Jeb traveled to China. *Had the accident changed Jeb's attitude toward what he does?*

"It's changed my attitude in that I'm going to be much more careful in the future," he said. "I became too comfortable, too confident, and I was pushing way too hard. Six feet is already close. But to try to push where you're coming within inches of things, I was stepping over what I should have been doing. And it basically spanked me, and I am very happy that I was able to make a mistake so massive and be able to recover from it. Because usually when you make a mistake like that—if you had told me before that happened that you could survive, I would say impossible, you'll die for sure . . ."

The rest of the answer went on to detail the internal conversation he'd had in the air, debating whether or not to pull his parachute. Finally he got around to a bromide of the kind TV talk shows have been dispensing since talk shows were invented. "What it taught me is," Jeb said in summation, "it taught me, you know what, no matter how bad you think it is, never give up, because it may not be as bad as you thought it was."

"I'm glad you made the choice you made," Conan said, over applause from the audience. "I have to ask, because we're completely out of time: how soon are you going to do this again?"

Jeb said he would be walking without crutches in about two weeks and jumping in about three months.

"I'd do it with the crutches," Conan cracked. "But that's just me. I kind of live on the edge."

Not everyone would find humor in Jeb's act, though. Karin Sako had visited him in Palm Springs, and he cajoled her into watching his crash footage from Table Mountain, which she resisted over concerns that it would be too upsetting, akin to witnessing Jeb's death.

Karin had scaled back jumping since becoming the mother of two children, allowing her to "look at it from some different dimension, not only as a friend, but the impact it has on the people around and the other people that are left behind. Of course you can say, 'Oh, he died doing what he loved doing, blah blah blah,'" she would say. "Yeah, that's true, but it's still hard, because you miss them and want them there."

But Jeb was still there. And when Karin broke down in tears while watching his crash, Jeb was confused. *Why are you crying? Why are you getting so emotional? I'm right here.* He happened to be reading *Shōgun*, by James Clavell, and was captivated by the samurai code of Bushido, particularly the act of seppuku, the ritualized suicide by which honor is restored. The manner in which one died held significance. Some would take that as a death wish. A reporter had actually asked him about that—whether he had a death wish. "Bro," Jeb said, "if I had a death wish, I would be one dead motherfucker, and it would have happened a long time ago. If you wanted to die doing the shit that I do, you'd die right away." Put that way, it was hard to argue with.

Chapter 21

THE RIGHT NUMBERS

Flying is the 2nd greatest thrill known to man.
Landing is the 1st.

—*Sign on the wall of a bar in Canton, New York*

*T*alk shows and reporters were one thing. But big-money sponsors remained leery of the risks associated with landing a wingsuit. They did not want to touch it. "The reaction was 'You're mad!'" Mark Sutton would remember. "'You're just going to kill yourself. Bug off and leave us alone.'"

The Civil Aviation Authority would require convincing, too, before it would permit using a helicopter. Failing that, Gary and Mark would use paramotors, a paraglider with motor-driven fan propulsion. On a project with scant funding, paramotors would be a cheaper option, and Gary was already deep in debt on his credit card for expenses, which would eventually reach £40,000 (about $65,000). He called the enterprise "very Heath Robinson"—the British counterpart to Rube Goldberg.

Gary had ordered 18,600 boxes, to be stacked on landing day in a configuration 12 feet high, 40 feet wide, and 350 feet long. The site was a field adjacent to a bend in the Thames, in South Oxfordshire, just across the river from Henley. As word spread concerning his plans, people began reaching out to help however they could. Eager to volunteer, they lent the feeling of an old-fashioned barn raising. They would need to be fed on landing day, though, and toilets would need to be provided. Much of the logistics would fall to Vivienne.

Despite a growing volunteer army, Gary maintained close counsel with only a few confidants. He was as anonymous as ever among wingsuit pilots, who weighed in online on him and his project. Gary never replied to their questions or corrected wrong assumptions. The only message he would reply to was sent to him personally by Robert Pečnik, wingsuit-design pioneer and operator of Phoenix-Fly, one of Tony's competitors. Pečnik urged Gary not to attempt a landing, arguing that a landing would not advance the sport. He begged him to reconsider. If Gary was injured or killed, it would only stir a storm of negative publicity, with the fallout affecting other pilots and manufacturers, Pečnik himself among them.

Gary wrote back and politely told Pečnik he was moving ahead. He could not back out even if he wanted to, not after the good vibes and the response from eager volunteers. Sponsors, friends, and family had supported him thus far, and he was loath to let them down.

Toward the end of March, Gary explained to the Civil Aviation Authority how he planned to rotate his body when he was about three or four feet above the boxes so that he would land on the fleshy part of his side, limbs pulled tight, teeth gritted. He would be wearing a neck brace and, beneath his suit, body armor of the sort used by motocross racers.

Once the CAA granted provisional approval, Gary and Mark set off for a week in Lauterbrunnen to launch from the High Nose, which, at nearly two thousand feet, would allow them to simulate the low altitude of landing. Gary and Mark stayed at the Horner, which was deserted except for a few hardcore winter jumpers. Deep with snow, and dark in the last days of winter, the valley was bereft of life. The crowds were up on the mountains, skiing at the resorts at Wengen and Mürren.

Up on the Nose, Gary would struggle. "It took him awhile to get the suit," Mark said. "He would exit steep and get nervous after exit, and the flight is not great and the landing is not great. That's the time when I noticed he was having a lot of trouble. It was at that time we made the decision to leave Lauterbrunnen and head to Walenstadt, and we knew that with a hill to fly to, we could replicate the flight."

On a snowbound and slippery Hinderrugg, they cleared a path to the

Sputnik exit, where Jeb had famously leaped to start the sequence in "Grinding the Crack." Someone had placed a sign reading WALENSTADT, 1:30, indicating the flying time to town. Gary and Mark would spend ten days jumping the mountain, and Gary never once aimed for the Crack. He pointed the Rebel at an area dense with evergreens to the right of the ravine, a bulbous feature beyond which the cliff falls away quickly. The trees were his box rig. He flew to them and stalled, edging ever closer, before diving away over the cliff to gain altitude and open his parachute. He repeated the sequence again and again, each time growing increasingly familiar with the range and geometry of attack.

One variable that no amount of simulation could account for, however, was the mind game during landing. How would he cope after exit? Once the pressure was on? And then once he passed the floor where he could safely deploy a parachute—somewhere around 150 feet—and the ground was rushing up at him? Would he freeze? Freak out? Overshoot the box rig? Flare early and come up short?

"Knowledge dispels fear," he said at the time. "I think paranoia is a very good state of mind, because that keeps you very focused . . . It's about accepting that fear and being with it . . . dealing with the mind mess that comes in between."

He had been in funky situations before as a stuntman and nailed it. He was, after all, One-Take Gary.

FROM SWITZERLAND Gary sent the GPS readouts from his flights to Tony. In his Florida workshop, he sat under fluorescent lights at his sewing machine, accompanied by John, Paul, George, and Ringo, who drowned out the din of cutters and machines drifting in his open door. It was on March 21 that Tony received a FlySight readout from Switzerland attesting to a 3:1 glide ratio and forward speeds of fifty to sixty miles per hour with the Rebel. Vertical speeds hovered at around thirty miles an hour, some lower.

Tony was working on an order for a suit for a pilot from Norway, who was killing time in his workshop. They took up the subject of Gary's speeds. "He's doin' fifty forwards, thirty-five down. He weighs *nuffin'!* He weighs a hundred thirty-five pounds. I weigh one-eighty last *munf.* You never see good fat skydivers."

Foot on the pedal, the needle drumming a seam on a blue scrap of fabric, Tony suddenly launched into a monologue on performance. "Exactly!" he said, punctuating some private thought. "I come out the turn. I had speed coming out that turn. Speed at that position generates more speed and more lift. If you tip up, you go forwards and up. Speed . . . more lift. You're still going down, yeah . . . I'm doing less than thirty miles an hour. Gary's doing twenty-five. When you de-arch—say, tracking—you go back up or slow down. When you're tracking, you point your toes and start doing this with your butt." He stuck out his rear end on the wheeled chair he was sitting on. "Trying to get Bernoulli's effect—that's the key to performance . . . Some people just don't get it. Then you just got to stick it out and go for it. Then you do a dive . . ."

Cauterizing the end of a section of white piping with a disposable lighter, he suddenly wheeled on his chair several feet to his laptop and pulled up fresh data. "GPS, and this is your readout . . . Gotta like music," he said, selecting something other than the Beatles for a change. He pointed to a graph on the screen. "Gives me overall on jump-average, thirty-three miles an hour, minimum of twenty-six . . . That's my speed. And this is time: four seconds, five seconds, six, seven . . ." Gary's average was twenty-five miles per hour. "Twenty-five is the best I've ever seen in competition with a dive," Tony said in wonderment. Those fresh numbers from Switzerland showed that Gary had the necessary speed dialed in to attempt a landing.

A wingsuit instructor from Skydive City had walked in earlier and caught the tail end of Tony's monologue. Gregarious and barrel-shaped, the instructor defied Tony's dictum about fat skydivers. "So, you working sewing all day or coming out jumping?"

"Sewing," Tony said, gliding his chair back to the machine. He had several orders to fill. One came from California. It was for an Apache, to replace the one Jeb had trashed on Table Mountain.

Chapter 22

RAINY DAYS

My slumbers—if I slumber—are not sleep,
But a continuance of enduring thought,
Which then I can resist not: in my heart
There is a vigil. . . .

—*George Gordon, Lord Byron*, Manfred

On Wednesday, March 28, Gary uploaded a fifty-second video to You-Tube called "Less Corrr Than Corliss." In the footage, he wears the Rebel, opening strains of "Sail" in the background as he peers around a large wooden sign with a cow and a farmer standing over the words WILLKOMMEN IN UNTERWASSER. Prancing around in his suit like some character from a Monty Python sketch, he glances around, finally launching from the ground face-first into a snow pile, a mock tribute to his and Jeb's shared ambition. The video closes with thanks and "get well soon" messages to Jeb and the words "The 'Bremont Wingman' lands for real April 2012."

For his part, Jeb was gracious. He would say at the time: "You do get a little bit kind of sad when you hear someone's going. I always kind of had a feeling because of how long it was taking me that eventually some raging psychopath who had bigger balls than me would come in and do one of those methods. I never expected someone to do a box-catcher method. I hope it works, because I'm excited to see it."

GARY WOULD RETURN to the UK from Switzerland inspired and confident. He had the suit and the skill. He had permission from the authorities. He had ordered boxes and secured land, and an army of volunteers stood at the ready. Weather conditions looked promising. And on Friday, March 30, Gary sent a message to supporters and volunteers with the subject line "april falls madness."

hi all, thanks for all your support and patience

training has been fantastic and it has all worked out with me achieving my goals, [except the landing]

i now have CAA approval and boxes, 18,600 of them arrive on monday

it seems i may have a window of opportunity to do the build and jump on wed/thurs next week (4th & 5th April), any help would be great

i can let you know on monday evening around 8pm if its a 'go' via email, and where to come

i will be in touch personally with those who have offered equipment/gear

i am very aware of the difficulty of doing things at short notice and that some of you will be able to come and share the experience/help out and some will not, i hope you can make it, please bring a friend to help out. I have no idea how many will be there but i would love for you all to come.

Organising the logistics for this is a bit of a 'mare' as I have no real idea how many people will turn up. I've laid on catering for 100, the CAA are limiting the site to 200 when jumping but there's camping space for everyone! i have also organised showers at the local sport centre for everyone I'm sure there will be enough food to go around but if you are able to help out by bringing some for yourself that would be a great help. Bar-B-Q's are allowed as long as they are on the gravel tracks and stand up on legs and you have an extinguisher

Once I've landed the first round is on me

cheers to you all
gary

Before departing for Switzerland, Gary had been interviewed by the *Sunday Times* of London, the UK's largest paper. The resulting story and photos were finally published on Sunday, April 1. The timing revived speculation that the stunt was merely an elaborate April Fools' gag. But that would be the least of the problems stirred by the story. By Monday, April 2, days before he hoped to land, Gary would be scrambling to deal with a series of crises.

THE TROUBLE BEGAN the morning after the story appeared in the *Sunday Times* as truck drivers delivered loads of cardboard boxes to Gary's landing site, a picturesque centuries-old farm along the Thames, across from the starting area of the Henley Royal Regatta. The drivers called from the road and asked Gary to meet them there.

Driving over Henley Bridge to Remenham Farm, Gary encountered two idling trucks outside the farm's gate. As he approached, his phone rang again. This time it was one of the landowners. In exchange for using the family's land, Gary had promised to make the landing a private event, over concerns about liability if a mob showed up and someone wound up injured. The newspaper story, however, had given away the location.

"I got a phone call from the family that owned the land," Gary would recall, "who said, 'As a result of the news piece yesterday we're pulling the land.'"

Gary stood in the road, stunned, a trapdoor flung open in his mind, and what emerged would not be pretty. He quickly called Nick English and explained in stern tones what had happened. "I said, 'Nick, this one's for you to deal with,'" Gary recalls, citing Bremont's insistence that Gary meet with reporters for advance publicity. "'It's your PR that's caused this to happen!' I threw my teddy in a corner. I was under pressure anyway."

"Over the phone he sounded very upset," Nick remembers. "When I met him, he was very stressed about it. It had all been accumulating for the few days before the jump. He had nowhere to put these boxes. The [semis] are half an hour away, coming down the hill to put the boxes, and he had nowhere . . . As a character, Gary is on edge. You can see the adrenaline running around him. He's that sort of guy. This was the only time I'd seen him under stress, which isn't bad, really, considering he's about to jump out of an airplane without a parachute. I think it would stress most people."

Nick suggested airfields he knew around England, but Gary was adamant they find a location near Henley. Friends and family had committed to helping unpack and stack the boxes. He did not want to alter plans at the last moment.

Calling on local contacts, Nick pulled some strings and within hours had secured a new landing site. "I got onto some local farmers and estate managers we knew, and they helped," he says. "So we ended up finding this great field near a village in Hambleden."

Three miles north of Henley, just over the border in south Buckinghamshire, near a bend in the Thames, the site was called Mill End Farm. Although not as picturesque from the point of view of video—the Thames did not drift darkly in the background—the farm offered an equally good location for landing.

That night, Gary composed a message to his many volunteers. He did not mention the day's turmoil, writing simply and briefly that the weather for Thursday didn't look good after all. Having put one problem behind him, Gary faced another storm on the horizon, a literal storm: the weather was changing fast.

The day after locating a new landing area, Tuesday, April 3, he wrote to his volunteer brigade:

> hi everyone, hope you are all well
>
> its [sic] seems i would be silly to say lets start building on friday
>> the weather is pretty unsettled with wind and some rain forecast
>> we could be lucky and get a good window of opportunity but who
> knows, i run the risk of lots of wet boxes being blown all over everywhere
>> i cannot afford that

thanks for your understanding

will be in touch

gary

MARCH 2012 had been the driest March in the UK since 1953, and the sunniest in England since 1929. In the papers and on TV, they talked of drought and water shortages and hosepipe bans. For the first two days of April, the pattern held; it was dry and unseasonably warm. Then, on April 3, everything changed. Thundershowers broke out ahead of a cold front moving south. Temperatures plummeted all across the country. Heavy drifting snow snarled high passes in Scotland. Snow fell as far south as the Midlands. Across most of England, though, it rained. And rained. And rained some more. It was the start of what would be the wettest April on record across the UK—and the coldest April in more than twenty years.

Gary could see it coming on the weather forecasts he and Sutton studied. On April 4, Gary sent what would turn out to be his final missive for more than a week. The subject line: "the madness goes on."

hi everyone

due to the weather or the unknown weather i have had to call it off this weekend

i am sure you all understand my concerns of setting a box rig [big box rig] that could get wet and blow away

i will now focus on a very real 5 day 'high' window and do it at the right time when everything will be a little more predictable

so go and have a great long weekend and thanks again if you had planned to come to help, i cannot do it without your support

will be in touch soon

best wishes

gary

"It's so British it's untrue," Mark would say about what happened next. As rain continued falling, a battle ensued to keep Gary's $32,000 investment in cardboard dry. "The rain was awful," Nick English recalls, "weeks and weeks and weeks of rain. He was worried about his boxes. There was no point in jumping on a wet mush. He spent ages covering them up, and the tarp would blow off, and we would go back and cover them up."

Flat-packed and stacked in a field at Mill End Farm, the boxes were at the mercy not only of the elements but of cows that roamed the pasture. They were protected only by a massive tentlike structure consisting of eighty tarpaulins, lashed and tied. But wind tore at the tarps, and rivulets of water searched out gaps, threatening to turn the cardboard to pulp.

Gary was joined by Vivienne, Mark Sutton, and Nick and Giles English in securing their investment. "Pretty much every day I was there retying, resealing, getting up there with a brush, brushing water off," Gary says. "It was a bonkers nightmare. It was a logistic operation just keeping them dry."

Vivienne checked on the boxes when Gary couldn't, scrambling on top of the stack in downpours, crawling along to inspect the tarps for gaps where water could get in. She spent a lot of time tying up loose sections. "The cows are in the field wondering what on earth is this great big mass of boxes, and what is that crazy woman doing on top?" For Vivienne, there was no question about what to do. "It was Gary and my money," she says.

The longer it rained, the further he postponed landing, the worse Gary's financial situation grew. Vivienne's long hours at the café were not enough to keep them afloat. Gary needed to return to work. And on April 15, he sent an e-mail update to a patient but increasingly dubious volunteer force. As usual, Gary struck a positive tone.

hi everyone, hope you are all well

thought i would drop you a line to update you
     as you know, the weather has been a little windy and therefore
not right to set a big box rig and jump

i need at least 3 stable days back to back, this does not look likely on the long range forecast for the next 10 days

i have a short break to morocco booked towards the back end of april

before i do the landing i must go back to switzerland or italy, for a few days to get fully up to speed again as i am not now current

thanks for your understanding and continued well wishes, i am humbled by all the great messages and vibes surrounding this stunt

look forward to seeing you all soon, [when the weather changes]

lots of love
gary

Behind the scenes, though, not all the vibes had been exactly great. "We'd go and meet with Nick and Giles and have a chat," Mark recalled. "We'd go to PR and everyone was going, 'Come on, you said you were doing it in April!' We know Jeb is out of the picture, but there's chatter someone might attempt a snow landing. This would be a good time to do it—in spring snow."

With raindrops exploding on the surface of the Thames, Gary and Mark sat in the café drinking coffee and talking for hours, examining their options from all angles. If somebody landed first, well, they had done the best they could. They couldn't take the landing abroad. All they could do was wait for a break in the weather. "He had to turn down a lot of work," Mark said about Gary. "Suddenly he has to go back to work to pay for all of the boxes. Everyone is going, 'It's all rubbish. You said you were going to do it, and nothing has happened.'"

Vivienne had been with Gary for seventeen years, through all of his projects. Although busy operating the café, she could see her husband's frustration. "Mark was the calm, level-headed one," she says. "Very philosophical. It will happen when it happens."

Mark saw in their circumstances a national ethic. "The British, in our psyche, we snatch defeat out of the jaws of victory," he said. "And it was going to be another one of those stories. It was like 'Remember that Gary? He said he was going to do it, then so-and-so did it.' One of the reasons he wanted to do this, he had skied very well and never won. He had represented Britain in kayaking, but he's never won. He'd felt like he'd always come second place. He felt like this was his time to turn around to other people who thought he was a nutter and go, 'I can do this,' and then turn around and say, 'I have done this.' Yes, he was very stressed somebody might take that opportunity away from him."

To cope, Gary resorted to running extreme distances. "He's very good at doing stress if it's a short period of time," Mark said. "If you turn around to him and say, 'Right, I want you to crash that car at eighty miles an hour' or whatever, he's very good at dealing with that. What he's not good at dealing with is the long-term stress of a situation he can't do anything about."

Gary would tie his shoes and blast out the door at a trot, disappearing on grueling long runs, chewing off twenty miles at a time. Sutton remained behind, crunching numbers, scouring forecasts, reaching out to his brother, a commercial airline pilot, for sophisticated weather projections. "He did it all the time when we were away," Mark said about Gary's rambles, "and he did it when we were back, and I think that gave him something else to think about and got him through to the next day."

A month passed as Gary fell into a routine of running, inspecting his boxes, and taking occasional stunt-work assignments. Finally, on May 13, nearly a month after his previous missive, he sent an update to his volunteer corps.

hi everyone,

i thought it was about time i got in touch with you again.

its been a long and now [due to weather] tedious journey, as you know, since the end of march the weather has been totally crap if you are wanting to build a huge box rig and fly into it

i am constantly looking for the right opportunity/weather break.

all i can say is that i do not know when this will be

looking at reports now there seems to be unsettled weather continuing in the UK, bit of a bummer as keeping 18,600 boxes dry
under tarp tents is not easy

i wish to avoid the jubilee weekend as this will be a big weekend
for many, big news for the press and it would be nice for me to get
a little coverage

thanks again for your support

best wishes
gary

ps. remember, there is a drought

GARY COULD finally afford to joke. He and Mark had just returned from a
trip to Brento to brush up on their wingsuit skills after five weeks off.

In Brento they had jumped five times, and they returned to the UK with
confidence at an all-time high. The landing was a stunt, and Gary knew
stunts. He also knew boxes, and he knew he could fly accurately to the
boxes and walk away unhurt. In his mind he had done so hundreds of
times. The only unknown concerned what would happen in his head when
he actually dropped below two hundred feet, too low to reliably deploy a
parachute, and he would have to either land or die trying.

ON FRIDAY, MAY 18, five days after Gary's most recent message to supporters,
Mark finally saw a promising weather forecast. The coming Monday, Tuesday, and Wednesday looked clear. Three consecutive days would allow
enough time to build the box rig, make test flights to satisfy Gary and the
Civil Aviation Authority, and finally go for it. But when the time came to
make a decision, Gary hesitated. After such a long wait, he wanted to be
certain. The next day, he convened with Nick and Giles and Vivienne and
decided to sleep on it one more night. If the weather report called for good
conditions in the morning, he would push the button.

On Sunday, May 20, the forecast held, and Gary blasted a message to his nearly four hundred volunteers. The subject line read "landing."

Hi guys,

Finally the landing is on! It would be great if you could all come to be involved and be a part of history being made!!

Time of arrival and planning

The plan is to gather on Wed at 07:00 at the landing site for breakfast with a briefing from 07:45. The box rig building will then commence and I plan to jump mid afternoon. We'll then need to strip out the box rig to make sure we leave the field as we found it so, I'd appreciate any help later in the day for dismantling before we move on to P-A-R-T-Y! The more people we have the quicker the process!!!!!!

If you have a friend that is fit and willing to help, then please bring them along (and let us have their name too). The location will only be sent to those attending and who respond to this email with the intention of coming as crew.

Catering & Requirements

We have made catering arrangements for 100 people but as we have no idea how many will make it, please do bring an extra sandwich and some water in case we have more than what we've catered for. Please also bring some sunscreen and something to sit on (as we're in a farmer's field!) and be dressed in comfortable clothing and footwear. If you have girlie hands, perhaps bring gloves.

Spectators

This is NOT allowed to be public event, so please don't encourage spectators or friends unless they are able and willing to be part of the box building team.

The message told of a campground nearby where lodging had been arranged, and of vouchers for catering, before concluding: "when it appears in the news and papers, you can say 'I was there!'"

The following day was Monday, and Gary sent out a final message revealing the location as Mill End Farm. On Tuesday he rose early, stopping at the Chocolate Theatre Café for coffees, which he'd delivered to his team at Mill End Farm by 7:30. There was Mark; Robin, the forklift operator; a jumpmaster and stunt coordinator named Dave Emerson; Chris Wright; and two locals named Tim and John.

The forklift ferried pallets of flat-packed boxes to where the rig had been mapped out on the grass, stacking twenty-two thousand pounds of cardboard along a one-hundred-meter line for volunteers to begin building on Wednesday. A representative from the Civil Aviation Authority arrived. So did Andrew Harvey, thundering out of the sky at the controls of his Hughes 500 helicopter, a powerful, fast, nimble, and stable five-seater.

Harvey had come on board the landing project only a month earlier. He jumped at the chance, agreeing to a fee that would cover only his operation costs. "This partner of mine in the helicopter world knew him and had met him a couple of times," Harvey says about Gary, who happens to be a licensed helicopter pilot himself. "And he was having problems finding a pilot in a helicopter who would do what he wanted him to do, i.e., drop him out of a helicopter without a parachute. I said, 'I'm game for that.' It sounds a bit more exciting than the normal sort of stuff when you're bogged down in Health and Safety," he says, referring to Health and Safety Executive, a government agency dedicated to preventing workplace death, injury, and illness. "Can't do this, can't do that, without informing in triplicate, wearing Health and Safety jackets. We're becoming so risk averse and pathetic over here. It was right up my street, really."

A shareholder in a company owned by his family, Harvey was beholden to no one. He consulted with his lawyer, who saw no reason not to join Gary's outfit. "It's nice to be part of something off the wall and a world first and it's waving two figures, not at safety but at Health and Safety. It's nice to do something that's risky that hasn't been stopped by the do-goods of society."

When Harvey turned up Tuesday, the big question concerned where Gary and Mark should exit the chopper. They had been given clearance to jump from no higher than 2,500 feet, and they were facing a variable headwind. Although provisions had been made for virtually every aspect of the landing, they still had to work out details of the flight. For example, how would Gary guide Harvey to the proper position?

Suits on and zipped, Gary and Mark shuffled onto the right skid, clutching the door frame under a shower of rotor wash.

Below, the rolling English countryside ran to the horizon—roads, green fields, dense woods, and the Thames bending and looping back, scrawling its signature on the land. As the sun rose, the air warmed, and red kites wheeled between thermal columns, scanning for small game and carrion.

Once in position, Harvey gave a thumbs-up, "which means 'Okay, guys you've got ten, fifteen seconds.' And I'm just running really slowly. They were outside the aircraft, and the responsibility handed to Mark as stunt master. 'It's your call now. Go, or sit back in the aircraft and strap back in and we'll go back down again.'"

Perched on the skid, the pilots communicated with Harvey through hand signals or shouting. "I don't want to say *telepathy*," Harvey says, "but it's almost facial looks and expressions. *Slow down* and *left a bit* by hand signals and winks and nods and everything else. I've got a headset on. I've got to ask the jumpmaster on the ground is it clear to drop. There are aircraft flying around."

Gary and Mark had honed a countdown process over months on cliffs around Europe. This time, though, Gary had to shout over the whirring blades.

"You ready, Mark?"

"Yeah!"

Mark had a sixth sense of when Gary would go by reading his body position.

"Set," Gary said. "Okay, here we go. Three, two, one . . ." Gary pushed free from the skid, followed a second later by Mark. It was clear that communication was something they would need to work on after the first test jump turned into a disaster. "He jumped off and landed 3,400 meters short," Harvey says.

"Sure enough, we got it wrong," Mark said. "We kept working on dynamics we had used for BASE jumping, but with wind, we kept coming up far too short. And that had a major implication on the jump itself."

Back on the ground, they huddled and worked out their communications and visual references. Harvey would hover over a hill separating the Thames from the A4155 road, lining up for a flight parallel to Skirmett Road, toward the box rig, north into the wind. The second time they came up only 150 meters short of where the rig would be laid out. A third time they landed closer yet, but with wind gusting, they called it an afternoon.

THE DAY WASN'T FINISHED, though. There were media commitments and administrative issues and tending to last-minute logistics. That night, Gary drove to London to fetch his son, Kali, at the airport. He had flown in from Austria, where he was training as a downhill skier.

Climbing into bed that night, Gary would not stop thinking. He did not know how many volunteers would show up, or whether they would build the rig in time, or how the wind would blow. His mind tended to race 24-7, and he was not a great sleeper under the best of circumstances. Still, this was different. Questions ricocheted around his head. *What are you doing? Have you done everything in your power to make this work? Have you missed anything?* Convinced he had dotted all the *i*'s and crossed all the *t*'s, he lay in the dark a long time, hoping desperately for sleep to come. He did not dare get up for a drink of water, or for any other reason, concerned it would keep him awake for good. He listened to the abiding quiet of the house and Vivienne's steady breathing beside him. It would be a long time till dawn, when, having not slept a wink, Gary rose in the blue light to get ready.

HE WAS AT MILL End Farm by 6 a.m. for a live interview with Sky News for breakfast TV. Volunteers parked on Skirmett Road and at a narrow lane lined with rosebushes at the north end of the field. There would be about 120 volunteers that day, tramping in the dew-wet field. They were stunt colleagues, friends and family, friends of friends. Hazel and Chris were there. So was Jon Bonny, Chris Wright, Nick and Giles, Lydia and Kali, all tearing open bundled boxes, pulling out the flat-packed cardboard, and folding it into cubes. Those boxes damp from rain they laid in the grass to dry. In short order, novice box builders became experts, and slowly the rig began to take shape, cubes stacked twelve feet high, forty feet wide, and a hundred meters long.

Nick English was moved by the spirit of fellowship in the field. "It was very Henley," he says, "and not Vegas, put it that way. It was done in a typical British understated way. 'Okay, let's go for it.' One of the situations from the CAA, I believe, is that you couldn't have spectators, so we had to keep it fairly quiet. But there were helpers there, a couple hundred people, but we couldn't invite everyone we wanted, which is a shame in a way that we couldn't make it more of a spectacle. But that's what made it special in a way, this village-type atmosphere. Something pretty incredible is happening in an understated, quite laid-back manner."

Andrew Harvey wondered if perhaps some weren't drawn by morbid curiosity. "It sounds wrong, but it's a British way of dealing with death, making it humorous and funny," he says. "It's a macabre British thing to want to go and watch him kill himself." But, he adds, "they don't *want* him to be killed."

The Civil Aviation Authority and its representative also did not want Gary killed or injured. Gary still needed to demonstrate that he could jump safely, or he risked being shut down.

Harvey considered their biggest obstacle a headwind from the north. The Hughes weighed only sixteen hundred pounds, and with three hundred pounds of humanity perched on the right skid before exit, she tended to slide around in the sky. With the headwind, Gary would need to fly a steep angle, which would translate into increased speed, requiring a hard flare to bleed off momentum for the final approach. He had not practiced any of this during BASE training and could not predict how far he would glide in the headwind.

Following their practice jumps that morning, Mark attempted to huddle with Gary to dial in their exit position and flight. But on the ground,

Gary was in a melee, questions coming from friends, Vivienne, and especially the media, who wanted interviews and updates.

"After you do a jump, you want to come down and go, 'Okay, where did we go wrong? How can we improve this spot where the helicopter goes? Is the wind picking up? How can we monitor that?' Instead of focusing on that side of it, he's getting dragged away to 'So, how are you feeling?' type of conversations for live TV."

Gary reveled in the distractions, soaking in the attention, schmoozing like a campaigning politician, thanking volunteers for their support. He wanted viewers watching on TV to think, *Oh, he's a nice bloke.*

Reporters beseeched Gary to give them a firm time for landing. But he refused. He didn't know when the box rig would be completed or when his training would be done. He would not bow to a TV timetable.

In the meantime, the rig and the temperature continued to rise on the field. It would be an unseasonable high of eighty-two degrees. Vivienne handed out bottled water to volunteers. A friend, Jamie Flynn, crouched in the field, repacking Gary's rigs between jumps.

Back in the air, on his fourth practice jump, Gary dove, taking a steep angle, putting him in an uncomfortable position. But he found his line and landed on target under canopy, right next to the box rig, which after six hours was nearing completion. It was 2 p.m.

AN HOUR EARLIER, Gary had gathered the volunteers and put the matter to a vote: They could break for lunch right then or they could finish the rig, eat lunch, and settle in to watch his attempt to land. Everyone agreed on the latter—forging ahead and finishing. Now they lined up for lunch, and Gary, Vivienne, Sutton, Dave Emerson, and Andrew Harvey huddled to discuss the landing schedule. The weather forecast had called for increasing wind beginning at 1, and they could feel it building. Gary settled on 3:30, relaying the time to Sky News, which had been feeding updates from Mill End Farm back to the studio all day long.

Fixing a plate, Gary sat under a catering tent to eat, but his churning stomach would not allow him to swallow. A vegetarian, he asked the catering crew to set aside some of the roasted-tomato-and-basil pasta and salad so that he would have something for later.

The box rig had been smothered in netting to prevent the boxes from shifting or blowing around in the wind. As a result, the representative from the CAA required Gary to remove his cameras, out of a concern they would snag on the net and cause injury. Mark, too, had been barred from jumping with cameras, over worries of "object fixation," a phenomenon in which a cameraman focuses so intensely on his subject that he loses altitude awareness and forgets to pull. The result: there would be no cameras in the air during the landing attempt, except those mounted in Harvey's chopper.

Throughout training, Mark had done everything by the book, opening at 390 feet and landing practically at the CAA representative's feet to casually stroll up for a chat. This was designed to assure CAA that everything was professional and under control. Hoping his act had made an impression, after lunch Mark approached jumpmaster Dave Emerson about having a word with the CAA man. Emerson came back with word that Mark could use cameras after all. Mark mounted three—a still camera activated by a mouthpiece and two video cams—one with a narrow focus and one with a wide-angle lens. With the wind kicking up a few knots and the clock reading 3:25, it was time to head to the chopper, which sat in the south field, fifty yards from a shade tree. The plan called for Mark and Gary to exit closer to the box rig than they previously had, to compensate for the headwind. During their final briefing, Harvey noted that Gary was "cooler than a cucumber. That may be a bit of bravado. He was laughing and joking."

"If it's all right, we'll go for it," Gary said.

"Sounds good to us," Harvey replied.

The pilots ran through a final check of zippers, clips, cameras, rigs, and pilot-chute handles. Gary checked everything twice, and Mark extracted a promise from his friend. Mark asked that, before reaching a fence line separating the field from the A4155, if Gary wasn't lined up properly, he make a decision to abort and pull.

"This was the first time we had been low, to the envelope, where you have to fly into the boxes or not," Mark would recall. "The canopies we were using were good enough. I was opening at about 275 feet or so. They were working really low. Everything was focusing on 'This had to be one hundred percent perfect.' He had to hit the right spot and walk away uninjured. He couldn't just force a bad situation, like a car crash where he had to be two feet to the left but it sort of worked. He had to be spot-on. So that was one of my major concerns."

Gary promised he would pull if things didn't line up properly.

"This is just an attempt," Mark reminded. "Don't be forced into it. We can come back and do it again."

Mark climbed in the back of the helicopter to go over signals with Harvey. Out the window, he watched Vivienne approach Gary. "Gary and Viv had this really lovely moment," he said. "Viv was very emotional but holding it together. Gary was very emotional but not showing it."

When Vivienne turned and walked across the field toward the box rig, Gary watched her go for a long time. She did not look back. That's when Gary told himself: *Snap out of it! Get yourself together, Gary! Time to go to work! Get your game on!*

Hopping into the chopper in the seat next to Harvey, he closed the door. "Let's go," he said.

Harvey would recall that Gary then gave him a "knowing look." Harvey sensed that Gary was going for it, no matter what. "I knew he was going to do it at that time," he says. "I don't know why. I can't tell you. It was just something in his eye I picked up."

AS HARVEY LIFTED the Hughes into the sky, Gary waved down to Dave Emerson, the jumpmaster. From up close, the box rig looked like something built from LEGOS. But from the air, the rig grew smaller, resembling a postal parcel wrapped in brown paper and awaiting an address. Friends and family assembled a distance to the left of the boxes, near the shadow of a tree line.

In the chopper, Gary focused on breathing, controlling his heart rate and emotions. His mind relaxed. And Harvey continued to have premonitions. Three-quarters of a mile from the rig, he brought the Hughes into a hover. They were 2,400 feet up, and he would later say that it was as if some force above *knew*. The chopper had been bucking in swirling wind all day. But then "she just sits as smooth as a baby's bottom," he says. "She didn't even twitch . . . it flew itself absolutely perfectly. And I know helicopters are inanimate objects, but she knew that was the *time*, because she was as good as gold. I can't explain. I wasn't flying any differently. I've flown the bloody thing for six thousand hours—for twenty-five years—these types of machines, and it just *poof!* It was really quite strange."

Gary, though, was counting on training, not divine forces, to carry him through. *This is it, Gary! You are known as One-Take Gary in the TV-and-film world. And yes, for sure, if it's not right, pull out.* But in his heart, he knew he would not bail.

Emerson cleared Harvey to release the pilots, and Harvey gave them thumbs-up. They had fifteen seconds to get it together and go. Shoulder to shoulder on the skid, they shouted over the machine clatter.

"You ready, Mark?!"

"Yeah!"

"Set! Okay, here we go! Three, two, one . . ." And just as they had practiced in training, the pilots left the chopper in tandem, Sutton tight to Gary, disappearing out of Harvey's sight.

Eager to witness firsthand what would be a historic feat, he rotated the chopper 180 degrees, looking left, careful not to catch the pilots in his rotors as he descended fifteen hundred feet per minute. The pilots moved faster still, bleeding off altitude.

Vivienne had scarcely made her way across the field to the box rig when she was alerted to turn to watch Gary exit the chopper. Right away she could see Gary veer back and forth as if caught in terrible turbulence.

Harvey could see, too, through his windshield that Gary was obviously unstable. It looked like he was in trouble.

FlySight readings later revealed that Gary averaged a glide angle of 2:1 most of the flight, even as he attempted to compensate for the twisting motion by flopping hard in the opposite direction. He looked as though he might flip at any second.

Mark thought Gary must be mentally overloaded, and he expected his friend to deploy his chute at any moment as they had discussed. But Gary never reached for his pilot chute as he approached five hundred feet of altitude. And crossing the fence line they had discussed earlier as the point of no return, something unexpected happened: he came out of the dive and suddenly stabilized.

Spectators on the ground recognized that Gary had crossed the point below which he could no longer abort. Nick English stood near the box rig, thinking, *It seems so natural, this chap falling through the sky . . .*

Gary heard a roar from the crowd, and a smile crept across his face. There was no ground rush, only an awareness of diminishing altitude as he homed in on the boxes. In the field approaching the rig, extra boxes had been arranged so that, viewed from above, they resembled an arrow pointing the way and the words GO GARY.

From the helicopter, Gary appeared to be moving too fast as he closed in on the boxes. With a hard flare, the FlySight would reveal, he reached an almost 8:1 glide angle, traveling at 69.7 miles an hour forward and less than 10 vertically. Watching Gary race over the boxes, Harvey had his doubts. "He might get this wrong," he recalls thinking. Mark had a similar thought. Gary appeared to be moving too fast, with too much glide. "He's going to fly straight off the end of the boxes and he's now too late to deploy," Mark remembered. That was when Mark noticed Gary's shadow on the boxes. His shadow directly below meant Gary was close to making contact.

For Gary, time seemed to expand, and he noticed details. He remembered not to tuck into a protective ball too early, which would cause him to drop out of the sky. He noted the way every eight feet, a two-foot gap between boxes would allow them to move on impact and soften his landing. The gaps created a grid. One second closer, though, and all he could see was brown. Tensing reflexively, the result of seventeen years of working on the Stunt Register, Gary dropped his left shoulder and pressed his chin to his chest.

The FlySight would reveal that he hit the boxes at seventy miles an hour, plowing through the cardboard for fifty feet, at a 6:1 angle, penetrating eight feet down into semidarkness.

Seeing Gary skid into the boxes near dead center, Mark savored the moment, before suddenly snapping out of his reverie, and pulling at 285 feet. Drifting slowly under canopy, he scanned the boxes for some sign of Gary. But Mark had no radio, and no way of knowing whether his friend was injured—or alive.

Swirling above in the chopper, Harvey scanned for some sign of movement, thinking that the landing appeared "bloody fast!"

Thirty seconds ticked by before Vivienne's walkie-talkie crackled. It was Gary. "I'm absolutely, one hundred percent okay," he said.

Vivienne raised her hands and screamed and yelled to the crowd that Gary was okay, and everyone screamed and yelled back.

Buried and balancing precariously four feet up on shifting cardboard, Gary had struggled to reach the radio in his pocket. He wanted to soak in the sensation and savor his achievement alone for a moment. It would not happen.

A cluster of men charged into the boxes, picking their way to Gary, who several minutes later, emerged from among the boxes, suit unzipped, a big grin on his face and not a stitch out of place. Vivienne was waiting to throw herself into his arms.

WEARING BOARDSHORTS, a purple Chocolate Theatre Café T-shirt, and a black baseball cap, Gary carried a magnum of champagne by the neck, half trotted across the field to where TV cameras and reporters waited. Someone called out, "How do you feel, Gary?"

"I'm in a strange space, if I'm totally honest."

Tearing down the boxes would take four hours and by 7:30 a celebration was under way at the Chocolate Theatre Café, where Gary and Mark fielded endless phone calls from reporters and news agencies seeking comment, photos, and video. New York Times reporter Mary Pilon called Tony in Zephyrhills, catching him at the store, where he was buying champagne to toast at his shop with his workers. "I'm as high as a kite," he said.

Jeb Corliss had watched Gary's landing online, his dream of building a multimillion-dollar runway now dead. He was back in Venice, bones mended but fighting an infected skin graft on his right shin that required forty-two hours in a hyperbaric chamber to aid healing. He was weeks away from jumping again.

"We had never heard of this guy," Jeb told the *Times* about Gary, speaking for his fellow pilots. "We thought it was crazy."

"It's one of the most amazing things I've ever seen in my life," he added. "Because of movies, people don't really understand what they witnessed. It's monumental for a human to land at those speeds. It took an enormous amount of courage."

Interviewed by *Popular Mechanics* in the coming days, Jeb would call the landing "the greatest stunt ever performed" and say that he bore no grudge against Gary. *Shōgun* still fresh in his mind, he invoked Bushido. "I go by the Samurai code—if you are vanquished by your enemy, you must give him respect," he said. "There's nothing I can say other than 'Congratulations, bro.'"

GARY WOULD LEAVE the party at the café by 10 p.m. and collapse into bed, but for another night, sleep did not come. He savored the feeling of having stuck it to those who had dismissed him as a wobbler. *What's this idiot doing?* they'd thought. *He's going to kill himself!*

On his feet again before dawn, Gary drove the M25 ring road to Stansted Airport, northeast of London, to drop off Kali for a return flight to Austria. He was on set by seven, working to recoup some of the $50,000 he had shelled out for the landing. The crew offered congratulations but it would be a long day of filling out paperwork and coordinating a rape scene on a moving train for actors dressed in Edwardian garb. Calls and messages poured in from media outlets hungry to line him up for interviews or appearances on their shows.

When Mark got a look at Gary that night after work, his friend "appeared shot to pieces" from exhaustion and excitement.

"No, forget it," Mark urged Gary about consenting to another live interview. "Go and eat, go back to sleep. Go to work tomorrow. You're on BBC tomorrow night. You've got to start looking after yourself."

But Gary did not sleep, and on Friday he was back on set. Over the weekend he sat for television newsmagazine programs. He had been in all the papers. Robert Pečnik sent congratulations as did a good many other members of the wingsuit and BASE fraternities.

By Monday, once the news cycle had mostly run its course, Gary was barely on his feet, sleepwalking through work. He had slept perhaps twelve hours since landing five days earlier and felt on the verge of a breakdown.

That night he swallowed a sleep aid. When the pills took hold, the spell was broken, and Gary fell into the profound and peaceful slumber of the dead. When he awoke the next day, Gary understood that he had landed, but he could not recall whether or not he had dreamed.

EPILOGUE

*I*t would turn out to be a big year for skydiving and parachute sports. The following month, on June 16, as part of a live special broadcast on ABC surrounding daredevil Nik Wallenda's wire walk over Niagara Falls, Jeb's flight through the cave at Tianmen Shan was designated the "No. 1 Megastunt" in history. One month later, on July 27, Gary and Mark took part in the opening ceremony of the London Olympics, which were directed by Danny Boyle, Gary's old friend from the movie *The Beach*, for whom Gary had done stunt work.

At the Games, Gary stood in as a stunt double for the queen, wearing a gray wig and a salmon gown. Mark dressed in a tuxedo and played James Bond. They parachuted from a chopper eight hundred feet over Olympic Stadium, opening parachutes emblazoned with the Union Jack, and landed on a nearby bridge. The notoriety put them back on television and in the papers for a while.

On October 14, Felix Baumgartner, the pioneering professional BASE jumper, rode in a capsule beneath a balloon 128,100 feet up into the stratosphere for the Stratos Project, sponsored by Red Bull. When he plunged out, Baumgartner set the record for the highest free fall and broke the speed of sound during descent, plummeting at more than 830 miles an hour. The same week, Jeb, Iiro, and Frank Yang returned to China for the debut of the World Wingsuit League, a three-quarter-mile wingsuit race they organized that began at the platform on Tianmen Shan. Although he was jumping again, Jeb could not compete due to lingering injuries to his knee. Some of the world's foremost pilots took part, including Joby, Tony,

Jeff Nebelkopf, Jhonathan Florez, Jokke, and Douggs; Julian Boulle wound up winning.

Jokke continued his career, backed by Red Bull, wowing viewers with footage flying fresh lines all over the world. Matt Gerdes formed a wingsuit manufacturing company called Squirrel Suits, Inc. and eventually settled in Seattle. Barry Holubeck relocated to Switzerland. Douggs, too. He and Roberta each found a niche, and their voices, hosting their own Web series.

For Gary, there was no great windfall resulting from his wingsuit landing. He struggled just to find stunt work in TV and film. Were employers thinking, *Wow, he's done that, he's done the Olympics, we can't afford him?* Or, *We won't even bother ringing him because he'll be so busy because of what he's done?* Gary didn't know.

He had been enriched in other ways. On May 25, 2013, a year and two days after landing, Gary brought some visitors out to Mill End Farm. The place still conjured powerful feelings. "I'm trembling," he said on a sunny day with raptors wheeling overhead. "I'm going all goose bumpy putting myself back there again. It's never something that's going to go away. It's wonderful." Driving back to Henley that morning, he mused on mortality, noting how first a man's mortal body goes, then he dies again once his name and deeds are forgotten. "You die a second time when people stop talking about you, when no one knows your name," he said. The first death was inevitable, but he was hoping to forestall the second. That's what the wingsuit landing had been about.

On August 14, Mark Sutton was killed in Switzerland, while he and Tony were flying wingsuits. They had jumped out of a helicopter together, and Mark struck a ridge in the Swiss Alps along the French border near Trient. He was forty-two. Sutton's death made news worldwide for a few days.

Two months later, on September 28, approaching two years after crashing at Table Mountain, Jeb returned to China to pull off a spectacular wingsuit stunt. He jumped from a helicopter and, at 122 miles per hour, sliced through a crack sixteen feet wide in Jianlang Mountain, in eastern China. "It's the craziest thing I've ever done," he said about the feat he referred to as the Flying Dagger.

He had been so frightened in the chopper that he began crying and considered calling off the jump altogether. He reminded himself that he would die anyway, eventually. And he knew that if he couldn't continue, he would be finished. He would never jump again. And then who would he be?

Two weeks later, at the World Wingsuit League championship, a Hungarian wingsuit pilot named Victor Kovats was killed when he crashed into Tianmen Shan during practice. He was one of a record twenty-two pilots killed that year.

The casualties continued into 2014. In March, Dan Vicary of New Zealand, Ludo Woerth of France, and Brian Drake, an American, jumped from a helicopter over the Loetschental valley in Bern, Switzerland, and miscalculated their line, crashing into an alpine field. Vicary, thirty-three, and Woerth, thirty-four, were dead when rescuers arrived. Drake, thirty-three, hung in a coma for days before dying. They had been among the most experienced pilots in the world.

Joby continued planning and training for another first: an attempt to climb Everest and launch from the summit with a custom suit designed by Tony, a multimillion-dollar spectacle to be broadcast live by the Discovery Channel. By April Joby had made it to base camp, at 17,598 feet, with a production crew. On the morning of April 18, he was in a tent when he heard a terrific roar from above. Joby stuck his head from his tent to watch an avalanche of ice and snow half a mile away slam into a group of Sherpa guides that had just set out to carry provisions up the mountain. Sixteen guides were killed, three of them working for Joby's expedition. It was the worst tragedy in the history of climbing the mountain, and it canceled Joby's project and effectively shut down the spring season on Everest.

On May 25, Jeff Nebelkopf jumped from a Cessna Caravan at 13,000 feet over the east coast of Florida with five other wingsuit pilots. He peeled off with another jumper for a flight to 2,500 feet, where the other pilot deployed a parachute. Around 1,500 feet Jeff pitched his pilot chute, witnesses on the ground would recall. A subsequent investigation would reveal it was slow to inflate due to a packing error. Jeff's parachute opened with line twists that caused his canopy to begin spinning. At the same time, an automatic activation device fired to deploy his reserve pilot chute at 1,000 feet. The reserve pilot chute and bridle wrapped around his main parachute's suspension lines, and his main chute spun more rapidly until Jeff impacted the ground hard, killing him instantly. He was forty-three and had been married less than a year.

There were happier outcomes, too.

Karina Hollekim endured fourteen surgeries on her shattered legs, and a year passed before she attempted first steps following her accident. Hers was a long, grueling recovery. In January 2010, on an early morning in Hemsedal, Norway, she settled onto a chairlift and skied again. She would never regain her form. Still, it was a triumph on rebuilt legs. In 2014 she gave birth to a son. "It has turned my life upside down," she would write about being a mother. "I guess that's what we love about this life . . . its ability to turn and change in an instant."

Loic Jean-Albert moved back to Reunion Island to raise a family and work as a commercial pilot. He still skydives with his parents and wife for fun, but he no longer BASE jumps.

In the first months of 2015, Jeb and Gary continued to jump, searching for support to make real their dreams of more spectacular stunts.

Sometimes while asleep we are falling, or flying, and when we wake we recall that sensation, accompanied by the most vivid imagery. Clinicians tell us that our brain's occipital lobe, which processes visual information, becomes highly active during sleep. In the meantime, our brain paralyzes our body to prevent us from acting out our dreams and causing injury, while struggling to interpret signals from our vestibular system, which controls balance and spatial orientation. All of which combines to create sensations our brains interpret as falling, or flying.

For most of us, those feelings are integrated into our dreams. For a few, that's waking life.

ACKNOWLEDGMENTS

Writing may be a solitary exercise, but no writer operates without considerable assistance, and this book owes a debt to a great many talented and articulate people, particularly Jeb Corliss and Gary Connery, gifted raconteurs both. Their generosity and patience while taking time to explain and share many personal aspects of their lives made them essential partners in this enterprise. Jeb sat through more than one hundred hours of interviews and allowed me to accompany him in the United States, Switzerland, China, and South Africa. Gaining access to a subculture as notoriously closed to outsiders as BASE jumping would have presented some obvious challenges, too, if not for his guidance.

Gary also endured dozens of hours of telephone interviews and reminisced about his landing while providing a walking and driving tour of Henley-on-Thames, Mill End Farm, and the surrounding English countryside. I also want to thank him for making his military records available.

Despite their reputation for secrecy, the BASE-jumping and wingsuit-flying practitioners I met were warm, friendly, and delightfully down to earth. I particularly want to thank the following people for indulging my many questions: Joby Ogwyn, Chris "Douggs" McDougall, Anne Helliwell, Todd Shoebotham, Nick DiGiovanni, Karin Sako, Tony Uragallo, Jeff Nebelkopf, Karina Hollekim, Matt Gerdes, Roberta Mancino, Barry Holubeck, Iiro Seppänen, Loïc Jean-Albert, Luigi Cani, Maria von Egidy, Gary Cunningham, Jokke Sommer, Stephan Mueller, Jhonathan Florez, Brian Drake, Julian Boulle, Taya Weiss, Steph Davis, Gary Kremer, Miles Daisher, and Mike Swanson. I especially want to remember Mark Sutton, whose many contributions were invaluable, and Mario Richard, who gave me a lift in Switzerland and offered to take me jumping; both men died within a week of each other in August 2013 while flying wingsuits.

While traveling, a writer is bound to meet many good-hearted people, and I'm thankful to the following for their fellowship and conversation: in Switzerland, Mark and Ursula Nolan; Dr. Bruno Durrer; Christian and Andreas Gubser; Gian Autenrieth, who gave the Web "Grinding the Crack"; Marc Dorian from CBS; and Kurt and Thorsten Hoefle.

In China, I discovered many curious people whose humanity heartens me when I recall those times. Frank Yang was essential in assisting hapless foreigners. I thank him for never leaving me behind, even when I deserved to be. The translation of Minos "the Wizard" Degel and Monica were essential. Gigi Fitzmorris demonstrated from whom her son derives his backbone and shared her family's fascinating and adventurous history. Nic "Moose" Good's droll wit and companionship kept a leash on my sanity. "Papi" Sommer and Mr. and Mrs. Eskoo Seppänen served as an example for supporting your children's dreams, no matter how unusual.

In South Africa, I want to thank the aptly named Good family, for their warm hospitality and hot meals. Thanks to Kristian Schmidt for unparalleled views of Camps Bay, and Teddy Msuku for a reminder to not take a moment for granted. Thanks also to the crew from HBO's *Real Sports:* Spencer Wilking, Tim Walker, Jon Frankel, Chris Everson, and Ken Geraghty. In Florida, thanks to the folks at TonySuits, Inc., especially Tony's lovely wife, Mary, for tolerating my intrusions during work time. In Britain, thanks to Vivienne Connery as well as Chris and Hazel Bullock. Jon Bonny, Andrew Harvey, and Nick English also provided essential assistance.

Some men of science patiently explained theorems related to what's necessary to fly and land a wingsuit, both from a technical and a mental standpoint. Roy Haggard, a true believer of unwavering confidence, convinced me early on that talk of a landing was more than mere bravado. Jean Potvin not only believed a landing could be achieved, but explained how aeronautics and physics said so, too. Marvin Zuckerman has made it his life's work to study the personalities who live on the edge, and occasionally cross over.

I would never have had an opportunity to begin this project if not for some folks at the *New York Times*. They not only consented to my wishes to write about arcane sports, but actually encouraged me. Many at the *Times* were helpful and kind, but I specifically want to mention Tom Jolly, Jason Stallman, and especially Bob Goetz, who not only saw the early potential in a story of a possible wingsuit landing, but pushed to get it on page one. Bob later read an early draft of the manuscript and provided valuable suggestions. Others who took the time to comment on drafts include Sachin Shenolikar and Nick Friedman.

For their understanding and support, when this project took me from family obligations, I thank my parents and siblings, Andrew Higgins and Emily O'Connor. My wife, Ann, is my first reader. Her patience and pep talks urged me on. Our wonderful sons, Ryan and Shane, inspire me every day.

At The Penguin Press, Laura Stickney first saw promise in my proposal. Colin Dickerman kept the fires burning for two years. Every page has benefited from the influence of Ben Platt, whose editing is as strong and concise as his name. I also want to thank Will Palmer for smoothing my copy and nailing down facts, and Ann Godoff for her support.

Special thanks are reserved for Todd Shuster, my agent extraordinaire at Zachary Shuster Harmsworth. Todd is a writer's best friend. He believed in me and the book before I knew I had anything worth writing about. He and Rachel Sussman taught me to craft a proposal, and Todd steered me through the publishing process. During the writing of *Bird Dream*, Todd's wise counsel encouraged me to push past obstacles. Performing his job with consummate poise, Todd occasionally made me laugh when I badly needed to.

NOTES

Everything in the book, from events to dialogue and other details, were either what I saw or heard myself or were told to me directly by people who saw or heard them, or were recorded somewhere, on video or in writing. Most details were corroborated by multiple sources. Nothing was made up.

Interviews with Jeb Corliss, Gary Connery, and many others numbered in the hundreds, and in the interest of keeping the notes as concise as possible, they are not cited; nor are well-established or uncontroversial facts.

This book benefited from the outstanding research of other authors. Some of the books I've relied on for the history, characters, and technical aspects of BASE jumping include *The Great Book of BASE* by Matt Gerdes and *Confessions of an Idiot* by Christopher McDougall. Michael Abrams has written a thoroughly researched and humorous history of wingsuits, *Birdmen, Batmen, and Skyflyers*, which was very helpful. Two books assisted greatly with understanding the neurochemical and psychological components of fear: *Transcending Fear* by Brian Germain and *Extreme Fear: The Science of Your Mind in Danger* by Jeff Wise.

Abbreviations
AP: The Associated Press
BBS: Birdmen, Batmen, and Skyflyers
GBB: The Great Book of BASE
NYDN: New York Daily News
NYT: New York Times

INTRODUCTION
Most of the material in this section was drawn from my firsthand observations and interviews while in Switzerland, July 2011.

1   **"Who are these":** *The New Oxford Annotated Bible with the Apocrypha* (Oxford: Oxford University Press, 1991), p. 949, Old Testament.

1   **Jeb's Iconic Jumps (Jeb had plunged):** A 10:00 compilation video from 2003 titled *A Year in the Life*, 2003; *The Ground Is the Limit*, 2005 documentary film by Iiro Seppänen.

3   **Hinderrugg:** The official spelling of the mountain, in English, according to the official Web site of Switzerland Tourism is "Hinterrugg," http://www.myswitzerland.com/en-us/hinterrugg-the-highest-of-the-seven-churfirsten-peaks.html.

3   *20/20:* "Superhumans: Bird Man," ABC *20/20*, July 22, 2011, a segment produced by

Marc Dorian about Jeb's July 16, 2011, flight at the Crack, http://abcnews.go
.com/2020/video/corliss-jeb-fly-bird-birdman-wings-super-2020-14140045.

3   **Wingsuits:** "Can We Fly?," Nancy Shute, *National Geographic*, September 2011
cover story; *BBS* by Michael Abrams (New York: Three River Press, 2006), pp. 3–10.

7   **high-rise hotels:** *A Year in the Life 2003, The Ground Is the Limit, 2005*, a documentary film by Iiro, Seppänen.

7   **Empire State Building:** "Been There, Leaped Off That," Bill Hutchinson, *NYDN*,
April 28, 2006, http://www.nydailynews.com/archives/news/leaped-article-1.638131;
"Cops Stop Fall Guy. Foil Empire State Jumper," Celeste Katz, Oren Yaniv, and
Leo Standora, *NYDN*, April 28, 2006, http://www.nydailynews.com/archives/news/
cops-stop-fall-guy-foil-empire-state-jumper-article-1.606079; "Metro Briefing, New
York: Manhattan: Parachute Attempt Stopped," Karim Fahim, *NYT*, April 28, 2006,
(http://query.nytimes.com/gst/fullpage.html?res=9E06E5DD103FF93BA15757C0A
9609C8B63.

7   **without using a chute:** GoFast Sports & Beverage Company press release, announcing
plans to land a wingsuit, November 23, 2004, http://www.zoominfo.com/#!search/
profile/person?personId=139317216&targetid=profile; "Flying Humans, Hoping to
Land with No Chute," Matt Higgins, *NYT*, December 10, 2007, http://www.nytimes
.com/2007/12/10/sports/othersports/10flying.html?ex=1354942800&en=fa831ea44c
1a5ff7&ei=5090&partner=rssuserland&emc=rss; "The Aerialist," *Outside* magazine, July 2011, 80; *BBS*, Abrams, pp. 268–75.

8   **"We laugh":** Jean Potvin, telephone interview, October 2007.

8   **"Anything's possible":** Roy Haggard, telephone interview, October 2007.

8   **"not possible":** Jeb Corliss, telephone interview, November 2007.

9   **viral:** "Grinding the Crack," Gian Autenrieth, ed., which can be viewed at YouTube
.com, http://www.youtube.com/watch?v=TWfph3iNC-k.

10   **Byron:** "Lake Geneva as Shelley and Byron Knew It," Tony Perottet, *NYT*, May 27,
2011, http://www.nytimes.com/2011/05/29/travel/lake-geneva-as-byron-and-shelley-
knew-it.html?pagewanted=all.

11   **thirty-five Swiss francs:** Hotel Horner website, http://www.hornerpub.ch/Neue%20
Seiteeeee/neue_seite_1eeeee_Hotel.htm.

12   **where jumpers go to die:** Ursula Nolan interview, July 2011.

12   **seven jumpers were killed:** Dr. Bruno Durrer interview, July 2011; Swiss BASE Association, Lauterbrunnen BASE Fatality List, http://www.basejumper.ch/index
.php?option=com_content&task=view&id=12&Itemid=26.

12   **"Reckless":** "Reckless Jumpers Annoy Valley Dwellers," Von Bruno Petroni, *Berner Zeitung*, Christopher Cotter, tr., http://www.bernerzeitung.ch/region/thun/
Ruecksichtslose-Jumper-aergern-Talbewohner-/story/28221050; "Village Appalled
by Thrill Seekers' Deaths," Lukas Eberle, *Der Spiegel*, http://www.spiegel.de/
international/europe/base-jumping-in-switzerland-village-appalled-by-thrill
-seekers-deaths-a-784896-2.html.

13   **High Nose:** Swiss BASE Association, http://www.basejumper.ch/index.php?option=
com_content&task=view&id=4&Itemid=58.

14   **Seven Summits:** Jobyogwyn.com, http://www.jobyogwyn.com/about/ and http://
www.prweb.com/releases/wingsuit/everest/prweb5255324.htm.

14 *Adventure Wanted:* http://natgeotv.com/me/adventure-wanted/about.
15 **fifteen-second plunge:** Swiss BASE Association, http://www.basejumper.ch/index .php?option=com_content&task=view&id=4&Itemid=58.
15 **Depression, a heyday:** *BBS,* Abrams, 39–109.
16 **memoir:** *Confessions of an Idiot,* Chris "Douggs" McDougall (Base Dreams, 2009).
16 **Red Bull Air Force:** Redbullairforce.com, http://redbullairforce.com/pilots.

CHAPTER 1: BEGINNINGS . . .
21 **For centuries:** "A Brief History of the Parachute," Byron Kerman, Popular Mechanics .com, http://www.popularmechanics.com/technology/aviation/safety/a-brief-history -of-the-parachute#slide-1; *Parachuting: The Skydiver's Handbook,* Dan Poynter and Mike Turoff (Santa Barbara, CA: Para Publishing, 2007), pp. 85–92.
22 **Frederick R. Law:** "'Hero' Leaps Off Bridge," *NYT,* February 17, 1912, http://query .nytimes.com/mem/archive-free/pdf?res=F20612F63C5813738DDDAE0994DA40 5B828DF1D3; "Parachute Leap Off Statue of Liberty," *NYT,* February 3, 1912, http:// query.nytimes.com/mem/archive-free/pdf?res=F40916FB3C5813738DDDAA0894 DA405B828DF1D3; "Wall Street Sees a 500-Foot Leap," *NYT,* April 9, 1912, http:// query.nytimes.com/mem/archive-free/pdf?res=F70D14F73F5813738DDDA00894 DC405B828DF1D3; "Leap Year 1912," Lisa Ritter, *Parachutist,* February 2012.
22 **Mike Pelkey:** "Skydivers Leap Off El Capitan," *Los Angeles Times,* July 26, 1966; "Base Jumping Pioneer Falls to His Death," United Press International, October 23, 2006, http://www.upi.com/Sports_News/2006/10/23/Base-jumping-pioneer-falls-to-his -death/UPI-75451161621501/; "Someone You Should Know . . . 15 Questions with Mike Pelkey," Cynthia Lynn, basejumper.com, http://www.basejumper.com/Articles/ Interviews_and_Profiles/Someone_You_Should_Know . . . 15_Questions_with . . ._ Michael_Pelkey_868.html; "Mike Pelkey: El Capitan BASE Jump 1966," Mike Pelkey, basejumper.com, June 18, 2007, http://www.basejumper.com/Articles/Stories/Mike_ Pelkey_El_Capitan_BASE_jump_1966_771.html.
24 **the name BASE:** *GBB,* Gerdes, pp. 164–77; interviews in Augest 2011 with Nick Di-Giovanni, Anne Helliwell, and July 2011 with Todd Shoebotham; "Who Needs an Airplane?," Jack McCallum, *Sports Illustrated,* August 26, 1985, http://sportsillus trated.cnn.com/vault/article/magazine/MAG1119795/1/index.htm; "The Acronym," Nick DiGiovanni, basejumper.com, June 19, 2007, http://www.basejumper.com/ Articles/Stories/The_Acronym_786.html; "Know Your BASE Jumping History," Nick DiGiovanni, apexbase.com, https://www.apexbase.com/base-jumping-history -by-nick-di-giovanni; "Stars: The 2012 National Skydiving Museum Hall of Fame Inductees," *Parachutist,* August 2012, p. 63; "BASE Jumping: How It Began," Nick DiGiovanni, officialbridgeday.com, http://officialbridgeday.com/bridge-blog/tag/ nick-digiovanni/; "BASE Jumpers Fall for Thrill-Seeking Lifestyle," Cynthia Dizikes, *Chicago Tribune,* April 22, 2011, http://articles.chicagotribune.com/2011-04-22/ news/ct-met-basejumping-20110421_1_base-jumpers-thrill-arrest; "Dropping in the Series," Stephen Kiesling, *Sports Illustrated,* October 9, 1989, http://sportsillustrated .cnn.com/vault/article/magazine/MAG1068903/1/index.htm; "Twin Tower Para-chuter," C. J. Sullivan, *New York Press,* June 4, 2002, http://nypress.com/twin-tower

-parachuter/; "BASE Jumping Historical Time Line," *Blinc Magazine*, http://www
.blincmagazine.com/forum/wiki/Timeline.

25 rain: The Weather Channel, Average Monthly Averages for Perris, CA, http://www
.weather.com/weather/wxclimatology/monthly/graph/92570.

25 lawns: "California Town to Spray-Paint Lawn Bald Spots," AP, March 18, 2009,
http://www.nbcnews.com/id/29759735/#.Upzy0if-Xwg.

25 parachute: "How a Parachute Works," United States Parachute Association.

28 "gear": *GBB*, Gerdes, pp. 62–75.

28 Basic Research: *GBB*, p. 167.

29 Bridge Day: Officialbridgeday.com, http://www.officialbridgeday.com/bridge-day
-history-facts.

29 X Games: *The Insider's Guide to Action Sports*, Matt Higgins (New York: Scholastic
Reference, 2006).

29 dying in such far-flung locales: BASE Fatality List, *Blinc Magazine*, http://www
.blincmagazine.com/forum/wiki/BASE_Fatality_List.

30 physiology of fear: *Transcending Fear*, Brian Germain (Brian Germain, 2007),
pp. 22–28; "Terrorists at the Tea Party," Amanda Ripley, *National Geographic Adventure*, August 2008.

30 BASE Fatality List: *Blinc Magazine*, Blincmagazine.com, http://www.blincmagazine
.com/forum/wiki/BASE_Fatality_List.

31 catechism: *GBB*, Gerdes, pp. 82–163; Todd Shoebotham interview, October 2011.

32 printed table: *GBB*, p. 262.

32 With the ground coming up: Technical, mechanical, and ethical aspects of BASE,
particularly the sequence and perils, were drawn from *GBB* and conversations with
Todd Shoebotham, October 2011.

CHAPTER 2: INTERNATIONAL LAUNCH

Much of the material in this chapter was drawn from interviews with Gary Connery from
January through May 2013, and from access to his military records.

35 3 PARA: http://www.army.mod.uk/infantry/regiments/parachute/24106.aspx.

36 Consolidated Rigging: *GBB*, p. 168; Consolidated Rigging, http://www.crmojo.com/;
"BEFORE YOU LEAP: Where, When, and How to BASE Jump . . . or Not," Anna
Bahney, *NYT*, October 25, 2003, http://www.nytimes.com/2002/10/25/travel/
before-you-leap-where-when-and-how-to-base-jump-or-not.html.

36 Deep Purple: http://www.billboard.com/artist/300672/deep-purple/biography.

38 Bad Gastein: *Sports Illustrated*, February 17, 1958, http://sportsillustrated.cnn.com/
vault/article/magazine/MAG1001833/1/index.htm.

39 Saslong: Saslong.org, http://www.saslong.org/?pagid=89&artid=36&lang=eng.

41 not the first: "Para Death Video," Mike Sullivan and John Kay, *The Sun* (UK), May
22, 1992.

CHAPTER 3: A CHILD CALLED X-RAY MUJAHIDEEN

Much of the material in this chapter was drawn from interviews with Jeb Corliss, Todd Shoebotham, Anne Helliwell, Gigi Fitzmorris, Shawn Stern, and Brian Terwilliger from July through October 2011.

47   Georgia O'Keeffe: OKeeffemuseum.org, http://www.okeeffemuseum.org/about -georgia-okeeffe.html.

50   *hikikomori:* "Hikikomori: Why Are So Many Japanese Men Refusing to Leave Their Rooms?," William Kremer and Claudia Hammond, BBC World Service, July 4, 2013, http://www.bbc.co.uk/news/magazine-23182523; "Shutting Themselves In," Maggie Jones, *New York Times Magazine,* January 15, 2006.

51   "counterphobia": "The Counterphobic Defense in Children," Elva Poznanski, MD, and Bette Arthur, PhD, *Child Psychiatry and Human Development,* vol. 1, no. 3, Spring1971,http://deepblue.lib.umich.edu/bitstream/handle/2027.42/43947/10578_ 2005_Article_BF01433642.pdf;jsessionid=FA0975354D9051F59C8A51D5F8BF4C 15?sequence=1.

51   insurance brokerage: "2 Execs Buy Benefit Adviser Pacific Resources," *Chicago Tribune,* February 13, 2012, http://articles.chicagotribune.com/2012-02-13/business/ chi-2-execs-buy-benefit-adviser-pacific-resources-20120213_1_employee-benefits -pacific-resources-adviser.

52   *MTV Sports:* "John Vincent Says He'd Jump Off Gateway Arch Again," Pat McGonigle, KSDK.com, February 25, 2013, http://archive.ksdk.com/news/article/ 365208/3/John-Vincent-says-hed-jump-off-Gateway-Arch-again.

53   "When I was sixteen": This and the following quote from Fitzmorris came from *Daredevils: The Human Bird,* Firecracker Films, which aired in September 2009 on Channel 4 in the UK, http://www.firecrackerfilms.com/documentaries/daredevils -the-human-bird/.

53   eight-thousand-square-foot house: Source was the following online real estate listings: http://losangeles.blockshopper.com/property/4466006010/6957_whitesands/ and http://losangeles.blockshopper.com/news/story/2400154629-Advisory_firm_ founder_sells_Malibu_5BD_for_9M.

56   Foresthill Bridge: Golden State Bridge, Inc., http://foresthillbridgerenewal.com/ history.html; "BASE Tandem Jumps in Foresthill Bridge Future," Gus Thompson, *Auburn Journal,* August 16, 2012, http://www.auburnjournal.com/article/media -life-base-tandem-jumps-foresthill-bridge-future.

CHAPTER 4: GIMME DANGER

59   "It's a hard": *The Things They Carried,* Tim O' Brien (New York: Broadway Books, 1998), p. 192.

59   A growing body: "Toward Behavioral Genomics," Peter McGuffin, Brien Riley, and Robert Plomin, *Science,* February 16, 2001, pp. 1232–49, http://www.sciencemag .org/content/291/5507/1232.full.

59   born that way: Much of the material about the biological roots of personality in this chapter are drawn from *Biology of Personality and Individual Differences,* Turhan

Canli, ed. (New York: Guilford Press, 2006), http://www.acofps.com/up/uploads/files/acofps-6fda57861f.pdf#page=56.

60 attention deficit hyperactivity disorder: "High Prevalence of Rare Dopamine Receptor D4 Alleles in Children Diagnosed with Attention-Deficit Hyperactivity Disorder" *Molecular Psychiatry*, vol. 8, January 2003, pp. 536–45, http://www.nature.com/mp/journal/v8/n5/full/4001350a.html.

60 novelty seeking: "Dopamine D4 Receptor Gene (DRD4) Is Associated with Novelty Seeking (NS) and Substance Abuse: The Saga Continues...," J. M. Lusher, C. Chandler, and D. Ball, *Molecular Psychiatry*, September 2001, vol. 5, no. 5, pp. 497–99, http://www.nature.com/mp/journal/v6/n5/full/4000918a.html#bib1.

60 "psychiatry's repeat offender": "The DRD4 Gene: Psychiatry's Repeat Offender," Edward R. Winstead, Genome News Network, September 22, 2000, http://www.genomenewsnetwork.org/articles/09_00/DRD4_gene.shtml.

60 There was little disagreement: The sections on dopamine, MAO, and the interplay between neurotransmitters and pleasure are drawn from several sources: *Biology of Personality and Individual Differences*, pp. 56–74; telephone interviews with Dr. Marvin Zuckerman, September 2012; "Skydivers and Risk-Taking Behavior," Vic Napier, *Parachutist*, December 2009; "Jumping at the Chance for Danger," Charles Duhigg, *Los Angeles Times*, July 2, 2004; "BASE Jumping: Not Suicide, but Sure Looks Like It," Michael Y. Park, Fox News, May 22, 2006; "What's the Lure of the Edge?," Richard A. Friedman, MD, *NYT*, June 20, 2005.

61 "sensation-seekers": Information on high-sensation seekers and Zuckerman's research were drawn from phone interviews with Zuckerman in September 2012, and his book *Behavioral Expression and Biosocial Bases of Sensation Seeking* (Cambridge, UK: Cambridge University Press, 1994).

62 Car accident victims: The concepts of "time dilation, reallocation of resources, and the range of reactions to fear" are explained in *Extreme Fear: The Science of Your Mind in Danger*, Jeff Wise (New York: Palgrave Macmillan, 2009), pp. 32–78.

62 "flow state": "Go with the Flow," John Geirland, *Wired*, April 1999, http://www.wired.com/wired/archive/4.09/czik_pr.html; "Superhuman," Steven Kotler, *Playboy*, February 2012, http://www.stevenkotler.com/articles/superhuman/.

63 unpredictability: "Addictive Personality? You Might Be a Leader," David J. Linden, *NYT*, July 23, 2011, http://www.nytimes.com/2011/07/24/opinion/sunday/24addicts.html.

63 Omer Mei-Dan: "Daredevil Doctor Dives into Denver," Mark Couch, *CU Medicine Today*, May 2013, http://www.ucdenver.edu/academics/colleges/medicalschool/administration/alumni/CUMedToday/profiles/Pages/Omer-Mei-Dan.aspx.

64 Such a moment: The jump from the tower outside Camarillo, and its aftermath, was assembled from phone conversations with Jeb Corliss (July 2011), Anne Helliwell (August 2011), Gigi Fitzmorris (September 2011), and Shawn Stern (October 2011) and "The Man in the Black Flying Suit," *Popular Mechanics*, June 30, 2010, http://www.popularmechanics.co.za/features/the-man-in-the-black-flying-suit/.

67 Kjerag: Stavanger B.A.S.E. Klubb, http://www.basekjerag.com/rogaland/stavanger/svg_base.nsf/id/5752837A5B65F24AC1256E0B00699EE8?OpenDocument.

68 *Captain Corelli's Mandolin:* http://www.imdb.com/title/tt0238112/.

69   Beachy Head: "Base: The Final Frontier," BBC News, November 22, 1999, http://
news.bbc.co.uk/2/hi/uk_news/532131.stm. A video of Gary's appearance on TV
and his launch from Beachy Head and the Hilton Park Lane can be viewed at http://
www.youtube.com/watch?v=71qHMnv-lNs.

CHAPTER 5: WINGS

73   **One day up on Brento:** The account of the Russian jumper with the homemade wingsuit on Brento was drawn from live and phone interviews with Jeb Corliss from
January 2008 through September 2011.

74   **His timing was impeccable:** "The Birdman of DeLand," Michael Abrams, *Forbes*,
May 26, 2003, http://www.forbes.com/forbes-life-magazine/2003/0526/054.html.

74   **Bird cults:** *Man and His Symbols,* Carl G. Jung (New York: J. G. Ferguson Publishing, 1964); *Myths, Dreams and Religion,* Joseph Campbell, ed. (Putnam, CT: Spring
Publications, Inc., 1988).

75   **"the Michigan Icarus":** Much of the material concerning Clem Sohn and the air
shows during the Depression, and the development of his wings, comes from *BBS*,
Abrams, pp. 41–52; and "Transport: Wing Man," *Time*, March 11, 1935. A newsreel
of Sohn flying his wingsuit over Hanworth, England, can be viewed at the website of ITN Source, http://www.itnsource.com/shotlist/BHC_RTV/1936/05/04/
BGU407210479/. Footage of Sohn's fatal plunge can be seen at the website for British Pathé, http://www.britishpathe.com/video/news-in-a-nutshell-bird-man-falls
-to-death-hard.

76   **Vincennes:** "'Bird' Man Plunges to Death," *International Herald Tribune*, April 25,
1937,   http://www.nytimes.com/2012/04/26/opinion/100-75-50-years-ago.html?_
r=0; "Transport: End of Sohn," *Time*, May 3, 1937.

77   **The culture:** The description of wingsuit flight in the postwar years was drawn
from sections of *BBS*, Abrams, including "Death's Angels," p. 94.

78   **U.S.P.A.:** *BBS*, p. 205, and USPA.org, http://www.uspa.org/aboutUSPA/history/
tabid/113/default.aspx.

78   **Domina Jalbert:** *Parachuting: The Skydiver's Handbook,* Dan Poynter and Mike
Turoff, p. 98; "They're Not Just Toys Anymore . . . Kites Go Scientific," Ben Kocivar,
Popular Science, March 1972.

78   **Deug:** The material related to Patrick de Gayardon's life and wingsuit designs was
drawn from *BBS*, Adams, pp. 211–20; phone conversations with Loïc Jean-Albert
in October 2007 and February 2008; "Wing Flight," Bruno Passe, *Paramag*, issue
129, February 1998, http://paramag.fr/contenus/archives/n129/article/article-us
.html; "It's a Bird . . . It's a Plane . . . No, It Isn't. It's Adrian Nicholas," Daniel Mi-
chaels, *Wall Street Journal*, September 30, 1999, http://online.wsj.com/article/
SB938646293927411674.html; the websites of Troy Hartman, http://www
.troyhartman.com/oldsite.htm; and Joe Jennings, http://www.joejennings.com/
patrick.htm; and X Games history, http://espn.go.com/extreme/xgames/xalmanac_
summer.html. A video compilation of Deug's stunts for the Sector No Limits cam-
paign can be viewed at http://www.youtube.com/watch?v=oUR8ZpYCRt0.

80   **Hawaii:** The episode surrounding Deug's death was drawn from "The Longest

Flight," Patrick Passe, *Paramag*, issue 132, May 1998; and Adrian Nicholas's obituary in the *Daily Telegraph* (UK), September 22, 2005, http://www.telegraph.co.uk/news/obituaries/1498884/Adrian-Nicholas.html; "Look! Up in the Sky . . . ," Stephanie Kendrick, *Honolulu Star-Bulletin*, May 4, 1999, http://archives.starbulletin.com/1999/05/04/features/story2.html.

CHAPTER 6: THE WORLD IS A PLAYGROUND

82 old guard: Descriptions of the schism in BASE come from interviews in July 2011 with Todd Shoebotham and Jeb Corliss, in August 2011 with Nick DiGiovanni, Karin Sako, Todd Shoebotham, Anne Helliwell, and Jeb Corliss.

83 tar-and-feathering: Interview with Nick DiGiovanni, August 2011, and "A Sport to Die For," Michael Abrams, ESPN.com E-Ticket, http://sports.espn.go.com/espn/eticket/story?page=basejump.

83 Felix Baumgartner: *BBS*, Abrams, pp. 248–51; "Profile: Felix Baumgartner," BBC News Europe, October 14, 2012, http://www.bbc.co.uk/news/world-europe-19942836; Redbull.com, http://www.redbull.com/en/athletes/1331578987345/felix-baumgartner.

83 Thor Alex Kappfjell: "Norwegian Who Parachuted from World Trade Center Pleads Guilty," AP, April 3, 1999, http://www.hurriyetdailynews.com/default.aspx?pageid=438&n=norwegian-who-parachuted-from-world-trade-center-pleads-guilty-1999-04-03; "Thor Kappfjell, 32, a Daredevil Who Leapt to Fame in New York," *NYT*, July 8, 1999, http://www.nytimes.com/1999/07/08/world/thor-kappfjell-32-a-daredevil-who-leapt-to-fame-in-new-york.html; video of Kappfjell's stunts can be viewed from the program *Extra*, http://www.youtube.com/watch?v=8qdHgtCMLMo.

85 Venezuela: Jeb described his adventures in Venezuela during phone interviews in June 2008 and live interviews, July 2011, and "The Man in the Black Flying Suit," *Popular Mechanics*, June 2010.

85 Canaima National Park: UNESCO.org, http://whc.unesco.org/en/list/701 and http://www.unesco.org/archives/multimedia/?id_film=172&id_page=33&s=films_details; "Conan Doyle's Lost World Gets Connected," Will Grant, BBC News, October 9, 2009, http://news.bbc.co.uk/2/hi/programmes/from_our_own_correspondent/8295819.stm.

86 *Real TV*: Interviews with Jeb Corliss in November 2008 and July 2011 and Jordan Stone in August 2012.

86 Milner Peak: Jeb Corliss described his and Yuri's jumps during live and phone interviews in July and September 2011. Summitpost.org, http://www.summitpost.org/milner-peak/151995.

87 Howick Falls: Descriptions of this jump and Jeb's hospital stay come from interviews with Jeb Corliss in June 2008, July 2011, and January 2012; and video from *A Year in the Life* and *The Ground Is the Limit*.

89 Cave of Swallows: Details of this expedition come from interviews with Jeb Corliss and his documentary, *A Year in the Life*; Atlas Obscura, http://www.atlasobscura.com/places/cave-of-swallows-sotano-de-las-golondrinas.

CHAPTER 7: DWAIN, SLIM, AND DR. DEATH

91   Dwain . . . Slim: Details and descriptions of Dwain and Slim are drawn from interviews with Jeb Corliss in July and September 2011; Iiro Seppänen in July 2011; Todd Shoebotham in October 2011, Nick DiGiovanni in August 2011; Karin Sako and Gary Cunningham in July 2012; and *Confessions of an Idiot,* Chris McDougall.

92   Dr. Death: Details about Dr. Nikolas Hartshorne are drawn from interviews with Jeb Corliss in July 2011; Karin Sako in July 2012; and the following sources: "Nirvana's Kurt Cobain Was High When He Shot Himself," *Seattle Post-Intelligencer,* April 15, 1994, http://articles.baltimoresun.com/1994-04-15/features/1994105028_ 1_kurt-cobain-cobain-suicide-heroin; "Police Say Evidence Consistent in Death of Alternative Rock Star," AP, April 15, 1994.

92   Video of Weston's monologues: http://vimeo.com/12608117.

93   Given his reputation: Interviews with Gary Cunningham, July 2012, and "A Sport to Die For," Michael Abrams, ESPN.com E-Ticket, http://sports.espn.go.com/espn/ eticket/story?page=basejump.

93   Perrine Bridge: "Huge," Tim Sohn, *Outside,* February 2006.

93   "For sure, Jeb": Iiro Seppänen live interview, September 2011.

94   Hongping Li: USC Trojan Athletics, http://www.usctrojans.com/sports/w-swim/ mtt/li_hongping00.html.

94   Iiro Seppänen: The material concerning the meeting between Iiro and Jeb Corliss and Iiro's background come from interviews with both men in July and September 2011, and from "Iiro Seppänen, a Rogue Magician's Tricks in the Night, and at Work," Pete Suhonen, *City* (Helsinki newspaper), May 7, 1996, Google, tr., http:// www.city.fi/ilmiot/iiro+seppanen/3301, and "Iiro Seppänen: Magician King," interview by Joona Rinne, *City,* August 4, 2006, Google tr. http://www.city.fi/ilmiot/ iiro+seppanen/158.

96   Skylon Tower: This episode and the others in Manhattan were drawn from interviews with Corliss and Iiro Seppänen in July 2011, and from "Been There, Leaped Off That," Bill Hutchinson, *NYDN,* April 28, 2006; Skylon.com, http://www.skylon .com/niagara-falls-attractions/observation-deck/.

97   Circus Circus: Descriptions of this jump are derived from *The Ground Is the Limit;* interviews with Jeb Corliss in June 2009 and March 2012; and Iiro Seppänen in July 2011; and a description of the casino was drawn from *Fear and Loathing in Las Vegas,* Hunter S. Thompson (New York: Random House, 1972) p. 46.

98   Eiffel Tower: This scene was drawn from interviews with Jeb Corliss in July 2011, and *The Ground Is the Limit.*

98   Golden Gate: The descriptions of the Golden Gate Bridge jump and the Stratosphere Tower in Las Vegas were drawn from *The Ground Is the Limit* and interviews with Jeb Corliss in July 2011 and April 2012 and Iiro Seppänen, July 2011. A video of the jump from the Stratosphere, narrated by Seppänen, can be found at Break.com, http://www.break.com/video/ugc/base-jump-from-stratosphere-tower-in-las -vegas-605541.

99   Bridge Day: The jump sequence was drawn from *The Ground Is the Limit* and from interviews with Jeb Corliss in July 2011 and Iiro Seppänen in September 2011. Description of Slim's injuries come from *Confessions of an Idiot,* pp. 163–64; "A Leap

Too Far: Leading Base Jumper Killed in Shanghai," Hamish McDonald and Philip Cornford, *Sydney Morning Herald*, October 9, 2004, http://www.smh.com .au/articles/2004/10/08/1097089572149.html.

CHAPTER 8: CHECK, PLEASE!

101 **in the winter:** The descriptions from the Extreme Air event and Karina Hollekim's subsequent BASE training were drawn from interviews with Karina Hollekim in July 2012, and Jeb Corliss in October 2008, and a documentary about Hollekim's life in BASE, *20 Seconds of Joy*, http://www.20secondsofjoy.com/; Omer Mei-Dan Extreme Productions, Ltd., http://www.extremegate.com/; The Northface.com, http://uk.thenorthface.com/blog/eu/en/karina-hollekim.

105 **Lauterbrunnen Valley:** The description of jumping in the valley with Weston and Hartshorne was drawn from interviews with Jeb Corliss in July 2011, and Karin Sako, July 2012. Details of Dr. Nikolas Hartshorne's death come from the following sources: Swiss BASE Association, Lauterbrunnen BASE Fatality List, http://www .basejumper.ch/index.php?option=com_content&task=view&id=12&Itemid=26; "A Sport to Die For," Michael Abrams, ESPN.com E-Ticket, http://sports.espn.go .com/espn/eticket/story?page=basejump.

106 **High Nose:** Swiss BASE Association, http://www.basejumper.ch/documents/SBA_ Valley_Jump_Info.pdf.

107 **Palace Hotel:** The circumstances surrounding the jump from the Palace Hotel were drawn from interviews with Jeb Corliss in January 2008, June 2008 and July 2011; Karina Hollekim in July 2012; and Gigi Fitzmorris in July and September 2011; in addition to the videos *A Year in the Life* and *The Ground Is the Limit*.

CHAPTER 9: SKYDIVER OF THE DECADE

110 **Loïc Jean-Albert:** Descriptions of Jean-Albert's early life and career are drawn from interviews with Jean-Albert, October 2007 and February 2008; *BBS*, Abrams, pp. 227–30; Flyyourbody.com, http://flyyourbody.com/en/content/25-about-us; Redbull.com, http://www.redbull.com/cs/Satellite/en_INT/Profile/Jean-Albert-Loic -021242746282381; and "Wing-Suit: A Suit That's a Wing," Bruno Passe, *Paramag*, http://home.nordnet.fr/~paramag/archives/n145/article1GB.html.

111 **Verbier:** Video of Jean-Albert's famous flight along the snow slope can be seen at http://www.youtube.com/watch?v=ZJTYzVd6LkU.

112 **Skydiver of the Decade:** *Outside*, August 2, 2010, http://www.outsideonline.com/ outdoor-adventure/aerial-sports/Loic-Jean-Albert.html.

113 **Perris:** Gary described his first wingsuit flying experience and his vision of landing during phone interviews, March 2012 and January 2013.

115 **Nelson's Column:** Descriptions of Gary Connery's plunge and arrest were drawn from interviews with Gary Connery, January and May 2013; and the following sources: "Protestor Parachutes off Nelson's Column," BBC News, May 9, 2003; "Diving for Dalai Lama," Tania Branigan, *The Guardian*, May 9, 2003.

CHAPTER 10: WHATEVER HAPPENS, HAPPENS

Details of Weston's life and his frame of mind before he arrived in Colorado were drawn from interviews with Jeb Corliss, January 2011, January 2012; and Karin Sako and Gary Cunningham in July 2012.

119 Go Fast Games: Descriptions from the Go Fast Games were drawn from interviews with Jeb Corliss, July 2011, January 2012; Karin Sako, July 2012; and Troy Widgery, May 2007. Additional details came from the TV documentary *Fearless, the Jeb Corliss Story*, http://www.imdb.com/title/tt0821251/.

119 Weston legend: "Base Jumper Was Meticulous," *Sydney Morning Herald*, October 7, 2003, http://www.smh.com.au/articles/2003/10/07/1065292560465.html?from=storyrhs.

119 magazine article . . . : "Aussie Skydiver Falls to Death," *Sydney Morning Herald*, October 7, 2003, http://www.smh.com.au/articles/2003/10/06/1065292522786.html.

121 "Oh, no!": Weston's final flight sequence and impact were drawn from HBO *Real Sports*, February 21, 2012.

122 Weston had struck the bridge: Details were drawn from *Fearless*; "Aussie Skydiver Falls to Death"; and "Stunt Attempt Proves Fatal for Skydiver," *Los Angeles Times*, October 6, 2003, http://articles.latimes.com/2003/oct/06/nation/na-briefs6.1.

122 Malibu: Descriptions of the memorial at Jeb Corliss's house were drawn from interviews with Corliss, July 2011; Karin Sako, July 2012; and Iiro Seppänen, September 2011; Nick DiGiovanni, August 2011.

123 Super Bowl: Apexbase.com, https://www.apexbase.com/film-tv-consulting.

123 "It's okay to die": HBO *Real Sports*, February 21, 2012.

124 Vibeke: "BASE Jumper 'Couldn't Open Chute,'" *Sydney Morning Herald*, July 21, 2005, http://www.smh.com.au/news/world/aussie-base-jumper-couldnt-open-chute/2005/07/21/1121539063068.html.

124 cave: The scenes from the cave in China come from interviews in July 2011 with Jeb Corliss and Chris McDougall; *Confessions of an Idiot*, McDougall, pp. 203–5; and *Journey to the Center*, a documentary about an expedition to Tiankeng, produced by Corliss and Iiro Seppänen.

124 Jin Mao Tower: Details concerning jumps from the building in Shanghai were drawn from *Confessions of an Idiot*, McDougall, p. 177; and interviews with Chris McDougall, September 2011; Gary Cunningham, July 2012; Jeb Corliss, July 2011; and Stephan Mueller, September 2011.

125 Slim: Details of the crash of Roland "Slim" Simpson at the Jin Mao Tower and his death were drawn from interviews with Gary Cunningham, July 2012; Chris McDougall, September 2011; and Jeb Corliss, July and September 2011; "A Leap Too Far: Leading Base Jumper Killed in Shanghai," Hamish McDonald and Philip Cornford, *Sydney Morning Herald*, October 9, 2004, http://www.smh.com.au/articles/2004/10/08/1097089572149.html; and "BASE Jumper Dies in Hospital," *The Age*, October 23, 2004, http://www.theage.com.au/articles/2004/10/23/1098474913262.html?from=storylhs.

126 Luigi Cani: Interviews with Luigi Cani and Jeb Corliss, February 2008; Joby Ogwyn, July 2011; and the official website of Luigi Cani, http://cani.tv/en/biography/.

127 "Go Fast!": The test and result of Jeb Corliss's and Luigi Cani's flight was drawn

from interviews with both men in February 2008; and the Go Fast! press release, http://www.zoominfo.com/s/#!search/profile/person?personId=139317216&target id=profile.

127 "I'm afraid": Cani's comment came from a phone interview in February 2008.

127 Robert Pečnik: His comments about the possibilities for landing a wingsuit were drawn from *BBS*, Abrams, pp. 274–75.

127 "Natural flying": Jean-Albert's quote can be found in *BBS*, Abrams, p. 274.

CHAPTER 11: "HOLY CHUTE!"

129 TV host: Details of Jeb Corliss's career as host of *Stunt Junkies* come from interviews with Jeb Corliss in July 2011 and Jordan Stone in August 2012.

129 *Fearless*: IMDB.com, http://www.imdb.com/title/tt0821251/.

130 *Stunt Junkies*: TV Guide.com, http://www.tvguide.com/tvshows/stunt-junkies-go -big-or-go-home/cast/278905.

130 Empire State Building: The descriptions of events surrounding the Empire State Building episode and its immediate aftermath were drawn from testimony and video and other evidence from a fall 2008 criminal trial and from multiple news accounts, including "Cops Stop Fall Guy. Foil Empire State Jumper," Celeste Katz, Oren Yaniv, and Leo Standora, *NYDN*, April 28, 2006, http://www.nydailynews .com/archives/news/cops-stop-fall-guy-foil-empire-state-jumper-article-1.606079; "Jumping Jerk Had Hopes of Fulfilling His Diving Dream," *NYDN*, April 29, 2006; and "Free Speech? Looks More Like Free Fall," Dan Barry, *NYT*, November 4, 2006.

135 Discovery fired: "*Discovery* Dumps Corliss," John Eggerton, *Broadcasting & Cable*, April 28, 2006, http://www.broadcastingcable.com/news/programming/discovery -dumps-corliss/28262.

135 Mel Sachs: "Mel A. Sachs, 60, Trial Lawyer with a Flamboyant Streak, Dies," Glenn Collins, *NYT*, September 1, 2006, http://www.nytimes.com/2006/09/01/ obituaries/01sachs.html?_r=1&.

136 legs like matchsticks: Descriptions of Karina's accident and aftermath are drawn from interviews with Karina in July 2012 and Jeb in October 2008; "Karina Holle- kim: The Lady Who Can Fly," Frances Booth, *Daily Telegraph* (UK), September 29, 2007, http://www.telegraph.co.uk/news/features/3634233/Karina-Hollekim- The-lady-who-can-fly.html); and Thenorthface.com, http://uk.thenorthface.com/ blog/eu/en/karina-hollekim.

137 Mark Jay Heller: "Mark Heller, Esq.," Michael Wilson and Serge F. Kovaleski, *NYT*, May 21, 2010, http://www.nytimes.com/2010/05/23/nyregion/23lawyer.html?page wanted=1.

137 State Supreme Court: "Empire State Building Stuntman Asks to Have Charge Dis- missed," Anemona Hartocollis, *NYT*, October 28, 2006, http://www.nytimes .com/2006/10/28/nyregion/28empire.html; "Free Speech? Looks More Like Free Fall," Dan Barry, *NYT*, November 4, 2006, http://www.nytimes.com/2006/11/04/ nyregion/04about.html.

138 London Eye: Details of Gary's launch from the London Eye were drawn from interviews with Gary in November 2013 and Vivienne Connery in September 2013;

and "Security Lapse at London Eye as Staff Fail to Notice Parachute Jump," *Daily Mail*, November 29, 2006, http://www.dailymail.co.uk/news/article-419518/ Security-lapse-London-Eye-staff-fail-notice-parachute-jump.html.

CHAPTER 12: THE WINGSUIT LANDING PROJECT

141 Ambrecht: "Foiled Daredevil Fares Better in Court," Anemona Hartocollis, *NYT*, January 18, 2007, http://www.nytimes.com/2007/01/18/nyregion/18jumper.html?_ r=1&; Judge Ambrecht's Decision, Supreme Court of the State of New York, County of New York, http://graphics8.nytimes.com/packages/pdf/nyregion/city_room/ 20080115_CORLISS.pdf.

142 *Cristo Redentor:* "The New Seven Wonders of the World," *Xinhua*, July 8, 2007, http://www.hindustantimes.com/world-news/the-new-seven-wonders-of-the -world/article1-235487.aspx.

142 Corcovado: Details concerning Jeb's and Luigi's flights over Corcovado are drawn from interviews with both men; video can be viewed at http://www.youtube.com/ watch?v=fzsNd5-0w2Y; and "Jump. Fly. Land," Carl Hoffman, *Air & Space*, November 2010, http://www.airspacemag.com/flight-today/Jump-Fly-Land.html?c =y&page=2.

144 Loïc: Comments are drawn from a phone interview with Loïc Jean-Albert, October 2007 and February 2008.

144 Maria von Egidy: Comments and background on Maria von Egidy are drawn from a live interview in January 2012 and phone interviews with Maria in November 2007; and "Will 'Flying Squirrel' Suit Let Skydivers Jump Without Chutes?," Sean Markey, National Geographic News, February 9, 2007, http://news.nationalgeographic .com/news/2007/02/070209-wingsuit.html.

145 Jean Potvin: Comments and background on Jean Potvin come from a telephone interview in October 2007, and Dr. Jean Potvin's home page, http://www.slu.edu/ colleges/AS/physics/profs/potvin.html.

146 ailerons: "Oldies and Oddities: Where Do Ailerons Come From?," Tom Crouch, *Smithsonian Air & Space*, September 2009, http://www.airspacemag.com/history -of-flight/Oldies-and-Oddities-Where-Do-Ailerons-Come-From.html; Glenn Research Center, NASA.gov, http://www.grc.nasa.gov/WWW/k-12/airplane/alr.html.

146 The key to a flare: *Parachuting: The Skydiver's Handbook,* Dan Poynter and Mike Turoff, p. 66; "Kiss the Runway," Bob Schmelzer, *Flight Training,* June 2011, http:// flighttraining.aopa.org/magazine/2011/June/Cover_landings.html; "The Last Six Inches: How to Make Perfect Landings," Mike Fizer, *Flight Training,* February 2012, http://flighttraining.aopa.org/magazine/2012/February/feature-perfect-landings .html; "Jump. Fly. Land.," Carl Hoffman, *Air & Space* magazine, November 2010, http://www.airspacemag.com/flight-today/Jump-Fly-Land.html.

147 Nordic ski jumpers: Eastern Ski Jumping & Nordic Combined Foundation, Inc., http://flighttraining.aopa.org/magazine/2012/February/feature-perfect-landings .html.

147 Roy Haggard: The personal information for Roy Haggard was drawn from interviews with Haggard in October 2007 and the website for Vertigo, Inc.; "Flying

Humans, Hoping to Land with No Chute," Matt Higgins, *NYT,* December 10, 2007, http://www.nytimes.com/2007/12/10/sports/othersports/10flying.html?_r=0; "Roy Haggard Named to Rogallo Hall of Fame," Tom Norton, *General Aviation News,* May 20, 2009, http://generalaviationnews.com/2009/05/20/roy-haggard -named-to-rogallo-hall-of-fame/; "Wing Nuts," *Chicago Tribune,* January 5, 2008, http://articles.chicagotribune.com/2008-01-05/news/0801040669_1_fly-landing -blue-sky.

147 **Vertigo:** Information on Vertigo was drawn from interviews with Roy Haggard in October 2007; linkedin.com, http://www.linkedin.com/pub/roy-haggard/9/57a/437; the Vertigo website (no longer online); and score.org, http://www.score.org/success -stories/vertigo-inc.

149 **Loïc was out:** Descriptions of Loïc's accident and decision to cease flying wingsuits were drawn from a telephone interview in February 2008 and "A Life in Flight," Bryan Schatz, *Adventure Sports Journal,* April 2, 2012, http://adventuresports journal.com/miscellaneous/a-life-in-flight.

CHAPTER 13: THE TRIAL

150 *New York Times:* "Flying Humans, Hoping to Land with No Chute," Matt Higgins, *NYT,* December 10, 2007.

150 *Today:* Video from Jeb's appearance on *Today* can be viewed at today.com, http:// www.today.com/id/22705333/ns/today-today_news/t/daredevil-sues-nyc -landmark-thwarting-jump/#.UrIStNJDvAx.

150 **Stephen Colbert:** Jeb's appearance on *The Colbert Report* can be viewed at colbertna tion.com, http://www.colbertnation.com/the-colbert-report-videos/147277/january -23-2008/jeb-corliss.

151 **countersuit:** "Would-Be Jumper Sues Empire State Building," Anemona Hartocollis, *NYT,* January 15, 2008, http://cityroom.blogs.nytimes.com/2008/01/15/would-be -jumper-sues-empire-state-building/?_r=1.

151 **police evidence:** "Lost Evidence Affects Empire State Jumper Case," Tony Lingefors, *The Epoch Times,* June 20, 2008.

151 **state supreme court appellate:** "Charges Reinstated Against Empire State Building Stunt Jumper," AP, March 4, 2008, http://www.nydailynews.com/new-york/ charges-reinstated-empire-state-building-stunt-jumper-article-1.284875.

151 **New York Times tower:** "Man Scales New York Times Building," Sewell Chan, *NYT,* June 5, 2008, http://cityroom.blogs.nytimes.com/2008/06/05/man-scales-new -york-times-building/; "Second Climber at Times Building in Custody," Sewell Chan, *NYT,* June 5, 2008, http://cityroom.blogs.nytimes.com/2008/06/05/yes -another-man-is-climbing-times-building/; "Third Man Climbs Times Building and Is Arrested," Sewell Chan, *NYT,* July 9, 2008, http://cityroom.blogs.nytimes .com/2008/07/09/third-man-climbs-times-building/.

152 **Bloomberg:** "Bill to Halt High-Rise Stunt Nuts," Frank Lombardi, *NYDN,* September 4, 2008; and the City of New York press release, "Mayor Bloomberg Signs Legislation Prohibiting BASE Jumping from City Buildings," September 22, 2008.

152 **Hearing, trial, and sentencing (hearing of criminal court):** Much of the material was

drawn from the author's observations, notes, and recordings; trial transcripts; and "Trial Opens for Empire State Building Parachutist," Samuel Maull, AP, November 15, 2008; "Prof Testifies in Empire State Stunt Case," UPI, November 18, 2008; "Empire State Stuntman Tells Jury He Feared Guards," AP, December 1, 2008; "Empire State Stuntman Convicted, Could Get Jail," Samuel Maull, AP, December 3, 2008; "Stunt Empire State Building Jumper Lands on Conviction," Barbara Ross, *NYDN*, December 3, 2008; "Empire State Stuntman Gets 3 Years of Probation," Samuel Maull, AP, January 23, 2009; "Chute-for-Brains Jumper Ducks Jail," Laura Italiano, *New York Post*, January 23, 2009.

CHAPTER 14: PAINT IT BLACK

158 Roberta Mancino: "Raising Her Profile by Showing Some Skin," James Vlahos, *NYT*, March 30, 2011, http://www.nytimes.com/2011/03/31/fashion/31mancino.html?pagewanted=all.

159 "The Human Bird": *Daredevils: The Human Bird*, Firecracker Films, aired Channel 4 (UK), September 14, 2009.

159 Kuala Lumpur: Details of Jeb's and Roberta's experience in Kuala Lumpur are drawn from interviews with both in September 2011; and "Falling Man," Bill Gifford, *Men's Journal*, June 11, 2010, http://archive.mensjournal.com/jeb-corliss.

160 Golden Knights: "Golden Knight, Soldier to Attempt Wing-Suit Record at YPG," James Gilbert, *Yuma Sun*, February 12, 2009.

161 Hervé le Gallou: "Base Jumpers: The Men Who Fall to Earth," Ed Caesar, *Sunday Times* (UK), March 8, 2009.

161 Dean Potter: "The Aerialist," Matt Samet, *Outside*, July 2011, http://www.outsideonline.com/outdoor-adventure/athletes/dean-potter/The-Aerialist.html.

161 "It's not crazy": Film Fest St. Anton, Austria, http://www.youtube.com/watch?v=ahNkbrotac.

162 Matti Hautamäki: Skijumpinginfo.com, http://www.skijumping-info.com/news/359-matti-hautam%C3%A4ki-finishes-long-and-successfull-career.html.

163 Bruce Beresford-Redman: "Estate of Reality TV Producer Bruce Beresford-Redman's Slain Wife Settled," Anthony McCartney, AP, December 11, 2013, http://metronews.ca/scene/881523/estate-of-slain-reality-tv-producers-wife-settled/. Results of Beresford-Redman's case were not available as of press time.

163 Hunter Defense Technologies: "Hunter Defense Technologies Acquires Vertigo, Inc.," Reuters, April 1, 2009, http://www.reuters.com/article/2009/04/01/idUS202657+01-Apr-2009+PRN20090401; "HDT's Vertigo Recognized by NASA PRNewswire," October 23, 2009, http://www.redorbit.com/news/space/1774443/hdts_vertigo_recognized_by_nasa/.

164 Tedx: Video of Jeb's speech at Tedx, USC, April 2010, can be viewed at http://stevens.usc.edu/Jeb_Corliss__Harnessing_Fear.flv.

CHAPTER 15: A FLYING PHILISTINE

167 TonySuits, Inc: Much of the material for this chapter was drawn from visits to TonySuits' manufacturing facility and interviews with Tony Uragallo in March 2012 and

Jeff Nebelkopf in September 2011 and January 2012; and Tonywingsuits.com, http://www.tonywingsuits.com/. Several wingsuit pilots also described the effect on their sport from developments in Tony's workshop.

170 **Mark Sutton:** Mark Sutton described his background in a telephone interview in June 2013.

171 **Bernoulli's principle:** NASA has published a pamphlet on Bernoulli's principle for students that offers a straightforward comprehensive explanation, http://www .aeronautics.nasa.gov/pdf/bernoulli_principle_5_8.pdf.

CHAPTER 16: BOXES AND BOXES

175 **"He's quite a striking character":** In separate interviews, Gary, in January 2013, and Mark, in June 2013, described their meeting in Italy, subsequent travels, and growing partnership in pursuit of a wingsuit landing.

175 Extremsportveko: Extremsportveko.com, http://www.ekstremsportveko.com/.

176 **"Grinding the Crack":** The video can be viewed on Jeb Corliss's YouTube channel, http://www.youtube.com/watch?v=TWfph3iNC-k.

CHAPTER 17: DRAGONS AT HEAVEN'S GATE

Details and descriptions for this chapter are drawn from my observations and multiple interviews with all of the wingsuit pilots present in China during September 2011 and from various media reports, including "Mind the Gap! Wingsuit Stuntman Shoots Through Narrow Slit in Mountainside at 75 MPH," Gareth Finighan, *Daily Mail*, September 24, 2011, http://www.dailymail.co.uk/news/article-2041434/Wingsuit-stuntman-Jeb-Corliss -shoots-narrow-slit-Tianmen-mountain-75mph.html.

CHAPTER 18: A MEETING OF THE MINDS

The bulk of this chapter derives from live interviews with Matt Gerdes and Barry Holubeck in September 2011, and Tony Uragallo in March 2012, and phone interviews with Gary and Vivienne Connery, Mark Sutton, and Nick English from January through September 2013.

CHAPTER 19: TOUCH-AND-GO

205 **Cape Town:** The contents of this chapter were drawn from observations and interviews with the pilots and others present in South Africa during January 2012. Another helpful resource was the episode of HBO's *Real Sports*, which aired on February 21, 2012, and featured Jeb's crash into Table Mountain.

205 **Table Mountain:** South African National Parks, http://www.sanparks.org/parks/ table_mountain/tourism/attractions.php#tablemountain.

CHAPTER 20: "THE REBEL"

219 **Zephyrhills:** Descriptions of Gary's training and Tony's attempt to develop a wingsuit for a landing attempt came from interviews with Gary, in January 2013, and Tony, March 2012, and Mark Sutton, June 2013.

220 XRW: "Project XRW," Taya Weiss, *Parachutist*, April 2012.
224 *Conan:* Jeb's appearance on *Conan* can be viewed at teamcoco.com, http://teamcoco.com/video/jeb-corliss-never-give-up.

CHAPTER 21: THE RIGHT NUMBERS
229 **Switzerland:** Mark and Gary described their flights in Lauterbrunnen and Walenstadt in January and June 2013, respectively, and I was present at Tony's shop in March 2012 when Gary sent e-mails containing his flight metrics and Tony read them aloud and discussed them with others in the shop.

CHAPTER 22: RAINY DAYS
231 **"Less Corrr Than Corliss":** The video can be viewed at Gary's website: Garyconnery.com, http://garyconnery.com/media-gallery/detail/15/119.
232 **"april falls madness":** Gary's messages to his volunteer corps appear with permission from Gary Connery. Descriptions of preparations for landing, including training, were drawn from interviews with Gary Connery, in January 2013, Mark Sutton, in June 2013, Vivienne Connery, in June and September 2013, and Nick English, May 2013.
235 **it rained:** Weather records for the UK came from the Met Office, the UK's National Weather Service, Metoffice.gov.uk, http://www.metoffice.gov.uk/climate/uk/2012/may.html.
240 **"landing":** Descriptions of the landing day were drawn from interviews with Gary Connery, January and May 2013; Mark Sutton, in June 2013; Vivienne Connery, June and September 2013; Andrew Harvey, Nick English, Chris and Hazel Bullock, and Jon Bonny in May 2013; "Gary Connery Lands Safely After 2,400 ft Helicopter Jump Without Parachute," Charlie Cooper, May 23, 2012, http://www.independent.co.uk/news/uk/home-news/gary-connery-lands-safely-after-2400-ft-helicopter-jump-without-parachute-7782213.html; "Stuntman Takes a Superhero Plunge," Mary Pilon, *NYT,* May 23, 2012, http://www.nytimes.com/2012/05/24/sports/englishman-connery-completes-successsful-wing-suit-landing.html?_r=0; "Skydiver Becomes First to Land Without Chute," Roddy Mansfield, Sky News, May 23, 2012, http://news.sky.com/story/20784/skydiver-becomes-first-to-land-without-chute; "Flying Suit That Enabled Landing Without a Parachute Was Made in Zephyrhills," Mary Kenney, *Tampa Bay Times*, May 24, 2012, http://www.tampabay.com/news/bizarre/flying-suit-that-enabled-landing-without-a-parachute-was-made-in/1231865; and "Behind the Death-Defying, Record-Setting Wingsuit Jump," James Vlahos, *Popular Mechanics,* May 26, 2012, http://www.popularmechanics.com/technology/aviation/diy-flying/behind-the-death-defying-record-setting-wingsuit-jump-9174357. Video of the landing can be viewed at itv.com, http://www.itv.com/news/meridian/2012-05-23/gary-falls-to-earth/.

EPILOGUE

253 "No. 1 Megastunt": "It Was a Great Spectacle, Despite ABC's Coverage," John Law, *Niagara Falls Review,* June 16, 2012.

253 opening Ceremony: "'Secret Agent' in the Coup that Made the Queen a Global TV Comedy Star . . . and the Daredevil Who Took a Royal Dive," Ian Gallagher, *Daily Mail,* July 28, 2012, http://www.dailymail.co.uk/news/article-2180214/London Olympics-2012-Gary-Connery-played-Queen-opening-ceremony.html.

253 Stratos Project : Redbullstratos.com, http://www.redbullstratos.com/.

253 World Wingsuit League: worldwingsuitleague.com, http://www.worldwingsuitleague .com/julian-boulle-wins-the-first-wwl-grand-prix/.

254 Mark Sutton: "Olympics Stuntman Mark Sutton Dies in Switzerland Wing-Diving Accident," James Meikle, *The Guardian,* August 15, 2013, http://www.theguardian .com/film/2013/aug/15/olympics-stuntman-mark-sutton-dies.

254 Flying Dagger: "Flight of the Year," *The Red Bulletin,* January 2014.

255 Victor Kovats: "Hungarian Wingsuit Flier Dies After Crash During China Jump," The Associated Press, NYDN, October 9, 2013, http://www.nydailynews.com/ news/world/hungarian-wingsuit-flyer-dies-crash-china-jump-article-1.1480340.

255 Loetschental: "Two Men Killed and One Seriously Injured in BASE Jumping Horror After They Plunged from Helicopter and Smashed into a Field" Kate Lyons, *Daily Mail,* March 31, 2014, http://www.dailymail.co.uk/news/article-2593106/Two-men -killed-BASE-jumping-accident.html; "Wingsuit Diver Brian Drake Dies After Accident in Switzerland," Ed Adamczyk, United Press International, April 10, 2014, http://www.upi.com/Top_News/World-News/2014/04/10/Wingsuit-diver-Brian -Drake-dies-after-accident-in-Switzerland/4601397150703/.

255 Everest: "Everest Climber Joby Ogwyn Still Shaken After Witnessing Tragedy" Emily Yahr, *The Washington Post,* May 1, 2014, http://www.washingtonpost.com/ blogs/style-blog/wp/2014/05/01/as-discovery-airs-mount-everest-avalanche -documentary-climber-joby-ogwyn-still-shaken-after-witnessing-tragedy/; "Joby Ogwyn Recalls Everest Disaster for Discovery Special" Patrick Kevin Day, *Los Angeles Times,* May 2, 2014, http://www.latimes.com/entertainment/tv/showtracker/ la-et-st-joby-ogwyn-recalls-everest-disaster-for-discovery-special-20140502-story .html.

255 Jeff Nebelkopf: "Skydivers Mourn Loss of Fellow Sebastian Jumper" Keith Carson, VeroNews.com, May 27, 2014, http://www.veronews.com/news/sebastian/public_ safety/skydivers-mourn-loss-of-fellow-sebastian-jumper/article_b39529a6-e5b7 -11e3-9f3d-0017a43b2370.html; "Sebastian Sky Diver Who Died Sunday was Professional Stunt Performer, Designer," Lamaur Stancil, *TCPalm,* May 28, 2014, http://www.tcpalm.com/news/sebastian-skydiver-dies-after-equipment; "Incident Reports" Jim Crouch, *Parachutist,* October 2014.

256 Karina Hollekim: "Falling Toward Grace" Jim Rendon, *Marie Claire,* January 25, 2013, http://www.marieclaire.com/world-reports/inspirational-women/falling-to ward-grace-5.

INDEX

CREDITS